OLD TESTAMENT LAW

DALE PATRICK

John Knox Press
ATLANTA

Library of Congress Cataloging in Publication Data

Patrick, Dale.
    Old Testament law.

    Includes bibliographies and index.
    1. Law (Theology)—Biblical teaching.   2. Bible.
O.T.—Criticism, interpretation, etc.   I. Title.
BS1199.L3P37 1984   241.5   84-4418
ISBN 0-8042-0133-1

© copyright John Knox Press 1985
10 9 8 7 6 5 4 3 2 1
Printed in the United States of America
John Knox Press
Atlanta, Georgia 30365

Acknowledgments

The idea for this book was germinated in a conversation between Richard Ray, then editor of John Knox Press, and the author at an annual meeting of the Society of Biblical Literature. Noting the dearth of scholarly literature on biblical law, particularly at an introductory level, we decided it would be desirable to publish a textbook that would survey the legal texts of the Pentateuch and familiarize the reader with basic concepts and theories of current scholarship into biblical law. It has taken a half-dozen years for the idea to grow into a complete manuscript, during which time Dick left his post as editor for the pastorate. I wish to give him due credit for inaugurating this project and thank the current staff for working it through to completion.

I had been prepared to take up this project by the Group on Biblical Law and Comparative Studies, a program unit of the Society of Biblical Literature. I had the honor of chairing this group for most of a decade. It was our good fortune to have among us leading scholars in the field of biblical law, and the rest of us benefited greatly from their tutelage. The younger members of the group contributed a restlessness and spirit of experimentation to our deliberations. This book attempts to synthesize the best of the scholarship bequeathed to us by our elders with the most compelling explorations of our youth.

Various members of the group not only were the community of scholars that incubated my thinking but were generous enough to read and criticize portions of the manuscript. Professors Ron Hals, Martin Buss, and Rolf Knierim reviewed the major chapters, while professors Jacob Milgrom and Tikva Frymer-Kensky scrutinized Chapter Six minutely. I corrected the mistakes they identified and modified my views when persuasive alternatives were proposed. Their collective contribution to the text is invaluable.

My wife, Mary, belongs on the roster of scholars who have a hand in the production of this book. We discussed many of the ideas as they were taking shape; her scholarship was especially helpful in the exposition of the New Testament love commandment in Chapter Seven.

Thanks are also due to a number of University of Missouri undergraduates who volunteered to be guinea pigs, to read the manuscript for comprehensibility and felicity. Their personal reactions, coupled with evaluations of what they learned, were incorporated into revisions, as it was crucial that the book be understandable and appealing to readers outside the circle of critical scholarship.

The book is dedicated to a close friend, Isaac Crosby, who taught philosophy and religion at Stephens College in Columbia, Missouri, while I was teaching at the University of Missouri. Whenever we got together to discuss theology, philosophy, or politics, we quickly became so engrossed in the subject that the hours vanished; we were soul brothers. Isaac was a soul brother of untold numbers in the community and in the worldwide church. His heroic struggle against bone cancer made us acutely aware of the grace with which God had favored us when this beautiful being was sent among us. We hoped against hope that the horrible disease could be controlled, and for a while it seemed that it was, but no sooner had we begun to whisper of a miracle than it erupted with devastating fury and wasted his body. This book is an unworthy tribute to Isaac, but it is all I have.

Dale Patrick

To
ISAAC CROSBY
In Memoriam
(1936–1983)

CONTENTS

Chapter One

INTRODUCTION

Law, say the gardeners, is the sun,
Law is the one
All gardeners obey
Tomorrow, yesterday, today.

. . . .

Law, says the priest with a priestly look,
Expounding to an unpriestly people,
Law is the words in my priestly book.
Law is my pulpit and my steeple.

Law, says the judge as he looks down his nose,
Speaking clearly and most severely,
Law is as I've told you before,
Law is as you know I suppose,
Law is but let me explain it once more,
Law is the Law.

(From W. H. Auden, "Law, say the gardeners")

Like these personages in Auden's poem, we all desire to define the word *law* and thereby pin down what the word means. Law is too important to take for granted. Law is necessary for civilized living. Through law, community is established and maintained; without it, people simply could not live together. Nor is law merely a practical instrument for social integration. It is a repository of religious and philosophic concepts and values that give coherence and purpose to communal living. Law enshrines and protects what a community holds to be sacred and partakes of the sacrality it guards.

But alas, when we try to define *law*, we are tempted to move beyond description to theories which reflect and enhance the position we fill in society. The gardener looks to the physical environment, the priest points to the symbols of religion, while the judge insists on law's perfect independence. Each raises his or her own experience of law to a universal concept. The priest and the judge are self-serving in their theories, for both make themselves out to be oracles of the law. The gardeners are comparatively innocent, but theirs is a childish innocence that does not recognize the difference between natural processes and human society. No one is able to transcend his or her own social role sufficiently to get at the thing itself.

Nevertheless, the judge is not entirely wrong for insisting that the "Law is—the Law." Surely our most primitive experience of law is that it commands us, that it claims our conscience and measures our actions. The judge may take this primitive experience and turn it to his or her advantage, but we would not grant authority to the judge if we did not recognize an undeniable truth in what he or she says. There is simply no escaping the fact that the "Law is."

Nor is the priest misdirected when he or she roots the law in the sacred. The sense of unconditional ought—of duty owed irrespective of our interests or desires—has the force of the voice of God. The people of antiquity were simply reasoning from their hearts when they attributed law to divine command. The Bible raises this sense of sacred duty to a primary experience of God. Even the secular person can imagine hearing the commanding voice from Sinai, though he or she no longer believes there is a Speaker.

The gardeners, too, have their truth. Even if the regularities of nature are not the same as duties imposed upon the consciences of free and responsible selves, our moral traditions are experienced as a "second" nature. The mores of the community into which we are born seem as objective and permanent as the physical laws of our world. Only as we mature and confront choices between ought and inclination do we begin to appreciate the distinction, and even then we normally live as though the social order were a natural one. Our narrow and biased views do in fact reveal dimensions of the mysterious phenomenon known as Law.

Laws and the Law

How do we recognize law when we meet it? We can begin to answer this question with the definition of *a* law. Perhaps the Law of a given social group is the sum total of its laws. Or perhaps the Law is more than the sum total of laws, more a consistent, comprehensive scheme of principles and values shared by a social group. The dictionaries and common wisdom alike seize upon the idea that a law is a *rule* about what we should or should not do and the sanctions that accompany such a rule. When it is said that parents "lay down the law" to their child, it means that the parents have set rules (usually in a harsh tone of voice) which carry threats for noncompliance. When a legislature passes a law, it provides a rule for the action of officials and citizens which courts are expected to enforce.

One might generalize from the definition of a law to the definition of the Law. The Law could be identified as the sum total of the rules in force in the social group under consideration. If we are thinking of a family, the Law would be every rule made for family members over time (and not rescinded) and every rule that could be logically inferred from the rules given. Likewise the Law of a society would consist of every statute "on the books." By this definition the Law is simply a collective noun like *sheep* or *swine*.

There are a number of serious problems with this collective definition of the Law. First of all, it does not include the necessity of consistency. A legal system must be consistent for decisions to be made and judgments rendered. A person cannot be held accountable for his or her actions if adherence to one rule would entail the violation of another. Any adequate definition of the Law must provide for a consistency precluding contradictory obligations.

Second, the definition suggests that matters not covered by rules are outside the province of law. Since life is infinitely varied and complex, no legal system would be able to govern more than a portion of the situations that might occur. This would mean that persons would have to proceed in numerous situations without any guarantee of rights or knowledge of duties. To minimize these situations, the lawgiver might multiply the rules endlessly, making the social order overly rigid and complex while failing to solve the problem.

Third, the idea that the law is the sum total of commands valid in a given community is too authoritarian. When a child challenges a rule laid down by a parent, the parent may pull rank with "because I said so." Nothing could be more arbitrary and contradictory to the idea of law. Genuine law, as opposed to arbitrary commands, must convince the conscience.

If the collective definition of law is defective, what alternative is there? I propose the following: Law is the order of justice and right to which individuals and groups should conform and which judicial authority should enforce. Rules will necessarily play some role in this order, but there also will be principles and values which form a consistent system, cover all possible situations, and belong to the collective conscience of the community. By this definition, explicit rules—laws—are only the tip of the iceberg of the phenomenon of Law.

To illustrate this definition, let us return to the family. Parents who depend upon rules to govern the behavior of their children will fail to nurture moral character in them. The family ethos should instill values and principles that the child learns to apply independently. When a child encounters temptation, he or she should know without a stated rule the kind of behavior expected. In this way the individual develops a conscience and the power to reason. At times there must be punishment to convey the seriousness of the moral life. Such punishment is legitimate whether a rule has been enunciated or not, for the child is expected to know right from wrong.

The English common law once provided an ideal example of a legal system with a minimum of rules (statutes) and a maximum of moral and legal reasoning and still does to a lesser extent. The Law was an order of justice and right built into the social order and inculcated by the entire social ethos. Statutory law played a minor role; monarch and parliament generally restricted themselves to policy and administration, depending upon legal precedent to chart the scope of rights and duties. Decisions of judges were preserved as examples of the legal reasoning later judges should imitate, but later judges could appeal to principles of justice and right against precedent cases. The Law was always "under review," for the ideal was that the court would give cognizance to the most cogent moral and legal reasoning, whether it followed precedent or created it.

Every legal system is an order of justice and right permeating the entire social organism. Rules or statutes may play a much larger role than they do in common law, but invariably the judicial art of reasoning from precedent, from the principle of consistency, and from shared communal values supplements the rules. The Law is more than the sum total of laws.

Moral and Judicial Law

With the definition of the Law presented in the previous section, a distinction between two categories of law, moral and judicial, can be explained in such a way that both categories can be understood as components of a legal system. Moral law is what a person or group should or should not do irrespective of the legal consequences, whereas judicial law (often termed *positive law*, an expression unfortunately implying fixed statutes) is what sovereign authority is duty-bound to enforce. The two overlap a good deal but not entirely: moral law includes duties that either cannot be enforced or are not, and judicial law covers adjudication where moral fault is not at issue.

An example will aid in explaining the distinction. Imagine yourself before a body of water witnessing a person drowning. What is your duty? Under normal conditions, you would be morally obligated to attempt to rescue the person. If this meant risking your life, you would still be so obligated as long as the risk was not inordinate and your chances of success were reasonably good. However, if the body of water was, say, a raging river or you were not a competent swimmer, you would not be expected to throw your life away. It would be considered moral supererogation to subject yourself to grave risk under the circumstances; if death ensued, it would be accounted heroic.

Though some circumstances would relieve one of moral responsibility for rescuing the drowning person, others would not. Above all, the identity of the person drowning is not a relevant moral factor. If the person were of a different race, a personal enemy, or simply a stranger, the same duty would be owed as to a close friend or family member.

In the Anglo-American legal tradition, the weight of precedent is against holding one legally responsible for failing to perform one's moral duty in a case like this. Neither the state nor the relatives of the deceased would be able to win a criminal or civil judgment for failure of duty. Duties of assistance are too hard to establish. In addition, the threat of punishment for failure to aid would discourage the reporting of accidents and perhaps even discourage acts of mercy.

There are circumstances, however, in which the witness of a drowning becomes legally as well as morally responsible. If the witness were a lifeguard overseeing the body of water, his or her employment would entail the duty of rescuing the drowning person. Either the state, the relatives of the victim, or the employer might punish or exact compensation for failure of duty, since the official position of the lifeguard translates moral duties into legal ones.

The fact that a distinction can be made between moral and judicial law should not be taken to mean that morality can be banished from the concept of law. Moral law is the basis of most judicial law; we punish people when they willfully harm other people or the health of the society, because their actions are wrong. We limit our enforcement of moral law because such enforcement might do more harm than good and the higher reaches of morality may be more than can be required of a citizen. The judicial system can only hold people to the minimum necessary to maintain the peace and well-being of the citizenry. In addition, it must establish and enforce conventions (like driving on the right hand side of the road) to facilitate the smooth functioning of social intercourse.

Law and Community

Legal systems are the creation of the community in which they operate. Each community has its own law, which is binding upon it alone. Thus, law is what a community, with its religion, values, political and economic systems, and experience of living, requires of its members. It is embedded in the fabric of the society and instilled by preaching and practice.

The community's will must be articulated through authorities—kings and parliaments to make statutes, judges to decide cases, clergy to inculcate the divine will, teachers to train the reason, and parents to nurture character in their children. Invariably class bias, parochial interests, and individual perversions are introduced into the law in the process of articulation and implementation. No communal law has the impartiality and beneficence that its apologists are wont to claim for it.

Our age may have learned this lesson too well and turned cynical about the majesty of the Law. The core of every communal law does claim the conscience in spite of the biases and perversions it contains, for rightness is felt to be intrinsic to the order of justice and right embedded in the community. People obey, not just out of fear of—punishment by the authorities, but because they believe the law to be good. When the discrepancy between the community's law and true justice and right becomes too great, persons of sensitive conscience will withdraw allegiance in the name of a higher law.

By "higher law" is meant what is truly just and right. Some may be skeptical of the concept of a higher law, but people actually appeal to it often. The very capacity to argue over what the law should be depends upon the existence of a scheme of principles and values to which both parties in the argument make appeal. The universality of this law is demonstrated by the capacity to visit foreign countries and conform without unreasonable adjustment to the law of each, honoring in those laws the order of justice and right to which all humans are subject.

The existence of a higher law has been the point of departure for philosophical reflection and religious celebration, the latter ascribing the order of justice and right to the will of God and the former arguing for a law of nature known by reason. Both lines of interpretation agree that the mores and laws of actual communities derive their legitimacy and majesty not from the authority of lawgivers but from the capacity to convince the conscience of their justice and rightness. One need not identify with either to recognize the truth of this insight.

The Scope of This Study

With the ideas of what to look for set out, the Law of Hebrew Scripture, known as the Old Testament among Christians, can now be examined. First, an explanation is in order concerning the document to be studied and the method of approach.

There is a built-in ambiguity in the study of Hebrew Scripture. The document is at once the tradition of an ancient society, Israel, and the Word of God for two living religious communities, Judaism and Christianity. As the tradition of an ancient society, the text can be studied for the legal system and scheme of values of that society. As the Scripture for Jews and Christians, the document can be studied for its representation of God and God's will for the people. The approach taken here is one guided by historical considerations, as it seeks to determine the meaning of the texts for the community that produced them. It conforms, however, in one respect to the theological approach, in that the scope of study is limited to the biblical material and its picture of the legal community.

The study is limited to the law of the Old Testament itself, leaving out the interpretive traditions that grew up in Judaism and Christianity. Hebrew Scripture is a literary work in its own right, with a unity and integrity that allows it to be studied apart from either the Talmud or the New Testament. The divine law presented in the Old Testament is the original statement of the will of the biblical God and the basis for the subsequent elaborations, adaptations, and transformations wrought in Jewish and Christian literature. In Chapter Seven I will take a brief look at the interpretation of the divine law in early Judaism and in the New Testament, and in the Postscript I will reflect upon the significance of biblical law for the twentieth-century reader.

Within the Old Testament study, attention is concentrated on a few specific texts, namely, the series of commandments and collections of legal statements found in the Pentateuch, or Torah (Genesis, Exodus, Leviticus, Numbers, and Deuteronomy). The series and collections (or "codes") constitute distinctive genres of literature. One might call them epitomes of the will of the biblical God, highlighting what is expected of God's people in their religious and social behavior. These epitomes are quite distinct from other genres of biblical literature, such as narrative, prophecy, psalms, and proverbs. In addition, they are anchored in the account of one specific event, the covenant making at Mount Sinai, portrayed as the act of founding Israel as a legal community.

Is it legitimate to limit the study to the series and codes of the Pentateuch? Did not the definition of law encompass much more than explicit rules and instruction? Readers of the Old Testament have certainly found divine law elsewhere. Teachers of Jewish tradition, in fact, designate all of the five books of Moses as *torah*, which

means "law" or "legal teaching." They found the earliest commandment of Scripture in the divine blessing to be "fruitful and multiply,
and fill the earth and subdue it" (Gen. 1:28), and from narratives
they drew forth legal teaching of all sorts. In like manner, moral law
could be drawn from practically every prophecy collected in the
books of writing prophets. Wisdom books, particularly Proverbs,
contain voluminous moral teachings and encouragement. Obviously,
Old Testament law is not limited to a few series and codes associated
with the event at Mount Sinai.

It is necessary, however, to limit the subject to a manageable size.
If I took up every text relevant to the moral and judicial law, the
book would grow to enormous dimensions. Nor is my delimitation
arbitrary. As I said above, the series and codes constitute distinct,
related genres of literature. These texts are presented in a context and
with a solemnity that indicate that they were meant to be law in a
special sense. They state the will of the biblical God for the people of
Israel at their founding. One might call them the *official* presentation
of the moral and judicial law of Israel, the people of God.

Another factor in my delimitation of the subject of Old Testament law to the series and codes of the Pentateuch is the neglect of
this set of texts in introductory literature. A survey of published material shows an ample number of introductory works on Israelite
prophecy, wisdom literature, and psalms but virtually nothing on the
series and codes of law (except on the Ten Commandments). This
study is designed to fill the gap in introductory literature.

The Objectives of This Study

This book is intended to be a course of instruction for beginners
and assumes no prior knowledge of the subject. It endeavors to instruct the reader in the methods of critical scholarship as well as to
examine the content of the texts themselves. Moreover, it familiarizes
the reader with series and codes equally rather than concentrating on
favorite ones. It is hoped that the reader will be prepared by this
course of study to pursue further in-depth study of specific legal
texts.

One task is to learn when and where the Pentateuchal series and
codes originated. The capacity to locate a text in a general historical

setting is a necessary condition for understanding the specific import of its communication. It is also necessary to reconstruct the literary conventions to which the authors were adhering and the social settings which cultivated such conventions and preserved the literary deposit.

The most important task is simply to become acquainted with the texts themselves. The heart of the book is an exposition of the statements of series and codes of the Pentateuch. Such exposition begins with deciding what range of action is governed by a rule of law and what sort of enforcement is envisaged.

It then must penetrate beyond the moral and judicial rules of law to the legal concepts and principles that inform them and even further to the world view and system of values that are inculcated through and protected by the presentation of law. This level of analysis involves thinking through the logic of individual provisions and the order of provisions, comparing a text to other biblical and extrabiblical material, and assessing the import of the rhetorical shaping of the presentation of law. Results are less certain as one relies more heavily on imaginative inference, so one must exercise caution and humility; yet the understanding of the full meaning of the text would be impoverished without knowledge of the intellectual and moral foundations of the explicit statements.

A final goal is to relate the presentation of divine law to judicial practice on the one hand and constitutional theory on the other. This involves the attempt to reconstruct the actual process of judicial reasoning in ancient Israel and to assess the role of the series and codes in that process. It also involves examining the narrative contexts of the presentation of law for the constitutional theory presupposed by it.

Set off in a postscript is a discussion of the relevance of biblical law to the modern reader. Some read the Bible as a witness to their God and a source of guidance for their lives; others read it with an interest in the world view and values of an ancient people and the roots of Western civilization. Each reader must learn history and understand texts. Each one must enter imaginatively into the thought process of the original authors and evaluate the cogency of their reasoning in the matter under scrutiny. Each one must follow the influence of a text on subsequent generations and recognize the interconnection of texts that have been gathered together to represent the law in its totality. Only when one reflects upon the meaning of biblical law for the modern reader is it necessary to lay out separate tracks for the divergent ways of appropriating biblical literature.

SUGGESTED READING

At the end of each chapter, I will recommend articles and books on the subjects covered in the chapter. All works mentioned in the chapter will be listed, as well as introductions, commentaries, monographs, and articles which would advance the reader's knowledge or present alternative viewpoints. These are primarily works in English generally accessible to an American reader; materials written in foreign languages or published in obscure journals are included only by reason of their singular importance. If the reader desires to pursue a subject more thoroughly, the bibliographies of the works cited can be consulted.

A noncritical introduction to Old Testament law:

Falk, Z. W. *Hebrew Law in Biblical Times, An Introduction*. Jerusalem: Wahrmann Books, 1964.

There are numerous books available on the concept of law. The following are a selection that I have found useful:

Lloyd, Dennis. *The Idea of Law*. Baltimore: Penguin Books, 1964.
Pound, Roscoe. *An Introduction to the Philosophy of Law*. New Haven and London: Yale University Press, 1922.

A general discussion of the religious dimension of law:

Berman, Harold J. *The Interaction of Law and Religion*. Nashville and New York: Abingdon Press, 1974.

Histories of the philosophy of law:

Friedrich, Carl J. *The Philosophy of Law in Historical Perspective*. 2d ed. Chicago: University of Chicago Press, 1963.
Morris, Clarence (ed.). *The Great Legal Philosophers: Selected Readings in Jurisprudence*. Philadelphia: University of Pennsylvania Press, 1959.

Treatments of technical aspects of law:

Black, Henry C. *Black's Law Dictionary*. 4th ed. St. Paul: West Publishing Co., 1968.
Levi, Edward H. *An Introduction to Legal Reasoning*. Chicago: University of Chicago Press, 1949.

Treatments of the nature and method of English common law:

Blackstone, William. *Commentaries on the Laws of England*. 4 vols. Adapted by R. M. Kerr. Boston: Beacon Press, 1962. This is a classic.

Pound, Roscoe. *The Spirit of the Common Law*. Boston: Beacon Press, 1949.

A contemporary description and defense of the common law theory and practice:

Dworkin, Ronald. *Taking Rights Seriously*. Cambridge: Harvard University Press, 1977.

Waltzer, Michael. Review of *Taking Rights Seriously*, by Ronald Dworkin. *The New Republic* 176, no. 26 (1977), pp. 28–31. A lucid account of Dworkin's argument.

Chapter Two

HOW LAW
IS STUDIED BY
CRITICAL SCHOLARS

The beginning student of Scripture should be introduced to the methods and kinds of evidence employed by modern biblical scholars before being invited to interpret the text. The uninitiated reader is inclined to take the text for granted and proceed to interpret it without awareness of the shaping of culture and history. In previous eras, the dogmatic and theological teaching of the synagogue and church supplemented a rather meager knowledge of history as this framework. During the last two centuries, the study of the Bible has gradually become an independent intellectual discipline with its own methods, evidence, and criteria of validation. This intellectual discipline can be called critical biblical scholarship.

A method of textual interpretation, or exegesis, is simply a set of related questions to be applied to the text and the systematic procedure by which answers are found. What is the correct text and how is it to be translated? Who wrote the text? In which historical setting did he write? What were the literary conventions under which he wrote? Whence did he derive his material and ideas? Under what authority did he write? Questions of this sort have prompted scholars to develop a body of evidence, kinds of argument, and interpretive hypotheses to provide answers.

Aside from the study of the textual traditions and Hebrew language—once called *lower criticism*—the most widely accepted and employed method for interpreting Old Testament literature is *source criticism* (sometimes called *literary criticism*). The source critic attempts to identify the authors of texts and locate them within history and culture. Once this has been accomplished, two other methods come into play: *form criticism* and *tradition history*. The form critic endeavors to determine the literary conventions under which the text was composed and the social context suggested by those conventions. The traditio-historical critic seeks to trace the oral and written sources of an author's information and ideas.

The literature of the Old Testament came into being in the midst of the large, complex civilization of the ancient Near East. Vast quantities of texts from this civilization have been unearthed, deciphered, and published and are now available to the critical biblical scholar as aids in philological, source, form, and traditio-historical interpretation.

The cumulative work of textual interpretation creates the basis for critical history. By critical history is meant the reconstruction of the life and institutions of the people under consideration, in this case ancient Israel. In this chapter the methods of textual interpretation will be examined in preparation for reading the legal texts, and the methods of critical history will be reserved for the chapters in which historical reconstruction is undertaken.

Source Criticism

Much biblical literature was written anonymously. The source critic seeks to identify the authors, if not by name at least by historical period, geographical location, cultural and political group, and distinctive personal characteristics. The critic uses the evidence of vocabulary and style and distinctive social, cultural, and theological ideas to determine authorship. In narrative literature, one may establish the contributions of several authors through the lack of narrative coherence and smoothness and attempt to reconstruct the original story of each. If it is possible, each story is associated with other narratives by the same author, and inferences can be drawn from the whole body of his work as to when and where he wrote.

The development and confirmation of hypotheses is central to source criticism. To account for the evidence, theories are constructed as to what authors contributed to a given biblical book or set of books, when and where they wrote, and how they can be distinguished from one another. A theory must also account for the collection and integration of these various sources into the present biblical text. As a hypothesis, each theory is under continual scrutiny, revision, refinement, and challenge by others.

Source Criticism of the Pentateuch. The texts of biblical law are restricted to the first five books of the Old Testament, known in Jewish tradition as the Torah and in modern scholarship as the Pentateuch. For much of the history of the synagogue and church, the authorship of these books was attributed to Moses. There are references within the Pentateuch to Moses' writing the laws revealed to him (for example, Exod. 24:3; 34:27–28; Deut. 31:9), but one must go to late Jewish authors and the New Testament to find the belief that he wrote the entire five books. Once this idea took hold, however, it held the mind of the synagogue and church in its grip for two thousand years. Occasionally there were scholarly or pious demurrers to the consensus, but it took the Enlightenment's rationalistic attack on all tradition to begin to dislodge it.

The beginnings of the source hypothesis that now holds sway in critical scholarship are in the eighteenth century. The person to be credited with discovering the clue to solving the mystery of Pentateuchal authorship is Jean Astruc, private physician to Louis XV. In an endeavor to explain to skeptics how Moses could have known of the events that transpired before his time, Astruc proposed the existence of sources for Genesis that Moses edited into their present form. To identify these sources, he analysed the pattern of divine names in Genesis. Some passages use the Hebrew name *YHWH* (vocalized "Yahweh," translated "the LORD" in the RSV), while others use *Elohim*, "God" (RSV), and a few have still other names, such as "God Eternal," "God Most High," "God Almighty," and "God of Bethel." From this evidence Astruc deduced two chief sources and about ten fragmentary sources for Genesis.

In the last quarter of the eighteenth century the German Old Testament scholar Eichhorn expanded the basis of Astruc's theory by associating style and content with the divine names. In this way a body of evidence began to build that would facilitate the development of the mature hypothesis approximately a century later. In subsequent years the sources were found to continue throughout the Pentateuch, and so Astruc's idea of Mosaic editing of Genesis and authorship of Leviticus-Deuteronomy fell by the wayside. At the same time, the two main sources of Genesis were subdivided.

In 1805, W. M. L. de Wette published a study of Deuteronomy

that was to prove momentous for the progress of source analysis. He was able to identify Deuteronomy as the book of law that was found in the temple in the eighteenth year of Josiah's reign (621 B.C.) and made the basis of his religious and political reform (recounted in 2 Kings 22:3–23:25). Deuteronomy calls for the recognition of only one legitimate place of sacrifice, and Josiah's reform is predicated upon such a provision. With de Wette's breakthrough, it was possible not only to distinguish Deuteronomy from the other Pentateuchal sources but to fix an absolute date for one source and a principle for dating the others, which was: those writings presupposing the centralization of the sacrificial cultus must come after the publication of Deuteronomy (hence, after 621), while those knowing no such provision probably precede it.

During the next three-quarters of the nineteenth century, evidence continued to accumulate and its interpretation was refined. The central problem was the development of a relative chronology, that is, determining the sequence of sources. The solution finally came in the form of a philosophical theory of development which placed the priestly and cultic regulations at the end of the evolution of Israelite religion. Julius Wellhausen is to be credited with bringing the developmental theory and textual evidence together to produce the classical synthesis of Pentateuchal source criticism, known now as the Graf-Wellhausen hypothesis. His most influential work is still available in English translation under the title *Prolegomena to the History of Ancient Israel.*

According to the Graf-Wellhausen hypothesis, the Pentateuch is a combination of four major sources and a number of independent blocks of material and editorial links and comments. There are three narrative sources whose authors are named for outstanding characteristics: the Yahwist (siglum J), the Elohist (E), and the Priestly writer (P). The Yahwist is named for his use of the divine name "Yahweh" throughout the work and the Elohist for his use of the divine name "Elohim" in Genesis and preference for that name in Exodus and Numbers. The Priestly Source also uses "Elohim" in Genesis but switches to "Yahweh" in Exodus 6:2 and uses it consistently in the rest of the Pentateuch. The name "Priestly writer" comes from his cultic interests and prosaic style. The fourth major

Pentateuchal source is the Deuteronomist (D), whose contribution is restricted to the book of Deuteronomy.

The order of writing, according to Wellhausen and the majority of subsequent source critics, was JEDP. Wellhausen dated J about 850 and E about 750, but many scholars—including this author—would place the Yahwist in the Solomonic renaissance (c. 950 B.C., Judah) and the Elohist in the prophetic movement associated with Elijah (c. 850 B.C., Israel). When the Northern Kingdom, Israel, was destroyed in 721, the northern traditions, which included E, migrated to Jerusalem and were combined with the Yahwist in the following century. The work of the Deuteronomist must have been executed in the century before its publication in 621. The Priestly writer seems to have been among the Babylonian exiles (hence, after 587 B.C.), and the publication of the work may perhaps be associated with Ezra's return to Jerusalem (between 458 and 398 B.C.) with the "book of the law of the God of heaven" (Ezra 7:12; see also Neh. 8). It is possible, however, that Ezra's "law" was the whole of the Torah.

Source Criticism of the Legal Texts.   With one major exception and a few minor ones, God's law for the people of Israel is delivered as a part of the revelation and covenant making that occurs on Mount Sinai. The Sinaitic account runs all the way from Exodus 19 through the entire book of Leviticus to Numbers 10. The major exception is the address of Moses to the people on the plain of Moab just before he dies, recounted in the book of Deuteronomy.

Within the large mass of Sinaitic materials, it is possible to distinguish the older account from P's with relative ease. The older Sinaitic material is much less extensive, consisting only of Exodus 19–24, 32–34. It includes the appearance of God to the people, the proclamation of the Ten Commandments, the delivery of the Book of the Covenant to Moses, the ratification of the covenant between God and the people, the making of a "golden calf" and the breaking of the tablets, the appearance of God to Moses upon the mountain, and the revelation of a second Ten Commandments. There are numerous problems of sequence and coherence, indicating the existence of several strands which include the Yahwist and Elohist and various isolated blocks of material.

The series known in synagogue and church tradition as the Ten Commandments, or Decalogue, is the first legal text in the Sinaitic account (Exod. 20:2–17). God proclaims these commandments directly to the people during a dramatic appearance before them. In Deuteronomy 5, the event is recalled and the same series repeated with a few slight differences in wording. In the Exodus text the series is introduced by a statement using the divine name "Elohim" (God) and is followed by a passage (20:18–21) also using this name. This evidence is sufficient to make a preliminary identification of Exodus 20:2–17 as Elohist.

There is another series that purports to be the Commandments revealed to Moses on Mount Sinai: Exodus 34:11–26. According to the present narrative, Moses breaks the tablets of the testimony written by God (Exod. 32:15–20). Consequently, he must make new tablets, ascend the mountain, receive and write down the Commandments again, and deliver them to the people (Exod. 34). Verse 28 explicitly asserts that verses 11–26 constitute a decalogue:

> And [Moses] wrote upon the tables the words of the covenant, the ten commandments [words].

Since chapter 34 uses the divine name "Yahweh" and contains expressions and ideas characteristic of the Yahwist, this series can be called the Yahwist Decalogue.

There is one other legal text in the older Sinaitic account: Exodus 20:23–23:19. This large collection of commandments and judgments covering a wide range of judicial and moral topics is called the "Book of the Covenant" in the Exodus text (24:7) and occasionally the "Covenant Code" (C) by scholars. Since this code cannot belong to either the Yahwist or Elohist, it must be an independent document inserted into the Sinaitic narrative in the process of editing the text.

The Priestly account (Exod. 25–31, 35–40; Lev. 1–27; Num. 1–10) relates the revelation and construction of the portable sanctuary known as the tabernacle, the imposition of regulations for the operation of this sanctuary and camp, the proclamation of law for the laity and priests, and directions for the arrangement of the camp on pilgrimage.

P preserves a mass of legal materials. One of the portions stands out as an independent body of literature: Leviticus 17—26. It has been given the name "Holiness Code" (H) by scholars for the distinctive formula that runs through it: "You shall be holy; for I, Yahweh, am holy" (Lev. 19:2; 20:7). Like the Book of the Covenant, H has laws governing a wide range of topics. It probably antedated P and underwent a revision when P incorporated it.

The remainder of the Priestly account of Sinai and the trek through the wilderness is a blend of narrative and law. It is difficult to decide which portions should be accorded the status of legal text. The sacrificial law (Lev. 1—7) and purification rules (Lev. 11—15) can safely be accorded the status of law, as can the regulations for the Day of Atonement (Lev. 17) and scattered passages in the book of Numbers.

Deuteronomy contains the one legal text that does not purport to be revealed by God through Moses on Mount Sinai to Israel. Chapters 1—31 have the form of an address of Moses to the people. Within the address of Moses, chapters 12—26 constitute a code of laws. As was said earlier, this code, and probably some portion of the sermonic framework, can be identified as the book of Mosaic Law found in the temple in the eighteenth year of Josiah's reign (621 B.C.) and made the basis of his reform. Although many scholars would limit the temple code to a small portion of Deuteronomy 12—26, these chapters exhibit, with a few exceptions, such an impressive unity in style, thought, and point of view that they can safely be treated as a single code.

This locates the legal texts to be studied and identifies the sources to which they belong.

Form Criticism

Once the authorship of a text has been decided, the twentieth-century biblical scholar finds it necessary to seek the identity of the oral or literary conventions employed by the author or preserved in the traditions from which the author drew. The assumption underlying this method is that a person speaks or writes according to social and literary conventions which are passed on by institutions and the cultural milieu. Just as people learn their native language by engaging in social intercourse, they learn when it is appropriate to say what. We learn, for example, when we should and should not tell a joke, and what type of joke is in good taste. Social setting dictates whether we should deliver a lecture or engage in small talk, and we learn how to do each by imitation and experimentation. More formal types of speaking and writing are learned through apprenticeship and disciplined instruction.

Form criticism as an independent method came into its own during the first decades of this century with the precedent-setting work of Hermann Gunkel and his associates on psalms, prophecy, and simple narratives. Their procedure was to classify units of literature according to type, identified by generic features characteristic of each kind of utterance, and to determine the setting in social and institutional life to which each type of speaking or writing originally belonged.

The big hurdle for the beginning student is learning to recognize the generic features that identify passages as being of the same speech type or form and to develop a classification scheme based upon these features. The method has been made more difficult by the fact that practitioners have differed among themselves as to what generic features are relevant to formal classification and how a classification system should be constructed. Some scholars, for example, seize upon the minutest details of style and rhetorical structure as a basis of classification, while others search for basic structures and general stylistic qualities as a guide to a relatively simple, synthetic classification scheme. Again, some scholars seek to understand the speech forms from the social settings in which they were used, while others concentrate on the texts and their interrelationship.

Despite the unsettled state of the art, the beginner can grasp some gross formal distinctions with ease. In the Sinaitic material, for example, one can distinguish the *narrative* portion of the account from the *legal corpora*. A narrative recounts the interaction of personages within a temporal framework; a legal corpus enunciates a series of timeless rules for the behavior of a designated group of people. The next step is to begin to classify types of narrative and legal corpora. The legal corpora in Exodus, Leviticus, Numbers, and Deuteronomy can be divided into two types: *series*, texts consisting of a relatively small number of rules formulated in similar style, and *codes*, texts consisting of a large number of rules covering a broad spectrum of subjects in some detail. A comparative study of the various codes and series of the Pentateuch and in the ancient Near Eastern milieu would yield other generic features. Now one can move to an analysis and classification of the building blocks of the legal corpora, the rules or *legal formulations*.

Form Criticism of Biblical Law. The form-critical investigation of biblical law made its first great strides at the micro level with the legal formulations. A number of attempts at identification and classification were made in the 1920s and 1930s. The German scholar Albrecht Alt brought earlier efforts together in an elegant synthesis in his monograph, "The Origins of Israelite Law" (in *Essays on Old Testament History and Religion*, 1966). His study has established itself as the point of departure for all subsequent form criticism of biblical law.

Alt reduced the multiplicity of styles and patterns of formulation to be found in legal texts to two basic categories: apodictic and casuistic law. The term *apodictic* suggests an unconditional, categorical assertion of right and wrong. It is an apt characterization of the prohibitions to be found in the Ten Commandments:

> You shall not kill.   (Exod. 20:13)

The person bound by the rule is directly addressed in an utterance which excludes a category of action without qualification. Alt maintained that some other formulations differing in style and sentence structure also fit the description of apodictic law:

> Whoever strikes a man so that he dies shall be put to death.   (Exod. 21:12)
> Cursed be he who slays his neighbor in secret.   (Deut. 27:24)

These two sentences differ from the commandment in their impersonal style and provision for punishment, but they resemble the latter in their categorical and unconditional quality.

The name of Alt's other category, *casuistic law*, was coined from the word *case*. A law of this type defines a specific case, distinguishes it carefully from other similar cases, and stipulates the legal consequences:

> When men quarrel and one strikes the other with a stone or with his fist
> and the man does not die but keeps his bed, then if the man rises again and
> walks abroad with his staff, he that struck him shall be clear; only he shall
> pay for the loss of his time, and shall have him thoroughly healed.
> (Exod. 21:18–19)

Not only is the style of this rule impersonal, but the rule is not
even concerned with moral right and wrong but with legal responsibility. Note how cluttered it is with qualifying phrases and
clauses defining the facts of the case and the duties of the party
held responsible. The overall pattern of casuistic formulation is
twofold: a *protasis* with a *when* and subordinate *if* clauses describing the case, and an *apodosis* stating the legal consequences of the
case described in the protasis.

Both apodictic and casuistic laws tend to be grouped together in
homogenous units. Apodictic law is invariably presented in series, of
which there are two kinds: comprehensive summaries of the fundamental violations of the social order, and concentrated treatment of
one specific topic. Serialization of grammatically similar and stylistically terse, emphatic sentences lends a poetic quality to apodictic law.
Units of casuistic laws are logically ordered; similar cases are treated
together and juxtaposed to cases with different rulings. Although
casuistic groups have a regular pattern, they would hardly strike one
as poetic.

Alt proposed a different cultural origin and setting in life for his
two categories of law. Since casuistic law with similar style and subject matter is found in ancient royal codes from around the Fertile
Crescent, Alt surmised that Israel borrowed this law from the indige-
nous culture after settlement in Canaan. The careful juridical reasoning of casuistic law suggested to him that it was formulated by jurists
for the instruction and guidance of subsequent judges.

Alt gave apodictic law a distinctively Israelite pedigree. The unconditional, categorical quality of apodictic series bespoke, he
thought, the spirit of biblical religion. Lacking the delicate weighing
of factors necessary for legal litigation, they could not be judicial law.
He traced them to a social setting "in which the whole people, and
through them their God, could adopt the imperative tone towards

individuals, and impose on them the absolute prohibitions, or threats of a curse or of death" (Alt, *Essays*, 125). This setting was the periodic assembly of the tribes to renew their covenant with Yahweh.

Critique and Reconstruction. Various components in Alt's synthesis have come under fire during the last two decades. Probably the strongest single assault was made by Erhard Gerstenberger. First, he insisted that the addressed commandments be kept formally separate from the formulations stipulating capital punishment or pronouncing a curse. Second, he demonstrated that the commandments were not unique to Israel but could be found in ancient Near Eastern (and biblical) wisdom books and cultic liturgies. From this fact he concluded that Israel adapted the form to the presentation of law. Third, he traced the form back to the patriarchal instruction of the clan during the pre-settlement era; it was adapted to various social settings after settlement, when patriarchal authority gradually passed to tribal elders and ruling elites. The formation of comprehensive series like the Ten Commandments stood at the end of the process.

Gerstenberger's critique of Alt's synthesis is certainly cogent. Alt's apodictic category must certainly be divided in two, and the commandment form must be associated with ancient Near Eastern parallels. On the other hand, Gerstenberger's theory of the original setting of the form—patriarchal instruction of the clan—smacks of romanticism. It is sufficient to say that religious and moral instruction was a common ancient Near Eastern practice, and Israel soon adapted the practice to the oral presentation of God's will.

I believe that Alt's category of casuistic law must also be divided in two. One species of casuistic law is *remedial*—the case is described in the protasis (*if* clause), and the legal remedy (usually a penalty for violation of rights) is prescribed in the apodosis. The other species of casuistic law is *primary law*—the protasis describes a legal relationship, and the apodosis prescribes the terms of the relationship (rights and duties before violation). The distinction between primary and remedial casuistic law would be only a minor refinement if it were not for the fact that primary law developed in the direction of personally addressed commandments in biblical law:

> If you lend money to any of my people with you who is poor, you shall not be to him as a creditor, and you shall not exact interest from him. (Exod. 22:25)

Here is an instance of a law whose formal casuistic structure is still recognizable but whose style has changed significantly. Not only has the style changed from impersonal to personal address, but the language is more emotive than in impersonally formulated casuistic law. These changes are typical of casuistic primary law within the Pentateuchal lawbooks.

The modifications of Alt's classification scheme can be summarized in a diagram:

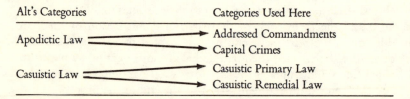

Alt's Categories	Categories Used Here
Apodictic Law	Addressed Commandments
	Capital Crimes
Casuistic Law	Casuistic Primary Law
	Casuistic Remedial Law

As one works through the texts of the legal corpora, there will be occasion to note a few other categories of law and law-related material which will not be dealt with at this point. The formal analysis of legal corpora will also be saved for a later time. The reader should have a basic grasp of the method of form-critical analysis and a working classification system for the study of biblical law. Refinements can be made as specific texts are examined.

The History of Tradition

The word *tradition* means simply "that which is passed on." One generally associates the word with stories, beliefs, rules, and customs transmitted without rational scrutiny from generation to generation by word of mouth or imitation. But one must not be too narrow. Oral traditions can be attached to texts to function as commentary and supplement. It is even legitimate to speak of written traditions in a culture that transmitted texts as it transmitted oral lore. (Remember, there were no publishers, copyrights, book distributors, or public libraries in antiquity.) Something is a tradition when it is the possession of a group, is passed from generation to generation, and is relatively stable but malleable.

The critical method known as the history of tradition is predicated upon the assumption that ancient Israelite authors received much of what they wrote from oral sources, and that their writings were preserved by groups as a part of a larger stream of ancestral lore. The task of the historian of tradition is to identify what a given author received, the group to which the received lore belonged, the geographical area to which it was attached, and the social formations and institutions to which it gave meaning and justification. The ways the critics go about answering these questions are difficult to specify, for tradition history is the least systematic of the methods discussed here. Though everyone can agree that oral tradition played an important role in early Israelite culture and that written works were handled as tradition, there seems to be minimal consensus as to the postulates and procedures by which to study the phenomenon. Consequently, there are few widely shared hypotheses to center the discussion.

Something can be said, however, about the aim and method of tradition history. The first task is to identify the tradition to which a text belongs. One can do so by identifying a linguistic idiom, literary style, speech form, idea, myth, or reference to a place or group that the text under scrutiny shares with other texts (including nonbiblical texts) by other authors; to account for the matter in common, one may postulate that it was transmitted in some identifiable channel (a group, place, or institution) to the authors of the different texts.

One can see that a text seldom belongs to only one tradition but rather is the intersection of a number of traditions. Perhaps it will share a linguistic idiom with one set of texts, an idea with another, and a place reference with yet another. One may postulate that the author had access to three different channels of tradition. The task of the traditio-historical critic is to locate the text in tradition by tracing the various traditions that intersect within it.

Another task is to fix the place of a text in a given tradition by examining all the texts with some matter in common and devising a hypothesis as to how they are related. Often the hypothesis includes a scheme of development. One may, for example, attempt to follow an idea from its origin to its dissemination and divers adaptations. A given speech form, which can be classified as one kind of tradition, has a history of modification within the changes of culture and historical conditions. Such a developmental scheme is speculative and should be kept under check, but it may prove valuable for further location of a text in tradition.

Tradition History of Biblical Law. There is no single hypothesis centering the traditio-historical study of law to the degree that Alt's hypothesis centers form criticism. However, there are numerous fruitful studies of Israelite law within the context of ancient Near Eastern legal tradition and within the framework of the covenant.

When a biblical legal formulation or corpora share technical wording, form, subject matter, legal principle, or similar ordering with an extrabiblical text from the ancient Near East, one can postulate a tradition flowing between the two peoples. The study of this sharing locates biblical law within the larger civilization to which Israel belonged and also helps to isolate its unique features.

Biblical law is presented as a constituent part of a larger complex of tradition, the covenant between Yahweh and Israel. Every series and code preserved in the Pentateuch is anchored in a covenant-making account, and these narratives prepare for the proclamation of the divine will to Israel or put it in force. Each legal corpus evinces the covenant setting in the speaker and addressee and in the provisions of the law and their homiletical amplification.

A complex of tradition is any grouping of texts that are bound together by some essential formal or material feature or features. The essential feature or features exercise a gravitational pull on consanguineous material, resulting in a contiguous collection or repetitive association in the biblical text. The Sinaitic literature is bound together by a number of common features: all the material depicts the same event at the same place (assuming Horeb to be the same as Sinai); the material employs common formulae and solemn expressions; the diverse strands follow a comparatively similar agenda; and the event is portrayed as having the same action, namely, the establishment of Israel as a legal community under Yahweh, its divine sovereign.

Deuteronomy records another event at another place, but the depiction suggests a "repetition" of the Sinaitic action. In that it shares the language and agenda of the Sinaitic materials and reproduces portions of the Exodus text, Deuteronomy certainly belongs to the covenant complex. Joshua 24, 1 Samuel 12, and Psalm 50 also recall the Sinaitic narrative sufficiently to be included in this complex of traditions.

In an epoch-making study, "The Form-Critical Problem of the Hexateuch," the renowned German scholar Gerhard von Rad argued that the Sinaitic covenant complex was originally independent of the story of the exodus from Egypt, the wandering in the wilderness, and the conquest of the land of Canaan. The Sinaitic tradition was transmitted at a festival of covenant renewal celebrated annually at the Feast of Booths in the city of Shechem. The agenda of the covenant-making narrative followed the agenda of the covenant-renewal festival; the materials ascribed to the Sinaitic covenant-making event actually developed in the course of re-enactment. By a cultic process of collapsing time, the material that came into being as a part of the repetition of the event was transferred to the original.

Von Rad's thesis was attacked from both the right and the left. Some scholars disputed his separation of the Sinaitic covenant-making complex of tradition from the exodus-wilderness-conquest complex. Others disputed the existence of a covenant-renewal ceremony. While points have been scored against the thesis by both parties, one can still agree with von Rad that the covenant material constitutes an independent complex of tradition which took shape in some sort of periodic public gathering.

This discussion should be sufficient for a beginning student to understand the reasoning that goes into statements locating a legal corpus in tradition and to recognize the specific theory of a covenant complex employed and developed here.

The Legal Documents of the Ancient Near East

The literature of the Old Testament was composed and preserved by a people that belonged to the large, complex civilization of the ancient Near East stretching from the Tigris and Euphrates valleys in the east to central Turkey in the north, and from the Mediterranean Sea into the Nile valley in the southwest. For the last two millennia, biblical interpreters have had to rely on what the Bible and a few Greek, Jewish, and Roman authors said for their knowledge of this civilization, as its writings and art were lost, buried in the debris of destroyed cities. During the last century, the archaeological excavation of Near Eastern sites has unearthed vast quantities of texts, works of art, artifacts, and construction that together reveal the true dimensions of the civilization and enable the biblical scholar to locate Israel in a historical and cultural context with a degree of depth and detail unimaginable in earlier eras.

No area of biblical studies has benefited more from the recovery of ancient Near Eastern literature than law. A number of ancient royal codes have been discovered and deciphered which have numerous points of contact with Old Testament legal texts. To supplement and correct the testimony of the codes, there are royal enactments, treaties and records, records of court decisions, and private contracts and letters. In addition to these, there are cultic rituals and wisdom instruction to fill in where judicial law leaves off. The evaluation and synthesis of this vast quantity of material is still far from complete, and new caches of texts are still being unearthed, but there has been sufficient advance in the understanding of ancient Near Eastern law and culture to apply it to every stage of the interpretation of biblical law.

There is no one method of comparative study. The ancient Near Eastern texts are useful in understanding Hebrew words, idiomatic expressions, and technical terminology and in identifying types of law. They contain antecedents to specific biblical laws and concepts and provide clues to the mentality of ancient Near Eastern moral instruction and juridical practice.

For the student of Scripture who has not mastered the languages in which the texts were written, *Ancient Near Eastern Texts Relating to the Old Testament*, edited by J. B. Pritchard, is indispensable. This is a massive anthology of ancient writings in English translation, including the translation of seven royal codes and a sampling of treaties, directives, and juridical documents in the section devoted to law.

In other sections there are letters, moral instruction, and cultic texts that also have a bearing on biblical law.

Three royal codes date from the Sumerian period of Mesopotamian history. Sumer was the complex of city-states at the mouth of the Tigris and Euphrates rivers sharing the same language, religion, and material culture. Sumerian culture flourished throughout the third millennium, then was subjugated by Akkad (near Babylon) for several centuries, after which it experienced a political and literary revival lasting into the second millennium. It is from the revival period that the three extant codes derive. The Laws of Ur-Nammu (c. 2100 B.C.) are named after the ruler under whose auspices the code was drawn up, who was the founder of the Third Dynasty of the city of Ur. The Code of Lipit-Ishtar is also named for the patron king, the ruler of the Sumerian city of Isin during the first half of the nineteenth century B.C. Both codes have poetic prologues and epilogues praising their respective kings and threatening divine retribution for defacement of the monument. A third code, the Laws of Eshnunna, derives from the Sumerian kingdom of that name from about the same time as Lipit-Ishtar. None of the three codes is preserved in the original, and all are fragmentary. Nonetheless, they are sufficiently well preserved to convey their scope, style, and content and the ideological purpose behind their creation.

Hammurabi (1728–1686 B.C.) was the great conqueror of the Near East in the second millennium, extending the sway of the Babylonian monarchy until it encompassed most of the Tigris and Euphrates valleys. The code drawn up under his auspices and named after him was a major cultural bequest to ancient civilization. What was probably the original copy of the code, a huge stone monument inscribed with the laws and topped by a bas-relief showing the sun-god Shamash commissioning Hammurabi to write them, was discovered by French archaeologists excavating Susa 1901–1902. It was one of the great archaeological discoveries of the century, the first of all the codes to be found, and in all probability the greatest code in ancient Near Eastern history. It comprises nearly 300 paragraphs covering public duties and a vast array of citizens' causes. In addition, it contains a long poetic prologue praising Hammurabi and an epilogue describing how he has established justice and cursing anyone who would alter his law or deface his monument.

The codes in our possession from the time after Hammurabi are not named after and cannot be ascribed to the act of a king, so that "royal code" may no longer be applicable. The collection known as the Middle Assyrian Laws derives from the ancient city of Asshur, situated on the Tigris River some 250 miles north of Babylon, from the twelfth century B.C. or earlier. This rather extensive collection was preserved on clay tablets, without prologue or epilogue. The collection known as the Hittite Laws derives from the ancient kingdom of Hatti, situated in central Turkey, from the fourteenth century B.C. These laws are important because they belong to a different linguistic and cultural tradition than the others. A third collection, known as the Neo-Babylonian Laws, derives from the years of the Chaldean empire (609–538 B.C.) and is the only one of the ancient Near Eastern codes from the Israelite period. It is much shorter than the rest, and only about half of it is preserved.

To reiterate, the codes just identified represent only a small portion of material relevant to legal studies. From the evidence of the actual practice of law, there is some question as to how closely the codes conform to practice. However, the codes are easy to consult and have additional value as major public monuments of their own time, vaunted by their creators and esteemed by subsequent rulers and the general populace. Thus, unlike juridical records, private contracts, and so forth, the codes were the product of conscious intellectual, literary, and artistic effort and constitute examples of "high culture." The codes found in Scripture were probably inspired by these and similar examples of the art of codification.

A Final Comment on the Art of Interpretation

The beginning student of Scripture should now be able to engage in the critical study of law. Learning to use the methods and comparative literature discussed in this chapter requires practice, but in time one will be able to follow the arguments of critical biblical scholars and assess them.

These methods need to be supplemented in the study of law by legal exegesis, that is, the interpretation of a text to uncover its legal doctrine. It was a scholar trained in Roman law, David Daube, who more than anyone else taught biblical scholars to read the texts for their legal concepts, principles, and reasoning. He researched biblical law with a subtlety and sophistication that has eluded critical biblical scholars. Although one should exercise care in adopting his readings, his use of legal reasoning can be imitated to expound the subject matter of the text.

SUGGESTED READING

For the policy informing this selection, see the statement introducing the bibliography at the end of Chapter One. Authors and works cited in Chapter Two:

Alt, Albrecht. "The Origins of Israelite Law." In *Essays on Old Testament History and Religion*, trans. R. A. Wilson, pp. 79–132. Oxford: Basil Blackwell, 1966.

Daube, David. *Studies in Biblical Law*. New York: Ktav Publishing House, 1969.

Gerstenberger, Erhard. *Wesen und Herkunft des "Apodiktischen Rechts."* Wissenschaftliche Monographien zum Alten und Neuen Testament, vol. 20. Neukirchen-Vluyn: Neukirchener Verlag, 1965.

————. "Covenant and Commandment," *Journal of Biblical Literature* 84 (1965), pp. 38–51.

Gunkel, Hermann. *The Psalms*. Trans. T. M. Horner. Facet Books Biblical Series, no. 19. Philadelphia: Fortress Press, 1967.

Pritchard, James B. (ed.). *Ancient Near Eastern Texts Relating to the Old Testament*. 2d ed. Legal texts trans. S. N. Kramer, Albrecht Goetze, Theophile J. Meek, John A. Wilson, and H. L. Ginsberg. Princeton: Princeton University Press, 1955.

————. *The Ancient Near East: Supplementary Texts Relating to the Old Testament*. Legal texts trans. J. J. Finkelstein, Albrecht Goetze, Erica Reiner, and H. L. Ginsberg. Princeton: Princeton University Press, 1969.

von Rad, Gerhard. "The Form-Critical Problem of the Hexateuch." In *The Problem of the Hexateuch and Other Essays*, trans. E. W. Trueman Dicken, pp. 1–78. Edinburgh and London: Oliver & Boyd, 1966.

Wellhausen, Julius. *Prolegomena to the History of Ancient Israel*. Cleveland and New York: Meridian Books, 1957.

Of the numerous introductions to the literature of the Old Testament, the following have distinguished themselves for their thoroughness, originality, or judiciousness:

Driver, S. R. *An Introduction to the Literature of the Old Testament*. Cleveland and New York: Meridian Books, 1956. Thorough and judicious source analysis.

Eissfeldt, Otto. *The Old Testament: An Introduction*. Trans. Peter R. Ackroyd. New York and Evanston: Harper & Row, Publishers, 1965. Exhaustive discussion of scholarly opinion.

Fohrer, Georg. *Introduction to the Old Testament.* Trans. David E. Green. Nashville and New York: Abingdon Press, 1968. A thorough discussion of the scholarly methodologies and hypotheses.

Kaufmann, Yehezkel. *The Religion of Israel: From Its Beginnings to the Babylonian Exile.* Trans. Moshe Greenberg. Chicago: University of Chicago Press, 1960. Offers original solutions to old problems.

Pfeiffer, Robert H. *Introduction to the Old Testament.* New York: Harper & Brothers, 1941. Gives clear reasoning for source divisions.

Handbooks explaining critical methods of biblical scholarship:

Habel, Norman C. *Literary Criticism of the Old Testament.* Guides to Biblical Scholarship, Old Testament Series (henceforth = Guides). Philadelphia: Fortress Press, 1971.

Klein, Ralph W. *Textual Criticism of the Old Testament.* Guides. Philadelphia: Fortress Press, 1971.

Krentz, Edgar. *The Historical-Critical Method.* Guides. Philadelphia: Fortress Press, 1975.

Miller, James Maxwell. *The Old Testament and the Historian.* Guides. Philadelphia: Fortress Press, 1976.

Rast, Walter E. *Tradition History and the Old Testament.* Guides. Philadelphia: Fortress Press, 1972.

Tucker, Gene M. *Form Criticism of the Old Testament.* Guides. Philadelphia: Fortress Press, 1971.

More advanced treatments of specific critical methods:

Hayes, John H. (ed). *Old Testament Form Criticism.* San Antonio: Trinity University Press, 1974. See especially W. Malcolm Clark, "Law," pp. 99–139.

Knight, Douglas A. *Rediscovering the Traditions of Israel: The Development of the Tradi-tio-Historical Research of the Old Testament, with Special Consideration of Scandina-vian Contributions.* rev. ed. Dissertation Series, no. 9. Missoula: Society of Biblical Theology & Scholars Press, 1975.

Koch, Klaus. *The Growth of the Biblical Tradition: The Form-Critical Method.* Trans. from 2d German ed. S. M. Cupitt. New York: Charles Scribner's Sons, 1969.

Nielsen, Eduard. *Oral Tradition: A Modern Problem in Old Testament Introduction.* Studies in Biblical Theology, no. 11. Chicago: A. R. Allenson, 1954.

Articles and monographs devoted to the analysis of types of legal formulations:

Begrich, Joachim. "Das priesterliche Tora." In *Werden und Wesen des Alten Testaments.* Beihefte zur Zeitschrift für die alttestamentliche Wissenschaft, no. 66. Berlin: Alfred Töpelmann, 1936.

Gemser, Berend. "The Importance of the Motive Clause in Old Testament Law." In *Supplements to Vetus Testamentum,* vol. 1, pp. 50–66. Leiden: E. J. Brill, 1953.

Gilmer, Harry Wesley. *The If-You Form in Israelite Law.* Dissertation Series, no. 15. Missoula: Scholars Press for the Society of Biblical Literature, 1975.

Liedke, Gerhard. *Gestalt und Bezeichnung alttestamentlicher Rechtssätze: Eine formge-schichtlich-terminologische Studie*. Wissenschaftliche Monographien zum Alten und Neuen Testament, vol. 39. Neukirchen-Vluyn: Neukirchener Verlag, 1971.

MacKenzie, R. A. F. "The Formal Aspect of Ancient Near Eastern Law." In *The Seed of Wisdom*, ed. William Stewart McCullough, pp. 31–44. Toronto: University of Toronto Press, 1964.

Patrick, Dale. "Casuistic Law Governing Primary Rights and Duties," *Journal of Biblical Literature* 92 (1973), pp. 180–184.

Rendtorff, Rolf. *Die Gesetze in der Priesterschrift: Eine gattungsgeschichtliche Untersuchung*. Forschungen zur Religion und Literatur des Alten und Neuen Testaments, no. 62. Göttingen: Vandenhoeck & Ruprecht, 1954.

Schulz, Hermann. *Das Todesrecht im Alten Testament*. Beihefte zur Zeitschrift für die alttestamentliche Wissenschaft, no. 114. Berlin: Alfred Töpelmann, 1969.

Sonsino, Rifat. *Motive Clauses in Hebrew Law: Biblical Forms and Near Eastern Parallels*. Dissertation Series, no. 45. Chico: Scholars Press, 1980.

Monographs and books devoted to the history of legal traditions:

Beyerlin, Walter. *Origins and History of the Oldest Sinaitic Traditions*. Trans. S. Rudman. Oxford: Oxford University Press, 1965.

Haran, Menachem. *Temples and Temple Service in Ancient Israel: An Inquiry into the Character of Cult Phenomena and the Historical Setting of the Priestly School*. Oxford: Oxford University Press, 1978.

Nicholson, E. W. *Exodus and Sinai in History and Tradition*. Growing Points in Theology. Richmond: John Knox Press, 1973.

————. *Deuteronomy and Tradition*. Philadelphia: Fortress Press, 1967.

Weinfeld, Moshe. *Deuteronomy and the Deuteronomic School*. Oxford: Oxford University Press, 1972.

Comparative studies of biblical law:

Boecker, Hans Jochen. *Law and the Administration of Justice in the Old Testament and Ancient East*. Trans. Jeremy Moiser. Minneapolis: Augsburg Publishing House, 1980. This work is also very useful as an analysis of types of legal formulation and study of the Book of the Covenant.

Meek, Theophile James. "The Origin of Hebrew Law." In *Hebrew Origins*, pp. 49–81. New York and Evanston: Harper & Row, Publishers, 1936/1950/1960.

Paul, Shalom M. *Studies in the Book of the Covenant in the Light of Cuneiform and Biblical Law*. Vol. 18 of *Supplements to Vetus Testamentum*. Leiden: E. J. Brill, 1970.

Chapter Three

THE
TEN
COMMANDMENTS

The series of prohibitions that is contained in Exodus 20:2–17 and Deuteronomy 5:6–21 has a unique status within the Bible and the religious communities which accept it as Holy Scripture. This series is by far the best known and most accessible legal text in the Pentateuch. Within the Sinaitic account, it is the first and most prominent proclamation of law; indeed, it is the only law spoken directly by God to the people. Moreover, it was set apart from the other laws by being inscribed on stone tablets and placed in the Ark of the Covenant. The series is known universally as the Ten Commandments. The title is apt, for there are ten utterances in the style of direct commands. The authors of Scripture preferred the term *words* to *commandments* and never attached the number ten to this particular series. Thus, the name "Ten Commandments" is an example of tradition improving on Scripture.

The following paragraphs will delve more deeply into the source-critical and form-critical questions surrounding the Ten Commandments and related series and then examine the Commandments individually.

Source Criticism

In Chapter Two I presented several reasons for identifying Exodus 20:2–17 as the Elohist Decalogue. The series is introduced by a statement using the divine name "God" (Elohim) and is followed by a passage (20:18–20) using the same divine name. In addition, this is the only legal text in the older Sinaitic account that could belong to the Elohist, for the other sources each have one.

Unfortunately, the Elohist identification is not so simple. The text of the Ten Commandments contains expressions that are otherwise distinctive to the book of Deuteronomy and the writings of the Deuteronomic school, for example, "Yahweh your God," "those who love me and keep my commandments," "that your days may be long in the land which Yahweh . . . gives you," and the whole of verse 10. Many source critics, including Welhausen himself, have surmised that the whole of the Ten Commandments was a creation of the Deuteronomic circle which had been inserted into E. Some go so far as to suggest that E had no divine law.

The thesis that the Elohist had no divine law can be refuted. The introduction (Exod. 20:1) uses E language and refers to a text of commandments. Isolated verses elsewhere have Elohist wording and speak of two tablets of stone containing such a series:

> And he gave to Moses . . . the two tables of the testimony, tables of stone, written with the finger of God.   (Exod. 31:18; also 32:15–16)

Since there is no evidence of an editor's using the divine name "God" in preference to "Yahweh," these passages demonstrate that the E account did have divine law, indeed had a series of "words" of direct divine origin that would fit on two stone tablets.

It is harder to account for the presence of Deuteronomic and even Priestly language (vs. 11) in the Ten Commandments. Either the present text has replaced an Elohist series, or the core of the present text is Elohist, and the Deuteronomic expressions are to be attributed to a rewriting by editors. Neither possibility is entirely satisfying. In the remainder of this book I will treat the text as the Elohist Decalogue, but the reader should be aware of the problems with this identification.

Related Series.   The material in Exodus 34:11–26 is identified as the Yahwist Decalogue in that the entire chapter uses the divine name "Yahweh" and contains expressions and ideas characteristic of the Yahwist. According to verses 27–28, the material in verses 11–26 contains the "words of the covenant, the ten words." Obviously this is the Yahwist legal text which parallels the Elohist's.

According to the present narrative, Moses breaks the "tables of the testimony," written by God, when he sees the golden calf (Exod. 32:15–20). Consequently, he must make new tablets, ascend the mountain, receive and write down the Commandments again, and deliver them to the people (Exod. 34). If the text is taken literally, the Decalogue which is most familiar was destroyed and lost forever, and the "words" in 34:11–26 are all that Israel ever knew. This is a very odd thought, for in fact the first series is known and honored over the replacement. Evidently an editor invented the story of the breaking of the original tablets to make way for another tradition, oblivious to the oddities that resulted.

The material in 34:11–26 differs markedly from 20:2–17. Indeed, it is hard to identify ten commandments between verses 11 and 26 despite the assertion in verse 28. In verses 11–16 there is a warning against adopting Canaanite ways. A commandment comparable to the first of the Elohist Decalogue is embedded as a parenthetical remark in verse 14. Verse 17 contains a parallel to E's second commandment. There follows in verses 18–26 a roughly organized series of cultic duties, six or seven in number, in an entirely different style. These verses have given the Yahwist series the nickname "cultic decalogue" in contrast to the Elohist's "ethical decalogue." However, verses 18–26 do not fit the description of commandments at all, and they do not have the necessary number.

There remain various insoluble puzzles and mysteries, and about the best that can be done is to decide which verses do and do not belong to J. I will tentatively adopt the position that the Yahwist Decalogue consists of only two commandments (34:14, 17) and that the series of cultic duties (34:18–26) is an insertion to fill out the text. I will discuss J's first and second commandments in this chapter and the cultic duties in the next in conjunction with the closely parallel text at the end of the Book of the Covenant (Exod. 23:10–19).

There are two other legal texts that to some degree parallel the Elohist Decalogue: Leviticus 19:1–18 and Deuteronomy 27:15–26. Leviticus 19 is a component of the Holiness Code. H, it should be recalled, was worked into approximately its present form during the earlier years of the Exile (598/587–538 B.C.) and incorporated into P. The portion of chapter 19 referred to resembles the Elohist Decalogue in (1) its commandment style, (2) its comprehensive scope and summarization of subjects, and (3) numerous actual parallels in content. In sheer number of commandments, Leviticus 19 is much larger, with twenty or more commandments grouped in twos, threes, and fours on the same or associated subjects:

> You shall not steal, nor deal falsely, nor lie to one another. And you shall not swear by my name falsely, and so profane the name of your God: I am Yahweh. (19:11–12)

The lawgiver portrays shady dealing as of a piece with overt theft and false swearing. The first and fourth commandments correspond respectively to the eighth (Exod. 20:15) and third (Exod. 20:7) commandments of the Elohist Decalogue.

The reader should not get the idea that Leviticus 19:1–18 is a simple, homogenous text of commandments paralleling the Elohist Decalogue. Verses 5–10 are in an entirely different style than Exodus 20:2–17 and cover different subjects. Moreover, some of the commandments in the appropriate apodictic style range far beyond the subjects covered by the Elohist Decalogue (e.g., vss. 13, 14). Thus, it cannot be said that this portion of Leviticus 19 constitutes another version of the Ten Commandments, but only that some of its provisions exhibit a parallel style, scope, and subject matter.

Albrecht Alt, in his study of Israelite legal forms, identified Deuteronomy 27:15–26 as a significant parallel to the Elohist Decalogue. The text contains a series of twelve curses for wrongful acts. The style differs markedly from the addressed commandments, but the regularity of the style resembles the regularity of a series of commandments. Moreover, the scope and actual provisions of the series are close to the Elohist Decalogue, yet differ sufficiently to discount any suggestion that one was copied from the other. Alt himself considered the text to be very ancient, perhaps the purest apodictic series in Scripture. Other scholars have not always followed him in this assessment. For this study it is important to affirm only that the text is several centuries older than the book of Deuteronomy.

The following table of the parallels among the texts discussed summarizes this discussion:

Exod. 20:2–17		Exod. 34:14, 17	Lev. 19:1–18	Deut. 27:15–26
I. 3	Other gods	14		
II. 4–6	Images	17	4	15
III. 7	Name		12	
IV. 8–11	Sabbath	(21)	3b	
V. 12	Parents		3a	16
VI. 13	Killing		(17–18)	24
VII. 14	Adultery			[20–23]
VIII. 15	Stealing		11 (13)	
IX. 16	False witness		15–16	(25)
X. 17	Coveting			[17]

The Question of the Original Form

It is necessary to address some theories regarding the Ten Commandments that have grown out of Alt's theory of apodictic law, particularly the proposed reconstructions of an original, pure version of the Ten Commandments. Such a reconstruction is arrived at by stripping away all motive clauses and excess words in the Commandments proper. Some proposals venture one step further and reformulate the positive commandments as prohibitions. The result looks something like this:

I am Yahweh your God, who brought you out of the land of Egypt, out of the house of bondage.

I. You shall have no other gods before me.
II. You shall not make for (me?) any graven image.
III. You shall not take (my?) name (of Yahweh?) in vain.
IV. Remember the sabbath day to keep it holy;
or = You shall do no work on the sabbath day.
V. Honor your father and your mother;
or = You shall not curse your father or your mother.
VI. You shall not kill.
VII. You shall not commit adultery.
VIII. You shall not steal.
IX. You shall not bear false witness.
X. You shall not covet (your neighbor's house?).

It is not uncommon for the scholar who proposes such a terse, homogenous original to suggest that it derives from Moses himself or at least from the period of the Judges (1200–1000 B.C.).

While such a reconstructed series satisfies a powerful urge for simplicity and symmetry, it is based upon highly dubious premises. In particular, one cannot assume that "pure" formulations, exhibiting greater brevity, order, and symmetry, stand at the beginning of a tradition only to be gradually "corrupted" in the course of transmission. It is just as possible for legal traditions to evolve *toward* brevity and symmetry. In other words, the Ten Commandments may well be a distillation of wordier and more heterogeneous traditions. It is also possible that the long, summarizing series are composites of original short ones (so Gerstenberger).

The Elohist Decalogue represents a level of abstraction that one would expect not at the beginning of Israelite legal history, but at a further stage of development, say, from the end of the period of the Judges through the first two centuries of the monarchy. There is in the Ten Commandments a highly sophisticated attempt to summarize the basic postulates of Israelite law. Their continued appeal several millennia later testifies to the quality of the achievement.

Undoubtedly scholars and students alike would find it desirable to give Moses credit for the Ten Commandments. It would be an honor to him to have received or composed this great text of moral precepts, and the text itself would gain prestige if it could be traced to him, but it is too much to expect the "founder" of the theocratic community of Israel to have foreseen the classical development of the movement he inaugurated. If Moses is to be credited with a component of the Ten Commandments, he may be identified with the first and second commandments. He is certainly responsible for the exclusivistic Yahwism that generated them, whether or not the actual wording can be attributed to him.

The Scope of the Commandments

The theories of an original, pristine Ten Commandments going back to Moses or the period of the Judges have not only shaped the view of their historical background but actually conditioned the interpretation of the content of the Commandments. In particular, they have encouraged the conviction that the Commandments summarize Israel's criminal law. Alt himself correlated the Commandments and the laws with the formula, "he shall be put to death." Others have gone even further and described the entire Israelite criminal law as violation of one or another commandment.

The conviction, however, that each commandment is to be correlated with a specific capital crime seriously distorts interpretation. Take the example of the eighth commandment against stealing. Since the stealing of property was not punishable by death in Israelite law and was treated as a civil action, interpreters have narrowed the commandment's original meaning to the stealing of persons—kidnapping—which was a capital crime. There is no warrant for such a narrowing in the wording itself. I propose that each commandment be read as governing a maximum range of actions. The prohibitions were, from the outset, abstractions intended to apply to a host of different actions. As history went on, new applications were found which were implicit in the original wording although not in the mind of the original author(s).

COMMENTARY

In the following consideration of individual commandments, the first words of the material to be discussed will be quoted at the beginning of each portion of the commentary.

/"I am Yahweh your God, who brought you out of the land of Egypt . . ."(20:2).

The Hebrew would allow the translation, "I, Yahweh, am your God," but parallel expressions in the Bible and ancient Near Eastern literature tend to confirm "I am Yahweh. . . ." Throughout the Near East, deities introduced themselves by name to identify which of the many was speaking. Though in biblical literature Yahweh alone speaks as deity, the same manner of speaking is continued.

Through introduction, Yahweh establishes his personal presence before his people, and the Commandments that follow are rendered as the address of an "I" to a "thou." By divulging the name, past encounters with this God are recalled to sharpen the drama of the present—the name not only evokes a presence, it also calls forth associations that give an identity to this presence. Thus, the self-introduction can be augmented by a recollection of the decisive deed by which Yahweh is known, namely, the deliverance from Egyptian bondage. The recollection of Yahweh's deliverance lends authority to his commandments. His deed has demonstrated that he is worthy of the benefactors' allegiance. He is a God to whom they can entrust their fate. His commandments can be trusted to be an expression of his gracious will toward his people. The people can be expected to obey out of trust in the goodness of what he commands and out of gratitude for all his saving benefits.

Although Jewish tradition treats the self-introduction as part of the first commandment, it appears to be an introduction to the entire series of ten. However, it is more closely linked to the first two commandments, since the first person "Yahweh" is limited to this part of the series. Thus, verses 2–6 constitute a distinct unit of "I–thou" address with an introduction (vs. 2) and a conclusion (vss. 5–6). The rest of the Ten Commandments speak of Yahweh in the third person, and this initial unit must bear the weight of establishing the whole as Yahweh's address to his people.

I. *"You shall have no other gods besides me"* (20:3).

The Hebrew wording is an idiomatic expression for possession: "There shall not be to you other gods before me." Like the English "have," the Hebrew idiom does not differentiate between ownership and the more personal, mutual sort of belonging. Since Israel is also said to "belong" to Yahweh, the idiom should here be construed as envisaging mutual relationship. The expression "before me"—literally "to my face"—is much discussed, but it is safe to say that the force of it is to exclude relations with any other deity.

Exodus 20:3 stands out from all other versions of the first commandment in its comprehensiveness. Exodus 34:14 forbids acts of homage to other deities, 22:20 condemns acts of sacrifice to them, and 23:13 warns against invoking them. Probably these more specific prohibitions exclude all commerce with other deities by the principle of *pars pro toto* (part for the whole). Exodus 20:3, by contrast, forbids any state of relation that might issue in illicit actions.

Exodus 34:14 offers the reason for the prohibition: Yahweh, whose name is Jealous, is a jealous God. Exodus 20:5 gives the same reason. Far from being a base, primitive motive, jealousy is the logical expression of the mutually exclusive relation existing beween God and God's people. Like a monogamous marriage, which involves mutually exclusive sexual access, the relationship between Yahweh and Israel excludes any competing relationship. Yahweh claims Israel as "my own possession" (Exod. 19:5), "distinct . . . from all other people" (Exod. 33:16). Having another people is out of the question. Likewise Israel can have no other God. Yahweh insists on sole claim to the prerogatives of deity among this people.

The relationship protected by the first commandment is actually a gift. Yahweh has offered himself to the people, and this prohibition defines who Yahweh is and what this means for Israel. Yahweh is the God who claims the attributes of deity to an exclusive degree. Israel is the people who must be known by their adherence to this God and must find their life in this one God, for that is why they were brought into being. Belonging to Israel means recognizing this God, and violating the exclusive relationship is an act of treason.

More than any other word of Scripture, the first commandment articulates the religious revolution that brought Israel into being. It is without parallel in the history of religions, and all other monotheistic religious traditions derive from it. To be sure, the wording grants the existence of other gods, but only to deny their efficacy. Yahweh is sufficient to all Israel's religious needs. Whatever help and guidance the supernatural can give, Yahweh can provide it, and whatever thanksgiving and praise and awe the supernatural calls forth belongs to Yahweh. Yahweh is, in a word, all that is divine for Israel. This principle underlies all biblical literature. Other deities are mentioned in the biblical narrative but are accorded no reality. Wherever divine words are communicated or divine acts are performed, it is this one God who speaks and acts. Only this one God is known in biblical tradition, and the tradition as a whole identifies the one to whom sole loyalty is due.

The first commandment protects Yahweh's sovereignty as well as his religious prerogatives in Israel by establishing a basis for the rest of the Commandments. If the power to command were not exclusively

Yahweh's, his commandments regarding human relations would not be incontrovertible. If there were more than one source of right and wrong in the community, it would be impossible to maintain an internally consistent and comprehensive law. Within the people of Israel, there could be only one divine authority from whom human authority was derived and under whose judgment it stood.

It was the task of each generation of Israelites to discover the implications of the first commandment. Going back to the Mosaic period in content if not in form, the commandment was a prime test of orthodoxy throughout biblical history. It is obvious from biblical narratives and prophecies and from archaeological evidence that it was often violated. Many Israelites did not recognize its validity. Even where the prohibition was accepted, it was not always clear what constituted "another deity" and what reality other deities had. It may have once been thought that other deities simply had other spheres of influence, but gradually Israelite intellectuals realized that only the most exalted theoretical monotheism was compatible with the first commandment. With this recognition, the first commandment became fused with the second.

II. *"You shall not make for yourself an idol . . ."* (20:4-6, author's translation).

The word translated here as "idol" originally meant a figure carved of wood or stone or cast in metal. Parallel texts use other words: "molten gods" (Exod. 34:17), "gods of silver . . . of gold" (Exod. 20:23), "graven or molten image" (Deut. 27:15). It makes little difference which word is selected for the iconographic representation of deity, for all such representations are meant to be excluded.

Exodus 20:4 continues: "or any likeness which is in heaven above. . . ." Given the awkwardness of the grammar and the absence of such a clause in the parallel texts, it is safe to assume that it is a later addition to the original prohibition. Although the wording seems to repudiate all artistic representation, the content demands that it be construed to mean that no images of creatures are to be constructed for worship. No creature is to be accorded the honor due God alone.

Originally, the second commandment was rather narrow in scope, excluding iconographic representation of Yahweh. Images of other deities would be excluded by the first commandment, but a separate prohibition was required to ban images of Yahweh. We can see this original meaning behind the condemnation of Gideon's ephod (Judg. 8:27) and the images, ephod, and teraphim made by Micah and stolen by the tribe of Dan for its sanctuary (Judg. 17–18), and it probably stands behind the condemnation of "golden calves" at various times in the narrative (Exod. 32; 1 Kings 12:28–30; Hos. 8:5–6; 13:2).

It is intriguing to ask why Yahweh rejected images of himself. Scripture itself is not without answers to this question. Some derive from the identity of Yahweh, others from the nature of idolatry. Deuteronomy 4:15–18 reasons from Yahweh's revelation itself:

> Since you saw no form on the day that Yahweh spoke to you at Horeb out of the midst of the fire, beware lest you act corruptly by making a graven image for yourselves, in the form of any figure, the likeness of male or female.

The point is that since Yahweh remained hidden behind a veil of flames in his revelation, there is no visage to reproduce, and an idol would have to be a copy of some other form, perforce an image of a creature.

The tradition does say, however, that Moses and other leaders and prophets "saw the form of God" (Num. 12:8; also Isa. 6). One account of the Sinaitic revelation even reports that the *elders of Israel* "beheld the God of Israel" (Exod. 24:10, 11). It cannot be said that Yahweh always remained veiled in his revelation. Yet a close scrutiny of these accounts confirms Deuteronomy at a deeper level. None of the accounts of appearances contain descriptions of God's visage, suggesting that the recipients did not and could not look directly upon God. Moreover, the appearances were fraught with such numinous dread that the recipient would not dare to attempt to reproduce what was seen.

One cannot find Old Testament support for the idea that God is a purely spiritual, immaterial being and therefore incompatible with any representation, but one can find a related line of thought:

> To whom then will you compare me,
>> that I should be like him? says the Holy One.
> Lift up your eyes on high and see:
>> who created these?   (Isa. 40:25–26)

To make an image is to offer a comparison between God and another being, and even the most exalted beings of the physical world—heavenly bodies—are mere creatures. God the Creator is not comparable to any creature; hence, an image is out of the question.

Modern interpreters have suggested one other motive for the prohibition. In the ancient world, the image of a deity was more than an artistic representation; the deity in some sense dwelt in the image, and the image was commonly addressed in prayer. By rejecting images, Israel rejected this sort of incarnation of deity. God was only visually accessible on God's own initiative. It took some time for Israel to carry through this principle thoroughly, but the second commandment inaugurated the movement and prodded it along.

Once the idea became firmly established in Israel that Yahweh was not to be represented iconographically, there was something of a fusion of the first and second commandments. If all idols are by definition of "other gods," then idolatry and apostasy become essentially synonymous. This fusion has already taken place in Exodus 20:5–6, for the warning "you shall not bow down to them or serve them; for I . . . am a jealous God" must refer to the worship of other gods as well as idols. The plural pronoun "them" must refer specifically to the plural "other gods" in verse 3; likewise, God's *jealousy* is intolerance of competing deities (cf. Exod. 34:14).

The fusion facilitated a very subtle critique of idolatry and polytheism. The first biblical author to capitalize on its possibilities seems to have been the prophet Hosea. Throughout his book, Hosea condemns Israel for pursuing the fertility god Baal (often spoken of as a plurality) as if this were a competing being. Yet in a summary statement of the sins Israel must confess, he depicts their apostasy as idolatry:

> "We will say no more, 'Our God,'
>   to the work of our hands."   (Hos. 14:3)

Baal was, by implication, the creation of his worshipers, which is to say an idol. Idolatry is forbidden because it is an act of "making a god," and Yahweh cannot be a human creation.

In later times, the meaning of the second commandment underwent another expansion of an entirely different sort. Putting faith in one's wealth, particularly valuable metal, became a violation:

> If I have made gold my trust,
>   or called fine gold my confidence;
> if I have rejoiced because my wealth was great,
>
> . . . .
> I should have been false to God above.   (Job 31:24, 25, 28)

It would not be surprising if the reader had heard a sermon or two on trusting in money as a form of idolatry!

One motive clause remains to be discussed:

> visiting the iniquity of the fathers upon the children to the third and the fourth generation of those who hate me, but showing steadfast love to thousands of those who love me and keep my commandments.   (vss. 5–6)

This is hymnic language describing the two sides of Yahweh's nature. Yahweh, as a just God, makes the iniquity of a person or group come back to haunt the perpetrators and their successors. To the modern reader, it seems unjust for later generations to suffer for acts of ancestors. Biblical literature itself is somewhat divided on this question. Whatever its ethical problems, however, the idea of guilt pursuing a family or community for generations is quite realistic. The final clause, "of those who hate me," may be intended to justify the idea by suggesting that the fated succession of generations share in their fathers' spirit.

Of a piece with justice is the love of God, promised to those who know God by heart and attend to the commandments. Since the presence of God is a gift and the commandments a protection of this gift, loving and obeying God is not a case of earning divine favor but of living in accordance with it. The statement goes behind the negative duty of exclusive recognition of Yahweh to the positive attitude of loyalty expected of Israel.

III. *"You shall not take the name of Yahweh your God in vain . . ."* (20:7).

The verb translated "take" actually means "lift up." It is a rather uncommon Hebrew expression, echoing perhaps the language of prayers and oaths, and could mean either causing the name to rise to heaven or causing it to be heard in public. The noun translated "vain" ranges in meaning from "empty" to "false." The adverbial expression used here seems to have the very general meaning, "for an empty or false purpose."

The scope of this commandment is linked to the various uses of the divine name in ancient Israel. One called upon the name in prayer and praise, pronounced the name in solemn oaths, and prophesied in the name, and whenever the name was used, it could be abused. In particular, oaths could be sworn with the intent to deceive, prayers could be uttered to manipulate God, and the name could be spoken in ejaculations of anger or passion.

Various parallels indicate that the third commandment was commonly applied to false oaths, as in Leviticus 19:12, "You shall not swear by my name falsely." There are two broad categories of oaths: promissory and assertatory. In a promissory oath, God may be called upon to be a witness to the promise and to act as a judge of performance. God was expected to enforce the provisions of the oath either through the acts of the injured party or through extraordinary means if the injured party were powerless to act. In an assertatory oath, God may be called upon to be a witness to the veracity of a person's testimony and, as the reader of the heart, the punisher of lies. One would be taking the divine name in vain if one swore by God to the veracity of false testimony or to the performance of deeds that one did not intend or was not able to fulfill.

Throughout human history, people have attempted to manipulate the power of the supernatural for their own good and to the detriment of enemies. Prayer itself attempts to move God (or the gods) to act, but genuine prayer submits one's case to God for a decision. One enters the domain of magic in believing that some utterances and rituals can cause good or evil irrespective of right and wrong. Within the Bible, the idea of a reservoir of supernatural power subject to human manipulation is rejected; God is the source of all power, which can be exercised only in conformity to divine will. The story of Balaam (Num. 22–24) shows Yahweh's veto of magical utterances. The attempt to coerce him into fulfilling one's desires would constitute a vain use of his name. He cannot be manipulated, and the attempt to do so is disrespectful of his majesty.

For some strange and mysterious reason, humans are given to ejaculating the most sacred names in anger or as emphasis. We call this "profanity," that is, using the sacred in a profane (and therefore disparaging) way. In Leviticus 24 the term *blasphemy* is used for this type of abuse of God's name:

> The Israelite woman's son and a man of Israel quarreled in the camp, and the Israelite woman's son blasphemed the Name, and cursed. (vss. 10–11)

The case functioned as the precedent in biblical literature for the execution of someone who utters God's name profanely as well as the precedent for countless sermons against profanity and "dirty" language.

The third commandment, like the first two, had the capacity to expand radically. The idea of "profaning the name" extended to a host of actions that brought God's name into ill repute. This was particularly true of things that happened around the sanctuary, such as child sacrifice (Lev. 18:21; 20:3), cultic prostitution (Amos 2:7), and priestly misdeeds (Lev. 22:2, 32). Once Israel was dispersed among the nations of the world, whatever they did or suffered could come under this commandment (cf. Ezek. 36:16–32).

The motive clause, "for Yahweh will not hold him guiltless who takes his name in vain," seems redundant. Perhaps the lawgiver wanted to remind the community that abuse of the divine name is a serious matter. By calling on the name, one becomes responsible to the one named for his or her utterance and sets in motion a process that may destroy the speaker.

IV. *"Remember to keep the day of solemn rest holy"* (20:8–11, author's translation).

The word translated "solemn rest" is *sabbath* in Hebrew, a descriptive noun as well as a proper name for the last day of the week. The word translated "keep holy" means "sanctify, hallow." Both the human addressee and divine speaker are made the subject of this verb within verses 8–11. One might say that God bestows the quality of holiness upon the day, and Israel is called to show proper respect for it and thereby join in the sanctifying act.

The length and style of the unit suggest that it is an example of *priestly torah* rather than an apodictic commandment. In the initial sentence a duty is commanded in the form of a positive rather than a negative command and is followed in verses 9–10 by a description of how the duty is to be fulfilled. The only prohibitive element of the unit is the negative nature of observance, namely, not working. The enumeration of those who are not to work is so extensive that it forms an independent subunit with the quality of a motive clause. Verse 11 also constitutes an independent unit explaining the origin of the day.

The specific duty imposed on the addressee is quite simple: not to work on the seventh day, that is, Saturday. Since the Bible counts the day as beginning at dusk, this means that no work is to be performed from sundown Friday evening to sundown Saturday. No definition of what constitutes work is provided, and this became the subject of numerous rulings in Jewish tradition. What verse 10 does do is enumerate those who come under the prohibition to prevent the addressee from assigning his or her work to others (children, servants, animals, or resident aliens).

The fourth commandment is the only example of a strictly religious practice in the Elohist Decalogue. To be sure, the first three commandments have to do with God, but they apply to all spheres of life and a variety of actions. The sabbath rest, on the other hand, is a specific practice with a religious purpose. It may have originated as a purely social institution (cf. Exod. 23:12), but religious meaning gravitated to it until it became Israel's religious institution par excellence. The command is to "sanctify" the day by setting it apart to God, making this day a sanctuary of time.

Further, the sabbath is unique among the sacred times instituted by God in its frequency and in its absence of mandatory worship. Because it was elevated to supreme importance and yet had no specific celebration attached to it, the day attracted a variety of meanings. In P, the sabbath is the "sign of the covenant" (Exod. 31:16–17, author's translation), the sacrament, one might say, of the everlasting union between God and the people which was the purpose of creation itself. In the Deuteronomic version of the Ten Commandments, the sabbath is a reminder of Israel's deliverance from Egyptian slavery (Deut. 5:15). In conjunction with this, the Deuteronomic version stresses the equality of master and slave on the sabbath.

Exodus 20:11 makes the sabbath rest a recollection of God's creation of the world. According to Genesis 1:1–2:4a, God created the world in six days and rested on the seventh, and the human community should imitate that pattern every week. The Creator's claim to sovereign rights over all creatures is symbolized by the removal of a segment of time from their disposal; humans are allotted sufficient time to accomplish their tasks, but by having this day taken from them they cannot live as if their time were their own.

V. *"Honor your father and your mother . . ."* (20:12).

The word translated "honor" frequently has God as its object, in which case it is translated "glorify." To honor parents is to accord them a respect and importance reserved for the sacred. In the same spirit, Leviticus 19:3 commands fear or reverence of parents. The element of affection is included in honor and reverence, but there is no hint of easy familiarity; the kind of affection commanded preserves the essential distance between generations.

Those who believe that the Elohist Decalogue derives from an earlier, purer series in prohibition style see this positive formulation as a replacement for a negative one. Other legal texts do in fact condemn a range of untoward acts toward parents: "striking" (Exod. 21:15; also Prov. 19:26), "cursing" (Exod. 21:17; Lev. 20:9), "despising" (Deut. 27:16), "disobeying and rebelling" (Deut. 21:18–21). While it would be possible to formulate any of these as a prohibition, none would have the comprehensiveness and power of the existing formulation. The positive wording rules out overt aggression altogether and at the same time creates a bond welding children to their parents.

The duty of honoring is much more suggestive than that of obeying. The duty of obedience diminishes as children become adults, but honor can and should persist long after the age of dependence. Indeed, it could motivate caring for parents when they can no longer support themselves, preserving their dignity even in the state of dependence. In that the commandment is addressed to children who owe honor to their parents, it is not a tool for wielding parental power. People are always the children of parents, and their obligation does not cease as long as they live. By showing honor to their parents they strengthen the system that bestows honor on themselves as parents.

The family is one of the primary human institutions. Within the biblical conception of life, it is created by God and subject to divine protection and regulation. Its origins are as old as the human race (Gen. 2:24; 4:1). Children are physically dependent for a long period of time and must acquire the capacity for economic, social, and cultural independence through a process of tutelage. As procreators—agents of God's creative act—parents have the right and duty to provide this tutelage to their children.

The fifth and seventh commandments of the Decalogue legitimate and protect the institution of the family. The fifth commandment bestows internal structure, while the seventh protects it from encroachment from outside. By nature the family is hierarchical. The parents are responsible for the existence of the family, its peace and order, and its participation in the larger community. The honor bestowed upon parents by the commandment is a guarantee of the sovereign authority delegated to them by God.

It is noteworthy that mothers and fathers are treated as equals under this commandment. Within the institutional structure of ancient Israel, only the family possessed such an equality of sexes. Men dominated the public institutions; the male heads of families participated in the council of elders that made legal and political decisions, and the defense of family interests in this arena devolved upon the patriarch. The family, however, derives its existence from the interaction of male and female, and both parties receive the honor due those responsible for its existence and maintenance.

The motive clause, "that your days may be long in the land which Yahweh your God gives you," describes the importance of the family for the continuance of the people of God. Respecting and revering those who have gone before and on whom an individual depends forges a chain through history. The identity of the people is passed on to the next generation by the children's holding in reverence those who have embodied it.

VI. *"You shall not kill"* (20:13).

This commandment opens the section of commandments dealing with relations among social equals, between a person and his or her neighbor, the first four of which are noteworthy for their extreme compactness. The word translated "kill" is much discussed by scholars. Some have argued that it means "murder," that is, intentional killing without legal authorization to do so, but the Hebrew word is used of accidental killing as well (as in Num. 35), so the less specific "kill" is a better translation.

As a commandment, the prohibition can only have in view the willful act of taking another's life. It makes no sense to prohibit accidents. Willful killing is not defined solely by the intent to kill, however, since an attack with the will to harm which inadvertently kills a person was treated as murder in Israelite law. This means that the prohibition against killing actually covers lesser crimes as well, that is, any act of violence against another person that might result in death. It is not a large step to the positive formulation of Leviticus 19:17–18:

> You shall not hate your brother in your heart, but you shall reason with your neighbor, lest you bear sin because of him. You shall not take vengeance or bear any grudge against the sons of your own people, but you shall love your neighbor as yourself.

Enmity is the motive force behind violent and murderous acts, and the best protection against this force is the cultivation of affection for those with whom one lives.

The prohibition against killing does not rule out participation in war or capital punishment. Killing is authorized by God for serious breaches of divine law and for wars that have divine support. In other words, one is not to kill on one's own authority, no matter how justified the cause might be. When a person kills as a member of a court, or as the avenger of the blood, or as a member of the army, that person acts as the agent of the One who has authority over life and death.

The Priestly Source interprets the prohibition against killing to be a universal law, a provision of the covenant made between God and Noah:

> Whoever sheds the blood of man, by man shall his blood be shed; for God made man in his own image.   (Gen. 9:6)

Every human person is sacred, the bearer of the image of God, and to kill a person is to violate God. Having taken life, the killer forfeits the right to life, and the human community is authorized to impose the death penalty. According to P, in fact, Israelite courts were not allowed to impose any penalty but death on a murderer (Num. 35:31), though Scripture reports a number of instances of pardon and equity judgments.

VII. *"You shall not commit adultery"* (20:14).

The word translated "commit adultery" covers violation of the sexual fidelity expected of married persons, which is distinguished from other forms of sexual immorality, such as "harlotry." By protecting the exclusive bonds between parents, it joins the fifth commandment in protecting the institution of the family.

There are various expressions of an ideal of monogamous marriage in the Old Testament, although this ideal stood in some tension with the legality of polygamy and the toleration of prostitution. The Yahwist's creation narrative articulates a monogamous ideal:

> Therefore a man leaves his father and his mother and cleaves to his wife, and they become one flesh.   (Gen. 2:24)

The radical union of man and woman in marriage assumes a mutually exclusive relation. Moreover, the woman is not defined narrowly as childbearer but broadly as "helper" (Gen. 2:20). Marriage is to form a community of mutual aid and comfort in which each partner finds fulfillment in the other. Procreation and the extension of the family through generations result from the union by the aid of God (Gen. 3:20; 4:1).

Despite the biblical ideal of monogamy, it was legally permissible for a man to have more than one wife; indeed, he was free to have as many wives, concubines, and mistresses as he could support. This arrangement introduced a double standard into marriage. A woman owed sexual fidelity to one man, but her husband did not owe her the same. Consonant with this legal inequality was the tendency to see a man as the "lord" of his wife or wives. In the realm of extramarital sex, the double standard permitted a married man to have sexual intercourse with unattached women. Although prostitution under either religious auspices or economic necessity was condemned in ancient Israel, it seems to have been tolerated. A man who had intercourse with a prostitute was not an adulterer under the law. However, extramarital sexual relations generally, though they were permitted, were morally condemned. The prophet Hosea goes so far as to remove the double standard in an ironic twist:

> I will not punish your daughters when they play the harlot,
>   nor your brides when they commit adultery;
> for the men themselves go aside with harlots,
>   and sacrifice with cult prostitutes. (4:14)

The fathers and husbands would like God to punish their wayward women, but God will not because it is they who corrupt them.

Even with these elements of a double standard, adultery was taken very seriously in Israelite law. Both men and women were subject to the death penalty when caught in the act (Deut. 22:22), and other cases were treated with equal severity. The strictness of the law is rooted in the sanctity of the institution being protected. Any violation, even an inadvertent one, was considered a grave sin (Gen. 20:9; 39:9). In fact, the institution of marriage is inviolable even by kings, as is shown in the accounts of David's affair with Bathsheba (2 Sam. 11–12) and Sarah's being taken mistakenly into foreign harems (Gen. 12:10–20; 20:2–18). It is an institution independent of and equal to the state, and the sovereign must acknowledge its binding force on himself and his subjects or come under divine judgment.

VIII. *"You shall not steal"* (20:15).

The verb translated "to steal" denotes the arbitrary seizure of persons or property. The absence of an object gives the prohibition a very broad and open-ended coverage. A number of recent critical studies have argued that originally only the capital crime of kidnapping was meant, but the word itself does not support this narrower construction, and the underlying belief that the Ten Commandments cover only capital crimes is gratuitous.

In a civilization that practiced slavery, people could be seized and sold into slavery. To avoid the intervention of the victim's family, he or she normally would be sold to agents who would transport the slave to a foreign nation to be sold. The dynamics of the international slave trade are vividly portrayed in the story of Joseph (Gen. 37, 39), whose brothers would have been subject to capital punishment under biblical law if their act had been detected.

Presumably the eighth commandment also covers seizure of personal property, namely, animals, goods, money, and perhaps even slaves. The right to security in one's possessions is protected in Israelite law as it is in any realistic legal order. The theft of property was treated as a civil injury in which the victim sought restitution with compensation from the defendant. The eighth commandment does not appear to cover seizure of real property (land and buildings), however. Arbitrary appropriation of real estate was certainly considered wrong, but it was not a case of seizure by stealth. To "steal" a plot of land or house, one must take it by either force or fraud. Since the use of force is out of the question within a settled legal community, theft of real property would involve fraud or undue economic pressure and would fall under the ninth and tenth commandments.

IX. *"You shall not bear false witness against your neighbor"* (20:16).

The words translated "false witness" are technical terms designating a person who offers false or deceptive testimony in a trial. The primary concern is testimony "against" another, that is, testimony that would deprive a person of life, property, or standing in the community. False testimony to protect someone would, of course, also come under the prohibition, but that problem does not appear to have worried the biblical lawgivers. The expression "your neighbor" refers to any member of the legal community, which presumably includes marginal persons.

This commandment constitutes something of a conclusion to the preceding ones. Following the proclamation of prohibitions of crimes and torts, it protects the citizen from being convicted of any of these falsely and the court process itself from becoming the vehicle of murder or theft.

The Israelite trial procedure depended heavily upon testimony and made little use of physical evidence. The concurring testimony of two witnesses was sufficient to convict a person of a crime or determine the outcome of a civil action. This rule invited abuse by those who stood to gain from another's injury or who were susceptible to hysteria, and collusion between witnesses, perhaps also with members of the court hearing the case, was easy and effective. Scripture contains an account of such abuse (1 Kings 21) and numerous complaints about it.

One might think that the third commandment would cover false testimony, but this is not the case, because testimony was not given under oath. Only when testimony and evidence were insufficient was there recourse to assertatory oaths. In such instances only the principals of the trial—the defendant or the two parties to a civil action—were required to swear to the truth of their testimony. The taking of oaths was intended to end a trial, and all parties had to accept it as satisfying their claims.

The ninth commandment thus brought testimony under the express judgment of God. In substance if not in form, false testimony was perjury. The court itself would enforce sanctions against false testimony. According to Deuteronomy 19:19, the person found to be giving intentionally false testimony to the defendant's harm was to be punished with the penalty that person sought to inflict on the defendant.

The ninth commandment underwent a broadening in the course of Israel's history. In Hosea 4:2, for example, lying testimony seems to have been expanded to all lying. Leviticus 19:16 associates standing forth "against the life of your neighbor" with going about "as a slanderer among your people." Injuring a person's reputation by malicious talk is of a piece with testifying to his or her injury in a trial. Leviticus 19:11 also seems to give a variation on lying testimony when it prohibits lying to one another in conjunction with stealing and swindling. Just as false or deceptive testimony in civil cases could be used to expropriate property, so could lying and deception be used in business and monetary transactions.

X. *"You shall not covet your neighbor's house . . ."* (20:17).

The exact meaning of the word translated "covet" is the subject of scholarly discussion. The prohibition of what might be called an affective state seems out of keeping with the rest of the commandments. Law addresses actions, not internal thoughts and feelings. This fact has led scholars to examine the use of the word throughout Scripture for evidence of its implying overt action as well as internal condition.

The tenth commandment also presents other difficulties. Taken literally, it is two prohibitions, and some church traditions (Catholic and Lutheran) treat it as two. In addition, the Exodus and Deuteronomic versions differ somewhat and raise the question of original formulation. I believe that the initial commandment in the Exodus version is the basic commandment, and the second, longer prohibition should be classified as a motive clause expanding the scope of the original.

The initial commandment concerns real property. Micah 2:1–2 provides insight into what it intends to cover:

> Woe to those who devise wickedness
>   and work evil upon their beds!
> When the morning dawns, they perform it,
>   because it is in the power of their hand.
> They *covet* fields, and seize them;
>   and houses, and take them away;
> they oppress a man and his house,
>   a man and his inheritance.

The prophet condemns those who devise ways to defraud people of their real property. "Coveting" here is not merely an inner state but a driving force that produces schemes and overt action. It is this sort of behavior that is prohibited by the tenth commandment. This fact would be clearer if the commandment had mentioned "inheritance" along with "house," but the mention of "house" is sufficient to establish that the commandment has to do with real property.

The extension of the commandment to cover the neighbor's wife, slaves, animals, and everything else takes it beyond the domain of real property. With the exception of "wife," these other items are personal property. The prohibition against coveting them must likewise have in view scheming to procure what one desires by actions which have the semblance of legality.

The inclusion of the neighbor's wife in the list of coveted things is puzzling, because in biblical law a married woman was not considered the property of her husband. Hence, the prohibition must refer to adultery, not arbitrary seizure, making the coveting of a neighbor's wife somewhat redundant (repeating the seventh commandment); all that is added is the subjective element. There is another problem produced by the inclusion of "wife" among the coveted things. The other commandments address both women and men, as in verse 10, which does not include "wife" in the list of persons and animals that should not work on the sabbath. The inclusion of "wife" here, making the commandment a matter for males only, introduces an inconsistency as to the addressee of the entire series.

It has been suggested that the author or editor drew the enumeration of coveted items from a traditional listing of persons and things subject to judgment along with a man (in curse texts and the like), and that "wife" was among them. The problem with this hypothesis is that children are invariably included in curse texts but are not mentioned here. It must be admitted that we do not know why "wife" is included in the list of the neighbor's possessions that should not be coveted.

SUGGESTED READING

For the policy informing this selection, see the statement introducing the bibliography at the end of Chapter One. For the analysis of the sources, forms of legal formulation, and history of tradition of the Decalogue and related series, consult the bibliography of Chapter Two.

There are many commentaries available on the book of Exodus. The two I recommend most highly are in the Old Testament Library series:

Childs, Brevard S. *The Book of Exodus: A Critical, Theological Commentary.* Old Testament Library. Philadelphia: Westminster Press, 1962.

Noth, Martin. *Exodus: A Commentary.* Trans. J. S. Bowden. Old Testament Library. Philadelphia: Westminster Press, 1962.

A useful summary of the scholarly discussion of the Ten Commandments:

Stamm, J. J., and M. E. Andrew. *The Ten Commandments in Recent Research.* Studies in Biblical Theology, 2d ser., vol. 2. Naperville: Alec R. Allenson, 1967.

There are numerous books devoted to the study of and meditation on the Ten Commandments. The following selection represents a spectrum of viewpoints:

Harrelson, Walter. *The Ten Commandments and Human Rights.* Overtures to Biblical Theology, vol. 8. Philadelphia: Fortress Press, 1980.

Nielsen, Eduard. *The Ten Commandments in New Perspective: A Traditio-Historical Approach.* Studies in Biblical Theology, 2d ser., vol. 7. Naperville: Alec R. Allenson, 1968.

Phillips, Anthony. *Ancient Israel's Criminal Law: A New Approach to the Decalogue.* New York: Schocken Books, 1970.

Some examples of precritical treatments by famous interpreters:

Farley, Benjamin W. (ed. and trans.). *John Calvin's Sermons on the Ten Commandments.* Grand Rapids: Baker Book House, 1980.

Goldman, Solomon. *The Ten Commandments.* Ed. Maurice Samuel. Chicago and London: University of Chicago Press, 1956. This work does take critical scholarship into account.

A selection of studies of the wording and content of the Commandments:

Alt, Albrecht. "Das Verbot des Diebstahls im Dekalog." In *Kleine Schriften zur Geschichte des Volkes Israel,* 3 vols., vol. 1, pp. 333–340. Munich: C. H. Beck'sche, 1953–59.

Andrew, M. E. "Falsehood and Truth: An Amplified Sermon on Exodus 20:16," *Interpretation* 17 (1963), pp. 425–438.

Dentan, Robert. "The Literary Affinities of Exodus XXXIV 6f," *Vetus Testamentum* 13 (1963), pp. 34–51.

Flusser, D. " 'Do not commit adultery,' 'Do not murder', " *Textus* 4 (1964), pp. 220–224.

Knierim, Rolf. "Das erste Gebot," *Zeitschrift für die alttestamentliche Wissenschaft* 77 (1965), pp. 20–39.

Moran, William L. "The Ancient Near Eastern Background of the Love of God in Deuteronomy," *Catholic Biblical Quarterly* 25 (1963), pp. 77–87.

———. "The Conclusion of the Decalogue (Ex. 20, 17 = Dt. 5, 21)," *Catholic Biblical Quarterly* 29 (1967), pp. 543–554.

Morgenstern, J. "Sabbath." In *The Interpreter's Dictionary of the Bible.* 5 vols. Ed. George Arthur Buttrick and Keith Crim. Nashville and New York: Abingdon Press, 1962–76.

Nicholson, E. W. "The Decalogue as the Direct Address of God," *Vetus Testamentum* 27 (1977), pp. 422–433.

Trible, Phyllis. *God and the Rhetoric of Sexuality*. Overtures to Biblical Theology, vol. 2. Philadelphia: Fortress Press, 1978. Pp. 1–5 in particular.

Zimmerli, Walther. *I Am Yahweh*. Trans. Douglas W. Stott. Atlanta: John Knox Press, 1982.

————. "Das zweite Gebot." In *Gottes Offenbarung: Gesammelte Aufsätze zum Alten Testament*. Theologische Bücherei, vol. 19, pp. 234–248. Munich: Chr. Kaiser Verlag, 1963.

Premier Old Testament theologies with sections on the Ten Commandments:

Eichrodt, Walther. "The Covenant Statutes." In *Theology of the Old Testament*, 2 vols., trans. J. A. Baker, vol. 1, pp. 70–97. Old Testament Library. London: SCM Press, 1961.

von Rad, Gerhard. *Old Testament Theology*. 2 vols. Trans. D. M. G. Stalker. Edinburgh and London: Oliver & Boyd, 1962–65. Vol. 1, pp. 187–219.

Zimmerli, Walther. *Old Testament Theology in Outline*. Trans. David E. Green. Atlanta: John Knox Press, 1978. Pp. 109–124, 125–126, 133–136, 138–140.

Chapter Four

THE BOOK
OF THE
COVENANT

The older Sinaitic accounts preserve a large corpus of laws from the earliest era of Israelite national history. After the Ten Commandments had been delivered directly to the people, Moses was elected to mediate between the people and God and ascended the mountain to receive this law. Later, when the covenant was ratified ceremonially, the "words and judgments" which he had received were written down (24:4) in a book known as the Book of the Covenant (24:7). It has become common to substitute *code* for *book* in the title.

Before embarking upon a commentary on the laws of the Book of the Covenant, I will return to some questions of authorship and form.

Source Criticism

Exodus 20:23–23:19 presents an assortment of commandments, case laws, duties, and motive clauses in serial fashion without significant break. This in its entirety constitutes the lawbook under consideration. The verse that immediately precedes the first law, 20:22, introduces the corpus; it is set apart from the unit 20:18–21 by a shift in the divine name from "God" (Elohim) to "the Lord" (Yahweh). At the end of the collection of laws there is a divine address (23:20–33) giving directions for the departure from Sinai and the conquest of Canaan. In all likelihood this text has been displaced from the narrative of departure (told in Num. 10 but foreshadowed in Exod. 33:1–17). This means that the lawbook ended simply and abruptly with the last law.

The Book of the Covenant cannot be ascribed to the two main early narratives, J (Yahwist) and E (Elohist). Both of these accounts assume that Moses received a decalogue inscribed on two stone tablets, and neither has a place for an additional revelation of divine law, certainly not one of such massive proportions. The Book of the Covenant is commonly treated as an independent document inserted into the Sinaitic narrative at some stage of the process of combining and editing the two older sources. There is evidence, however, that portions of Exodus 19 and 24 belong to the same source. In other words, the Book of the Covenant had a narrative framework which is now integrated into the JE narrative. The verses in chapter 24 that refer to this lawbook by name surely belong to this framework. These verses are a part of a ratification ceremony that rounded off a covenant-making account.

The verse that introduces the Book of the Covenant is linked by vocabulary, style, and thought to a unit in Exodus 19:

> Yahweh said to Moses, "Thus you shall say to the people of Israel: 'You have seen for yourselves that I have talked with you from heaven.'"   (20:22)

> Yahweh called to him out of the mountain, saying, "Thus you shall say to the house of Jacob, and tell the people of Israel: You have seen what I did to the Egyptians, and how I bore you on eagles' wings and brought you to myself."   (19:3–4)

Clearly these two passages are parallel in style and thought and can be ascribed to the same author. This conclusion is further supported by links in vocabulary, style, and thought between 19:3–8 and 24:3–8. Both texts are drawn to the word translated "covenant" and share a distinctive pattern of divine offer and human acceptance. Indeed, the words of acceptance form a litany running through the material:

> All the words that Yahweh has spoken we will do.   (19:8; 24:3, 7; cf. vs. 8)

This evidence adds up to the conclusion that the Book of the Covenant once had a narrative framework consisting of the initial negotiation of the covenant (19:3–8), the revelation of covenant law (20:23—23:19), and the ceremonial ratification of the covenant (24:3–8).

All three of these texts are embedded in E material, suggesting that this account was combined with E before it was combined with J. Since E was, in all likelihood, a northern writing which was

brought to the kingdom of Judah after the Northern Kingdom was
destroyed by Assyria (721 B.C.), one may suppose that the Covenant
Code with its framework was also a northern document which was
combined with the Elohist prior to the fall of the Northern
Kingdom.

Dating the lawbook is rather difficult. The provisions presuppose
an Israel settled in Canaan practicing farming and herding. Hence, it
cannot plausibly be traced back to Moses. Since Deuteronomy relies
on and adapts this code, one can surmise that the code is several
centuries older than D (which is to be dated between 700 and 621
B.C.). This would place it either in the period of the Judges
(1200–1000 B.C.) or the early monarchical period (1000–800 B.C.).
By a process of elimination, the former can be inferred; a king would
have seized the opportunity to promulgate the code to enhance his
prestige (as ancient Near Eastern kings did) if it had been drawn up
during his reign. Since the Book of the Covenant is silent regarding
the monarchy, it is likely that there was no king at the time of its
origin.

Form Criticism

Unlike the Ten Commandments, the Book of the Covenant is
not a nice, tidy series of utterances in the same form and style. It
contains examples of every form discussed in Chapter Two. The
forms, however, are not distributed randomly about the book but
are bunched together in relatively homogenous sections. Exodus 21:1
is an important clue to the formal order. There Yahweh commands
Moses to proclaim "judgments" (author's translation) to the people
of Israel. Between 21:2 and 22:20 are casuistic and related types of
law in impersonal style. The laws of this type govern criminal delicts
and civil torts that would come before a court for adjudication. By
"judgments," then, the text must mean this judicial law.

The passage that precedes "judgments" (Exod. 20:23–26) and the
portions that follow it (22:21–23:9; 23:10–19) contain forms of law
that address the people personally; that is, prohibitions in a style
identical or similar to that of the Ten Commandments. In addition,
there are examples of casuistic law addressed to the owner of duties

and examples of instructions in cultic practice (torah). These personally addressed types of law are much more prone than the impersonal
to being augmented by motive clauses.

This basic division of the Book of the Covenant between impersonal and addressed portions may mean that the present book is the
result of a wedding of two independent blocks of material. According to this view, the "judgments" once constituted a document created by jurists, similar in character to the royal codes of the ancient
Near East. The addressed portions would derive from some other
setting, probably an oral proclamation of moral and religious
teaching.

It would be a mistake, however, to stress the difference in form
and origin of the "judgments" to the detriment of the unity of the
code as it now stands. Moses is told to "set the judgments before" the
people, a phrase indicating oral proclamation. Moreover, there is a
scattering of personal address in the impersonal section. Such variants
can only be explained on the assumption that the lawgiver is presenting the judgments orally to an audience. Thus, the *whole* of the Book
of the Covenant as it now stands has the telltale signs of an oral proclamation of law to the community under its authority.

COMMENTARY

The following outline is given so that the reader will have as it
were a map of the forest about to be entered. It should be noted that
the passage references are to the English Bible; the Hebrew Bible
numbers the end of chapter 21 and all of chapter 22 differently: the
English 22:1 = the Hebrew 21:37; English 22:2 = Hebrew 22:1; and
so forth.

OUTLINE OF THE BOOK OF THE COVENANT

   I. The Law of the Altar (Exod. 20:23–26)
  II. The Judgments (Exod. 21:1–22:20)
      A. Slavery (21:2–11)
      B. Capital Crimes (21:12–17)
      C. Injury to Person by a Person (21:18–27)
      D. Death of Person or Animal by an Animal (21:28–36)
      E. Theft, Damages, and Ownership Disputes (22:1–15)
      F. Seduction of Woman Not Betrothed (22:16–17)

It is recommended that the reader have a Bible at hand, as a full translation of the text will not be reproduced. The first clause of the passage to be discussed is quoted at the head of the commentary on it; the remainder is to be read from the Bible in hand.

The Law of the Altar. The Book of the Covenant begins with a series of laws governing the construction of sanctuaries devoted to Yahweh. It falls into two parts, a couplet prohibiting idols (vs. 23) and a series of rules for the construction of sacrificial altars (vss. 24–26). These two parts are of different ages and by different hands: the couplet is formulated in second person plural address, the series in second person singular; the couplet assumes a fairly wealthy and sophisticated civilization (idols made of precious metals), whereas the series belongs to a simple, rustic one.

"You shall not make gods of silver . . ." (20:23).

This couplet is a significant example of the second commandment, applying the prohibition of idols specifically to the sanctuary devoted to Yahweh. Since the Hebrew word for "God" can also mean "gods," the prohibition can mean both "a *God* of silver/gold" and "*gods* of silver/gold." Thus, both representations of Yahweh and of other deities are ruled out in the same expression. The designation of images as "god/gods of silver/gold" is quite striking and is suggestive of the way by which an image became identified with the deity represented.

"An altar of earth you shall make . . ." (20:24–26).

These verses enjoin the making of altars and prescribe the way they are to be constructed. The heart of the altar law is the promise

of God to be present and to bless the community at altars marking
the divine presence:

> In every place where I cause my name to be remembered I will come to you
> and bless you.

There is a multitude of legitimate altars (in contrast to Deut. 12);
each is a place where Yahweh has caused his name to dwell, perhaps
by revelation (cf., e.g., Gen. 12:6–7; 13:18; 18:1; 28:10–22; Judg.
6:11–24).

The divine presence and blessing are granted in response to the
sacrifices offered upon the altar. There is no explanation of how sacrifice has the capacity to procure divine favor; it is simply assumed.
The passage does summarize the types of sacrifices in use at the time:
"your burnt offerings and your peace offerings." A burnt offering, or
holocaust, was a sacrifice in which the entire victim was burnt,
whereas a peace or well-being offering was one in which a portion of
the victim's fat was burnt and the remainder of the flesh was eaten
by the offerer and the offerer's family. The phrase "your sheep and
your oxen" covers the kinds of animals used in Israelite sacrifice.

The rules for the construction of the altar place a premium on
simplicity. The altar is to be built of sod ("earth") or alternatively of
rough field stones. The use of hewn stone is expressly forbidden, for
"if you wield your tool upon it you profane it." To "profane" a
stone is, evidently, to violate the integrity it has in the natural state.
The possibility of using quarried stone is not even envisaged. Verse 26
prohibits the construction of steps at the base. This means that the
altar was to be built sufficiently low for a person to reach the top
while standing on the ground. The explanation, "that your nakedness be not exposed on it," is obscure and has occasioned much scholarly discussion. Perhaps this statement simply means that those
standing around the altar could see under the garments of the one
who had ascended the steps. It might, however, be concerned with
standing on a portion of the altar, for the steps would share in the
holiness of the altar proper. In this case, "nakedness" would mean the
finitude of the creature in the presence of the holy.

The rules of construction laid down in this law reflect a very
early period in Israel's history. What is envisaged is an open-air altar

of the most primitive construction without a temple compound or other accouterments of settled life. The major cultic centers of the monarchical period ignored these rules; the altars at Jerusalem, Bethel, and elsewhere were made of hewn stone and even bronze, and some at least had steps. Yet it was the ideal of a simple sanctuary which inspired prophets like Amos and Hosea to criticize the lavish cult of later times (cf. Hos. 10:1–2; Amos 3:13–15).

The Judgments. The large, central portion of the Book of the Covenant is headed by a superscription:

> These are the judgments which you shall set before them.

The term translated "judgments" (*mishpatim*) sounds like a technical term for the category of law known since Alt as casuistic. Most of the laws in 21:2—22:20 belong to this category, and those that do not are sufficiently similar to fit under the heading. There is warrant for treating this section as an internally homogenous, self-contained corpus. One should not overlook the fact, however, that the superscription is a commission addressed to Moses which looks toward the oral presentation of the judgments to the people of Israel. This means that one cannot divorce the corpus of judgments from the rest of the code or from the Sinaitic setting without doing violence to the very verse that sets it apart.

"When you buy a Hebrew slave . . ." (21:2–11).

The first section governs two types of slavery. The first paragraph (vss. 2–6) concerns the enslavement of a male for his labor, the second (vss. 7–11) the enslavement of a female for marriage. Both are examples of the category I call casuistic law governing primary rights and duties. A primary right is an entitlement to be or do something; others owe duties to one's rights. Primary rights and duties exist in themselves prior to any breach of rights. Remedial rights come into play when rights have been violated and the injured party seeks relief, compensation, or punishment from the court.

Most casuistic law is remedial: it describes a violation of rights in the protasis, or *if* clause, and prescribes the remedy (compensation and/or punishment) in the apodosis. In these slave laws, however, the protasis names a legal relation and the apodosis describes the terms of the relation. In verse 2 the first clause of the apodosis grants the buyer the right to six years' labor, and the second clause grants the slave the right to freedom after six years of service. The next section (vss. 3–4) enunciates the rights of the slave and master at the conclusion of the legal relation. The third (vss. 5–6) states the conditions and procedure for nullifying the slave's right to freedom. In the law for female slavery, verse 7 describes the relation, specifically excluding the right to freedom granted in verse 2. The following verses (8–11) impose duties on the one who purchased the woman and state the conditions under which she would be granted freedom.

The kind of slavery described in verses 2–6 is known in later history as *indentured service*. A person who was financially insolvent would sell himself or his son to a fellow Israelite for the stipulated period of time. The term "Hebrew" in the law once designated a distinct social class ("outcast" or "outlaw") in the ancient Near East, but by the time this law was composed it had come to approximate "Israelite." In other words, both laws govern relations between members of the same group of people and explicitly forbid selling the slave to foreigners (vs. 8).

Verses 3–4 could all be subsumed under the rule that a male slave goes free in the same marital state as he entered service. If the slave were married at the time of his purchase, the master would have been able to calculate that fact when he entered the arrangement. The slave could not contract a marriage while enslaved unless his master provided a woman, and the law assumes that the master would give a slave, for a free woman would not have been his to give. This assumption explains the reason she remains the master's slave when her husband gains his freedom (vs. 4). The rule, though logical in itself, had the harsh consequence of breaking up a marriage when the slave fulfilled his service and undoubtedly was an inducement for the male slave to renounce his right to freedom.

When the slave renounces his right to freedom (vss. 5–6), he must clearly and formally declare his desire to remain a slave, not just express a casual wish, as the master might seize any pretext for making the arrangement permanent. The formal ceremony before God in the sanctuary would have consisted of an oath. This would guarantee the deliberateness of his decision to remain a slave and bind him to that decision for the rest of his life. There was also a ceremony performed at the master's house in which the slave took on a mark (a pierced ear) that signified his belonging to the household.

The institution of female slavery differs substantially from indentured servitude. First, it appears to be limited to a young, unattached woman sold by her father. Second, the woman is acquired as a concubine—perhaps a better term is *slave wife*. To be sure, she was also expected to perform work, but the law is silent on this aspect of the arrangement.

When a man purchased such a woman, he entered into an obligation to her analogous to betrothal. If he decided not to marry her, he could not sell her to a foreigner and had to allow her to be redeemed, that is, bought back by her family. Of course, if her father sold her under financial duress, it is hard to see how he would have the money to pay the redemption price. Although the law does not say so, her master probably did have the right to sell her to another Israelite or give her to a slave if she was not redeemed. This would explain why the lawgiver inserts a prohibition against selling her to a foreigner. Many translators suggest that he "broke faith" with her by not going through with the marriage, but it is possible that selling her to a foreign people is the act of breaking faith.

If the man purchases the woman for marriage with his son (vs. 9), he must treat her as a daughter within the household until she is married. Presumably this means that he is not to have sexual intercourse with her or treat her in a demeaning way.

Finally, the slave wife is protected under the conditions of polygamy (vss. 10–11). Although she undoubtedly did not enjoy the full rights of a free married woman, she could at least claim a basic standard of fairness—adequate food and clothing and the possibility of bearing children. If these rights were abrogated, her duties were dissolved and she could leave a free woman. One may assume that this would require the judgment of a court and that her father, brother, uncle, or some righteous man of the community would have to champion her cause in court.

The two types of slavery described in 21:2–11 are hardly an exhaustive description of slavery in Israel and other ancient Near Eastern societies. Even within these laws it seems that children born to slaves were themselves counted as slaves (vs. 5). This assumes something much more permanent than indentured servitude. It is also known that captives of war were permanently enslaved and that an international slave trade existed. A person enslaved in a foreign country would have little chance of gaining freedom. Israelite society most likely had permanent slaves of foreign origin, though very little is heard about them in the laws.

The institution of slavery was the natural outgrowth of the economic, social, and political structure of ancient Near Eastern societies. These laws do not assail the institution but attempt to regulate it and to protect the slaves from their masters. In the initial address (vs. 2) and various admonitions in the law, one can hear the appeal of the lawgiver to the master to honor the rights of his slave. The very act of enunciating slave rights laid the foundation for a more radical critique of the institution in later law.

"Whoever strikes a man so that he dies . . ." (21:12–17).

The style of the four principle laws (vss. 12, 15, 16, 17) is distinctive. Each law begins with a participial phrase as the subject of the sentence and repeats the same verbal clause, "[he] shall be put to death." Grouped together as they are, they strike the reader as something of a series. Alt surmised that this series was an example of apodictic law, but one should not be too quick to follow him. Like casuistic law, these laws are impersonal and judicial, whereas apodictic commandments are personal and moral (nonjuridical).

The law prescribing capital punishment for killing articulates the consensus of Scripture on this crime. As I stated in the commentary on the sixth commandment, P considers this law to have been given to Noah, hence, a universal law of human life. Each human bears the image of God, and so killing is an attack upon God. By a logic of equivalence ("life for life," Exod. 21:23), the killer forfeits the right to life. Israelite law is distinctive in its insistence on the death penalty for *all* murder; other codes of the ancient Near East allowed payments when a member of a superior class killed someone of an inferior class (Pritchard, *ANET*, Code of Hammurabi, Par. 207ff; cf. Hittite Laws, Pars. 1–5, 174). With Israel, however, class differences could not enter into the fundamental evaluation of a human person. This is one place where biblical monotheism had revolutionary import.

The law governing murder has been augmented by an addendum explaining the administration of the law. In the form of Yahweh's addressing the court personally, it outlines the distinction between intentional and accidental homicide and how each is to be handled. The clauses defining accidental slaying are cryptic:

> If he did not lie in wait for him, but God let him fall into his hand.... (vs. 13)

This statement sounds as if the court demanded overt evidence of premeditation to demonstrate intention. The description of murder also suggests the need for evidence of conscious deliberation:

> If a person schemes against another to kill him treacherously.... (vs. 14, author's translation)

This is equivalent to our phrase, "malice of forethought."

The addendum gives the impression of greater leniency than in fact obtained. If, for example, the case dealt with in verse 18 ("When men quarrel and one strikes the other with a stone or with his fist ...") had resulted in death, it would fit the definition of accidental homicide (vs. 13). It is my opinion, however, that it would have been treated as murder, although there was no scheming, and the blow itself was not intended to kill. The general tenor of verses 18–27 suggests that an act intended to harm someone, even if done in a moment of passion and without the intent to kill, would be counted as murder if death resulted. This would be the logical conclusion of a rigorous ethic that counted the desire to harm under all circumstances morally reprehensible.

In its description of the handling of the case, the addendum assumes the institution of blood vengeance, by which a male member of the victim's family was obligated to seek out and execute the killer. Verse 13 promises sanctuary to one who would be killed by the avenger of the blood. When the avenger sought the killer at the sanctuary, a trial could be convened to determine whether the person taking sanctuary should be removed to be executed by the avenger or allowed to remain.

The remark "I will appoint for you a place to which he may flee" raises a problem. Other texts speak of a series of six cities of asylum spread about the land, three in Canaan and three in Transjordan (Num. 35:13–15; Deut. 19:7–9; Josh. 20:7–9). The Exodus passage, however, uses the singular, and whether it means the six cities of asylum or each and every sanctuary is impossible to decide on the basis of the text.

The remaining three laws governing capital crimes do not require extensive commentary. Two (vss. 15, 17) concern the rights of parents. Both physical attack and verbal abuse of parents by their children (presumably minors in the home) could be punished by execution. Unlike the law governing murder, execution would not have been mandatory; indeed, it is doubtful that parents exercised this option with any frequency. Biblical literature reveals a great deal of parental affection for children. If executions ever did occur, they would not have involved the larger community.

The other capital crime, kidnapping, is of a more public character. The law assumed the existence of an international slave trade, where victims were seized and sold to caravan traders, who would convey them to foreign slave markets. Once in a foreign country, the victim would have little possibility of regaining his or her freedom by legal process or escape. Verse 16 inserts a clause to extend the crime of slave trading to include a trader found in possession of a victim. In other words, a person proven to have sold a person and one caught in possession of someone would both be counted as liable. A person charged with this crime would have been judged by a court and executed by the community.

A rather striking aspect of this series of capital crimes is the diversity of legal processes and agents and types of execution. The murderer was executed by the avenger of the blood after a hearing on his or her right to sanctuary. The kidnapper was executed by the community after a trial establishing guilt. The child who struck or reviled his or her parents could have been executed summarily by the parents. This diversity indicates that the formula "[he] shall be put to death" is more in the nature of a divine authorization than a specific legal penalty. Such a momentous act as taking life required God's approval; no individual or community could take this responsibility upon itself. This principle distinguishes divine law from human. Only the Lord of life can sanction the taking of life.

"When men quarrel and one strikes the other . . ." (21:18–27).

The next three segments of the judgments (21:18–27, 28–36; 22:1–15) are collections of casuistic remedial law. Casuistic law, as defined earlier, is the type of legal formulation with a protasis describing the case under consideration and differentiating it from similar cases, and an apodosis prescribing the legal consequences. Remedial casuistic law stipulates a remedy (compensation or punishment) for violation of primary rights.

The first segment of casuistic remedial law (21:18–27) is related to the section governing capital crimes, particularly the law governing killing (21:12–14). There are four paragraphs beginning with "when" (vss. 18, 20, 22, 26), each describing a case of striking which for one reason or another is not settled by the law of homicide.

The first paragraph (vss. 18–19) considers a case of striking that did not result in death. If a free citizen injures another in a fight, that person is not liable as a criminal: "he that struck him shall be clear [of bloodguilt]." Presumably the mention of "stone or . . . fist" means to exclude a case in which a lethal weapon (sword, etc.) was used. If someone picks up a stone in a fight, it is a matter of momentary passion, not a premeditated attack to kill or injure. Nevertheless, if death resulted, the assailant probably would have been prosecuted as a murderer (see above). In any case, where there is no evidence of premeditation and the result is injury, the case is given a civil remedy—compensation for loss of income during convalescence. The form of compensation is left up to the parties and the court. The final clause ("and shall have him thoroughly healed") indicates that the assailant is liable not only until the victim can walk abroad but until the victim can earn a living.

The second paragraph (vss. 20–21) concerns a master's killing his slave. Such a case would not fall automatically under murder. The apodosis ("he shall be punished") may mean the death penalty, thereby bringing the killing of a slave under the general law of homicide, but the wording is vague and could have meant some lesser penalty. Moreover, the subordinate case ("but if the slave survives a day or two, he is not to be punished") restricts the master's criminal liability to immediate death. The reasoning is this: a master has a right to strike (whip, beat with a staff, etc.) his slave to force him or her to work, but he has no such right in respect to free citizens. When he strikes his slave, it is presumed that he does not intend the latter's death but only seeks to coerce fulfillment of duty. If his corporal punishment results in convalescence and/or death, it is in the nature of an accident and he suffers economic loss. If the liability of a master for the death of his slave were unlimited, it would effectively remove his freedom to coerce the slave and would make the institution unfeasible.

The third paragraph (vss. 22–25) rules on injury to a pregnant woman and takes the opportunity to declare a general principle of remedial law. The protasis, "When men strive together and hurt a woman with child, so that . . . ," suggests that the blow to the woman need not be intended. In other words, the rule holds whether the woman was intentionally or accidentally harmed. If the blow results in a miscarriage, the case falls under the category of civil tort rather than criminal delict. The unborn child, in this case, is not considered a person protected by the law of homicide. The loss is to the parents, and they have the right to financial compensation. There is some question (because of the last clause, which could mean either "he shall pay as determined by the judges" or "in accordance with an assessment") whether the woman's husband was free to soak the liable party or whether judges or arbiters could force restraints.

Verses 23–25 take the occasion to introduce a rule for assessing criminal liability for harm to persons:

> If any harm follows, then you shall give life for life, eye for eye, tooth for tooth, hand for hand, foot for foot, burn for burn, wound for wound, stripe for stripe.

Although this commandment, known as *lex talionis*, is attached to this one case, it really applies to all cases of death and injury. It is noteworthy for its shift to personal address and its graphic, poetic quality. The addressee is the court that imposes penalties. The principle is simple and logical: a person should suffer to the same degree that the person caused suffering. How literally the *lex talionis* was read and applied in ancient Israel is not as clear. There are very few penalties involving mutilation in biblical law; that is, while the phrase "life for life" was taken literally, it is not certain that eyes were put out, teeth broken out, hands cut off, and so forth. These may be poetic equivalences that were translated into monetary compensation. On the other hand, the Holiness Code applies the principle of retaliation with utmost literalism (Lev. 24:19–20). Despite this counter-evidence, I seriously doubt that mutilation for bodily injury was intended. There is no hint of it, for example, in the case treated in verses 18–19, and verses 26–27 apply the rule of compensation to injury of slaves.

It should be noted that the *lex talionis* derives from pre-Israelite ancient Near Eastern legal tradition. It was a principle for assessing penalties that struck the ancient Near Eastern mind as eminently reasonable and fair, though it has come to be a symbol of legal barbarism.

The fourth paragraph (vss. 26–27) returns to injury of slaves. Though a master had the right to beat his slave, if he caused permanent injury he lost his rights over his chattel. The examples of "eye" and "tooth" suggest that the topic came to the lawgiver's mind when he introduced the *lex talionis* and that he sought to formulate the principle of equivalence in compensatory terms. The result is a strikingly enlightened provision protecting the person of the slave.

"When an ox gores a man or a woman . . ." (21:28–36).

This segment of casuistic remedial law considers the liability of an owner of an ox for the harm it does to humans (vss. 28–32) and animals (vss. 35–36), and the owner of a pit for injury to animals (vss. 33–34). The topic is the natural follow-up to death and injury due to human assault, though it moves even further from criminal law.

The first paragraph (vss. 28–32) rules on several cases of an ox goring a human to death. In every case the ox shall be killed for causing the death of a human being. Although the destruction of the ox could be justified on purely rational grounds (namely, to avoid repetition), the type of destruction (execution by stoning) and the taboo attached to the meat indicate that the ox was regarded as a "guilty party." It appears to be a case of fictitious guilt—that is, the animal is treated as a criminal in lieu of a morally responsible agent. In addition, the ox has violated the hierarchy of being which places humans over animals (see Postscript).

The liability of the owner varies according to circumstances. If the ox was not accustomed to gore, the owner is not criminally liable; there is, however, no mention of compensation for the victim's family. If the ox was accustomed to gore, the owner should have taken measures to prevent its harming anyone. As evidence that the ox was known to the owner to do this, the court would seek testimony that "its owner had been warned" (vs. 29). If the owner was found to have been negligent in restraining the ox, he or she was liable to the death penalty, but since it was not a case of intentional killing, the owner could be "ransomed" instead of executed (vs. 30). The more logical penalty would have been monetary compensation for harm due to negligence, but biblical lawgivers abhored the idea of setting a monetary value on human life (see Postscript).

Verses 31–32 consider the goring of children or slaves. Although one would expect the death of a child to be treated in the same way as that of a free adult, it was necessary to say as much in an ancient Near Eastern context to avoid the application of literal equivalence, namely, the execution of the ox owner's child (cf. Code of Hammurabi, Pars. 229ff). In case the victim was a slave, the ox owner must compensate the slave owner according to the going price for slaves. The slave is the one exception to the rule that humans cannot be assigned monetary value.

To avoid the thought that an ox's killing another ox is in any way comparable to its killing a human being, the lawgiver breaks the topical sequence with the case of an animal that falls into an uncovered cistern or well (vss. 33–34). The negligent party was liable to the animal's owner to pay the price of a new animal. It is worth noting that the ruling lacks any element of extra compensation for the distress caused to the animal's owner or punishment for negligence. In fact, the animal that has been killed goes to the pit owner!

The final paragraph (vss. 35–36) returns to the goring ox. The case is like that of the cistern, not that of the death of a human being. The ox which is the victim of goring is to be used for food (as in vss. 33–34), but here it is divided between the two parties, who also divide the payment received for the goring ox. Since the ox did not kill a human but another animal, it could be sold rather than slaughtered. The ruling operates on the principle of shared loss and compensation (as in vss. 33–34). The subordinate case (vs. 36) applies the ruling of verses 33–34 to the case of an ox that is known to gore: the owner of the ox must replace the victim and in return gets the meat of the victim. Presumably, the owner is allowed to keep the goring ox if he or she so desires or sell it to pay the owner of the victim.

"If a man steals an ox or a sheep ..." (22:1–15 [Hebrew: 21:17–22:14]).

The third segment of the collection of casuistic remedial law covers loss or damage of personal property due to theft, negligence, or accident. The material has a somewhat disorderly appearance, but it is possible to discern three basic, though unequal, units: (*a*) animal theft (22:1–4), (*b*) damage to crops (22:5–6), and (*c*) goods or livestock lost or injured under contract of bailment (22:7–15). The relatedness of this material can be recognized if one realizes that what we call larceny was treated as a civil tort rather than as a crime against the state. Hence, all the cases under consideration would involve a suit with a property owner as plaintiff and a person charged with stealing or damaging property as defendant.

(a) The first paragraph treats theft proper. Verses 22:1, 3b–4 stipulate the terms of settlement for animal rustling, and verses 2–3a break the thought sequence to consider guilt for killing a thief. The best way to proceed is to discuss 22:1, 3b–4 together and then comment on 22:2–3a.

The primary focus of the livestock rustling law is not upon establishing guilt or classifying acts but upon setting the terms of settlement. In other words, the law proceeds from the assumption that the thief has been convicted. The basic principle for settlement is *restitution with compensation*—the owner must get back what was lost and be

compensated for his or her distress. The compensation also functions
as a punishment of the thief and an attempt to render repeated rustling unprofitable (if the rate of apprehension were, say, one in three,
it would be unprofitable).

Several factors enter into the computation of compensation. If
the stolen animal has been slaughtered or sold, the compensation is
computed according to the value of the animal. The rate (fivefold
for cattle, fourfold for sheep) is quite steep, presumably because the
animal is unrecoverable and the chances of apprehension and conviction are proportionately lower. If the thief has been caught in possession of the animal, he or she has only to return the animal and add
another. If the thief cannot afford to compensate the plaintiff, he or
she is liable to being sold into slavery. This rule suggests that at least
some thieves were poor people, who resorted to theft out of dire
necessity. A sympathetic court could have granted the rustler the opportunity to work off the debt. The harshness of the penalty would
discourage false pleas of poverty.

In the middle of the unit, the lawgiver takes the occasion to rule
on a problem that would arise in conjunction with theft. If the owner exercised the right to defend his or her property against an intruder, would the owner be held guilty of murder? The answer is
surprising. As one would expect, an owner is not guilty of murder
for killing an intruder after dark, when one cannot recognize the
culprit or know whether the intruder has a weapon and one's own
safety is in question. The rule for the killing of a daytime intruder,
however, states that the killer is liable to prosecution as a murderer.
This means, in effect, that the life of a thief is protected in the very
act of intrusion. Nothing testifies more strongly to the biblical appre-
ciation of the value of the human person over property. Of course,
there would be less danger during the day, when the owner would
be able to recognize and apprehend the thief on the spot or have him
or her apprehended. Nevertheless, this is an amazingly humane principle of law.

(b) Verses 22:5–6 depart from the law of theft entirely to take up
damages to a farmer's grain or vineyard from grazing and burning.
The verse dealing with grazing has a number of textual difficulties.
The most likely rendering is:

> When a man causes a field or vineyard to be *grazed*
> or lets loose his livestock and they feed on another's field
>   [he shall make full restitution from his field
>   according to its yield;
> but if the whole field has been grazed over]
>   he shall make restitution from the best of his field
>   or the best of his vineyard. (author's translation)

The word *grazed* most commonly means "consumed by fire," but it must mean "consumed by grazing" here. The clauses in brackets are restored from the Greek translation known as the Septuagint.

The initial protasis has two clauses to cover both intentional and unintentional grazing. In other words, neither intent to graze another's field nor negligence need be proven to merit judgment. The animal owner in all cases must restore to the owner of the crop the loss suffered. If the field was partially grazed, the defendant must make up the difference between its actual yield and what it would have yielded without grazing, and if the crop was a total loss, the defendant must make good the entire yield (computed as the "best" possible one). The law of burning likewise ignores the question of guilt—a fire tender must make good any loss caused by a fire he or she ignited.

(c) The remainder of this segment of casuistic remedial law deals with goods and animals held in trust or hired by another. Verses 7–8 and 10–13 cover goods and animals that disappear while held in trust. The verse between these two laws (vs. 9) generalizes the principle articulated in verses 8 and 11. The final law (vss. 14–15) treats the analogous problem of death or injury to hired animals.

Verses 7–8 involve a case in which a person deposits goods with another and they disappear. If a thief is apprehended, he or she would simply be prosecuted according to the law of theft, which in the case of personal goods stipulated double compensation. If no thief is found, the bailee (the party holding goods in trust) must take an oath before God to the effect that he or she did not appropriate the goods. Since an oath called down divine sanctions upon the swearer, the bailee would (in theory) refuse to take the oath if he or she were guilty, thereby admitting guilt and coming under the law of theft. If the bailee took the oath, the depositor would have to accept it and

make no more legal claims upon the bailee (vs. 11). Whether the
bailee had to pay the depositor the value of the goods is unstated.

The case of an animal held in trust (vss. 10–13) involves several
contingencies. The description of the case in verse 10 includes death,
injury, and disappearance without a witness. No ruling is necessary
for injury, so the remainder of the law proposes remedies for disappearance and death. If the animal disappeared without a witness, the
case is handled in the same way as that of lost goods. Although the
initial clause "an oath by Yahweh shall be between them" sounds as
if both parties took an oath, it is clear from what follows ("to see
whether he has not put his hand . . .") that the bailee alone is involved. The following clause requires the owner to be satisfied with
the oath without restitution. Verse 12, however, seems to stipulate
that if the animal were *stolen* from the bailee, he or she must restore
it. This does not seem consistent, for it would encourage the bailee to
plead ignorance of the loss. Perhaps the text (read reflexively rather
than passively) means to say that if the bailee *himself* or *herself* appropriated the animal, that individual was liable to the rules of restitution with compensation laid down in 22:1, 4. If the bailee asserted
that the animal had died or was killed by a wild animal, evidence
had to be produced to that effect (vs. 13). If the court could be
persuaded of that claim, the bailee was absolved of liability.

Verse 9 generalizes the principle of oath taking to cases of disputed ownership. Although the initial words "For every breach of trust"
sound as though the verse still dealt with bailment, the remainder of
the protasis would apply to any case in which the owner of an
animal claimed to identify the animal in the possession of another
person. Hence, it relates to the law of theft in 22:1–4: whenever one
lost an animal and thought that one had found it in another's possession, the case could be brought before God. Presumably, the party
charged would first submit to an oath. If this did not resolve the case,
there seems to have been a follow-up procedure by which God declares one or the other party "guilty" (perhaps by sacred lot). Either
the one charged would be declared guilty or the one bringing the
charges would be held responsible for false charges; twofold compensation would be exacted in either case.

The final paragraph of the section (vss. 14–15) deals with animals borrowed for purposes of work or perhaps stud service. If the animal is injured or dies, the borrower must provide the owner with a new animal to replace it. The one who initiated the transaction is liable. The expression "make restitution" seems to have various meanings in these laws—sometimes only the supplying of a replacement, sometimes the return or replacement of the original plus one, three, or four additional animals as compensation. In this case, it must mean simple replacement. Verse 15 puts two qualifications on the borrower's liability. If the owner is present when the animal is injured, the borrower is no longer liable. The owner most likely would be driving his or her own animal and would have to take the blame for injury. If the animal has been rented for work, the risk for injury or death has been calculated into the rental fee; hence, the owner, not the borrower, assumes the risk.

"If a man seduces a virgin . . ." (22:16–17).

The only example of marriage law in the Book of the Covenant stands isolated at the conclusion of the collection of casuistic remedial law. Some scholars think that it belongs to the section on property theft and damages, but it can just as well be classified as a separate section. Despite assertions to the contrary, women were not classified as chattel of their fathers or husbands in ancient Israel.

The case before us deals with sexual intercourse between a man and a woman who is not betrothed. Although the word translated "seduce" suggests consent, that may be irrelevant to the legal classification. The status of the woman, however, is quite relevant. If she were betrothed, it would be a case of adultery or rape (see Deut. 22:23–27). Since she is unattached, the man incurs the responsibility of marriage by committing an act reserved for marriage.

The "marriage present" or bridal price he is obligated to pay was a fee that a prospective husband was expected to pay the parents for their daughter. Though the purpose of the institution is unclear, the bridal price is not a purchase. It probably functioned to solidify family ties and at the same time "compensate" a family for the loss of a member. It seems to have fallen into disuse in later times, for the Deuteronomic parallel (Deut. 22:28–29) substitutes a fixed fee as compensation for violating her.

The seducer owes the bridal price whether he marries the woman or not, and he is obligated to marry her if her parents are willing. However, her father has the right to refuse (and might very well, given the circumstances), just as he had the right to reject a marriage proposal.

"You shall not permit a sorceress to live" (22:18–20).

These verses cover three violations of the religious and moral order of the community. There is some question whether the section belongs with the judgments or in the following section of addressed laws covering moral questions. I would put them with the judgments because stylistically they resemble the laws governing capital crimes (21:12–17)—so much so that Alt considered the two sections to be fragments from the same series—and because these laws provide legal remedy for violation (namely, execution), whereas the laws in the following section do not.

Verse 18 can be translated, with a slight emendation, as: "Whoever practices sorcery shall not live." The emendation yields an impersonal style characteristic of Exodus 21:12, 15, 16, 17 and 22:19, 20. I do not know why it reads "shall not live" rather than "shall be put to death." The participle translated "whoever practices sorcery" is feminine in Hebrew, suggesting that women were more prone to this sort of action than men; undoubtedly male practitioners came under the ruling as well. Indeed, the law was probably intended to cover not only the specific practice known as "sorcery" (using magical spells and charms for sinister purposes) but all magical and occult practices.

It is possible that sorcery was understood in ancient Israel as a crime against other persons. Several ancient Near Eastern codes (Code of Hammurabi, Par. 2; Middle Assyrian Laws, Tab. A, Par. 47) have provisions against sorcery on the assumption that it harms persons. Biblical tradition, however, shows less interest in the harm black magic might do to others than in its violation of the religious principles on which Israel is to base its life.

The condemnation of sexual intercourse with animals (vs. 19) is repeated several times in Scripture (Lev. 18:23; 20:15–16; Deut. 27:21). Presumably it is so roundly condemned because it is an extremely degrading act that violates the image of God in humans. Israel had precedent for this provision in the Hittite Laws (Pars. 187–8, 199–200).

The final law of this series (vs. 20) embodies the thrust of the first commandment. Sacrificing to a deity is the most overt form of recognition and honor possible, and, clearly, sacrificing to other gods than Yahweh would be intolerable in a community based upon exclusive loyalty to him and under his sovereignty. If Israel had practiced religious tolerance, they would have quickly come to resemble the polytheistic societies around them. The expression "shall be utterly destroyed" has occasioned some comment. It was applied mostly to the enemies who fought against Israel in the war of Yahweh, or holy war, but it is infrequently applied to Israelites (Lev. 27:29; Deut. 13:16; Judg. 21:11; cf. Josh. 7). Whether its use here implies some unusual form of execution is impossible to say. It has been suggested that it means that Israel is to wipe out the memory of the guilty person, even to the point of executing the person's family as well (as in Josh. 7), but this would be a rather speculative and dangerous inference to draw from such meager evidence. All that can be said with certainty is that the offense was considered by the lawgiver to be the worst sort of violation of the religious order.

Moral Commandments and Primary Law. No superscription sets off the next division of the Book of the Covenant from the judgments, but the shift in mood, style, and subject matter is unmistakable. Most of the judgments are impersonal and relatively technical, but now God addresses Israel personally on subjects of a moral and religious character. The form is commandment or casuistic law protecting primary rights. There are no legal sanctions; instead, motive clauses seek to persuade compliance. The division falls into three relatively coherent parts: (*a*) the rights of the weak (22:21–27), (*b*) religious prohibitions and duties (22:28–31), and (*c*) court process and duties of assistance (23:1–9). The following exposition will take up each in turn.

"You shall not wrong a stranger . . ." (22:21–27).

These laws protect the rights of the weaker members of the legal community, exemplifying the concept that every person in the com-

munity is endowed with inalienable rights by the people's Lord. The
test of any legal system's respect for rights is its respect for the rights
of its weakest members. In this section Yahweh becomes the patron
of marginal persons, granting and guaranteeing the rights of those
who lacked the capacity to compel others to respect them.

The passage begins with two prohibitions in a distinctive, inverted commandment style. They are rather vague: do not "wrong,"
"oppress," or "afflict" the persons named. The word translated
"stranger" (sojourner or resident alien) designated a class of people
who did not enjoy the full rights of citizens. In early times even
Israelites might belong to the class if they were living apart from
their clan, and non-Israelites living permanently within Israel were
always so classified. These people were expected to conform in a general way to the religious and moral milieu but did not enjoy all the
privileges. They had no family estates passed from generation to generation. They may have been permitted to own real property by
purchase, but the biblical texts suggest that they commonly earned a
living by day labor. Without inherited land, a sojourner could not sit
among the elders and may not have been allowed to institute suits
before the court and thus was vulnerable to exploitation, fraud, and
social ostracism.

The widow and orphan (fatherless) were vulnerable because
they had no adult male to provide a living and defend their interests. In a society where the male head of a household performed
public duties, a household without a male head was dependent upon the extended family and the good will of the community for
survival. Likely the widow and orphan of a well-to-do man were
not so destitute, but the law speaks for the many who were: they
are to be protected in the little that they have and subsidized by
the community. God offers divine protection by threatening to
hear their outcries against their oppressors and to render poetic
justice.

Verses 25–27 depart from the prohibition form to casuistic law
governing primary rights and duties. The legal relationship under
consideration is a loan to a poor person. The lender, the stronger
party of the relationship, is forbidden to cause social disgrace or to
earn interest out of the distress of the needy. Presumably Israelite law

allowed loans on interest for business ventures but did not allow such when the loan was necessary to keep an impoverished person solvent.

When the loan came due and the borrower did not repay, the lender could distrain some movable possession of the debtor to enforce payment. The lawgiver does not condemn the practice of distraint, but he does require moral restraint, that is, the lender should not create further hardship by keeping the distrained item when it is needed (vss. 26–27).

The lending law concludes with God's promise to hear the poor in their distress. When an afflicted person cries out to God in prayer, by God's gracious nature the prayer will be heard. By implication, God will intervene on the behalf of the poor against the oppressor, namely, the lender; hence, the threat of judgment made in verse 24 is implied in verse 27 as well. What is striking is that judgment is characterized as an act of grace toward the oppressed—an important theological idea.

"You shall not revile God . . ." (22:28–31).

Exodus 22:28–31 is distinguished by a threefold "to me" (vss. 29, 30, 31) in a series of duties to God. It is somewhat of a mystery as to why these laws are so separated from the last division of the lawbook (cf. in particular 23:19a; also 34:19–20).

Verse 28 stands out from the rest as a prohibition (with inverted word order as in 22:21, 22) that refers to God in the third person, though God is the speaker of the lawbook. In content, the unique parallelism of an action toward God and an action toward a human tends to identify the human authority structure with God's. Indeed, it must be kept in mind that human authority within Israel was derived from God's authority and possessed something of the sanctity of its source. The word translated "revile" is the same as the word in 21:17, where parents are the object; here, it probably means any form of overt verbal abuse or disparagement. The parallel word "curse" suggests stronger utterances intending to bring harm to a person. The word translated "ruler" varied in meaning with the era, referring to judges during the early period and to kings and officials later. 2 Samuel 16:5–8 is an example of the sort of verbal abuse of a leader that would come under this rule.

Verses 29–30 deal with "first things." A special quality of sanctity attached to the first crop and firstborn. Since anything set apart as sacred could not then be put to profane or everyday use, it had to be given to God, redeemed, or deconsecrated. In the case of annual crops, a token was offered before regular harvest began and another when processing commenced. This seems to be the principle alluded to in verse 29a, "You shall not delay to offer . . . from the outflow of your presses." I take this to mean that a token portion of juice was to be dedicated to God at the sanctuary at the beginning of each season of pressing.

Verse 29b commands the dedication of each firstborn male child. If only this commandment had been given, one would have to conclude that Israelite law prescribed child sacrifice, but every parallel passage fills out the law with a prescription for the redemption of the firstborn: "All that opens the womb is mine. . . . All the first-born of your sons you shall redeem" (Exod. 34:19–20). To redeem a child, a lamb was substituted, and the same rule of substitution applied to a firstborn ass, because it was not an offerable animal.

Verse 30 states the rule for dedicating firstborn oxen and sheep (probably including goats). The young are allowed to nurse for a week and then are delivered to the altar. If the animal is without blemish, it is sacrificed either as a holocaust or a donation to the priests (the text is silent on this matter). The law does not say what is done with blemished firstborn nor explain what is to be done if the firstborn is female.

The final verse of this unit begins with a general admonition to be "men holy to me" (author's translation), recalling the theological designation of Israel as a "holy nation" (Exod. 19:6) and "holy people" (Deut. 7:6). Here the admonition is applied to the specific question of dietary contamination. Israelites are not to eat the carcass of an animal killed by wild beasts. No explanation is given, and some scholars surmise that it is because its blood was not properly drained, but this notion is contradicted by the parallel law in Deuteronomy 14:21 (sojourners and foreigners are allowed to eat the carcass, but no biblical lawbook allows the eating of blood). Note too that oxen killed in accidents may be eaten (21:33–36).

"You shall not utter a false report . . ." (23:1–9).

Finally, two series of commandments on trial morality (vss. 1–3, 6–8) are separated by two laws governing duties of assistance (vss. 4–5) and followed by a verse (vs. 9) which rounds off this entire division of the Book of the Covenant.

Verses 1–3 are a series of five prohibitions addressed to a witness before the court and represent something of an elaboration of the ninth commandment (false witness). The initial prohibition simply forbids any false testimony, whether conscious lies or unfounded rumors. The second covers conspiracy to witness falsely. Verse 2 considers the more subtle dangers of social pressure—the witness is to resist the temptation to go along with the majority or color his or her testimony to suit their desires. In verse 3, the witness is advised not to tailor his or her testimony according to personal prejudices, particularly not in favor of a poor person.

Verses 4–5 impose duties of assistance on anyone who happens into a situation needing assistance. If one observes a stray work animal, one must capture it and return it to its owner, and if one observes an ass down under its burden, one must assist the owner in getting it to its feet. The tone is strongly homiletical and emotive. For example, the ass is identified as belonging to one's enemy; it is assumed that one would assist a friend. The treatment of the capture and return of a loose animal in the Hittite Laws (Pars. 71, 79, cf. 45, 86, 107) explains a good deal about the origin of this law. There it is subsumed under the topic of livestock theft. One can imagine suits in which an animal owner charged someone with theft, and the defendant pleaded that the plaintiff's animal had been caught running astray. The case here has been severed from this theft context and associated with another duty of assistance, and both have been couched in the language of moral duty.

Verses 6–8 constitute a series of prohibitions addressed to the judges: they are not to decide out of a bias against the poor or in disregard of their rights; they are to examine the testimony carefully to avoid conviction upon false charges; they are to make an extreme effort to avoid executing an innocent person, for they will be held accountable to God for innocent blood. This suggests the rule that any doubt of guilt should count in favor of the accused, for it is more important that the "righteous [not] fare as the wicked" (Gen. 18:25) than that the wicked be punished. Finally, the judges are warned against bribery, the blatant cause of injustice.

Scripture offers several descriptions of the Israelite judicial system, but concrete and secure knowledge is lacking. Exodus 18:13–27 envisages courts of original jurisdiction made up of "able men from all the people, such as fear God, men who are trustworthy and who hate a bribe" (vs. 21). If one bypasses the rather confusing introduction of military organization into the picture, one can surmise that a group of righteous men heard all cases within their territorial jurisdiction, deciding the cases within their competence and seeking Moses' decision (if necessary, with the aid of divine revelation) in difficult ones. After Israel settled, the local court consisted of selected men living in a given town or city, and court sessions were held in the city gate. What is not known is how many judges there were in each city, how they were selected and trained, how many heard a given case, or how they conducted the trial and voted. There is also continuing debate as to who played Moses' role during various periods in Israel's history.

Verse 9 repeats the prohibition against oppressing the sojourner that began this division of the lawbook (22:21), providing a pleasing symmetry. Even the same motive clause is used, "You know the heart of a stranger, for you were strangers in the land of Egypt." Israel's own historical experience should make the people particularly sensitive to the outsiders in their midst. This distinctively biblical appeal draws upon memory to motivate moral action. By recalling the Exodus in particular, Israelites are reminded of the relativity of all national, class, and economic distinctions and, by implication, of their dependence on God.

Sabbatical Times and the Festival Calendar.   The last ten verses of the Book of the Covenant are concerned with "times," some with a social and others with a cultic rationale. The style of formulation can probably be identified as priestly torah, that is, a duty which is commanded, followed by an explanation of how it is to be fulfilled. The explanations here are rather rudimentary and homiletical, suggesting that the section was not intended so much to prescribe practice as to encourage performance of duties already known. Particulars would be a matter of local tradition and priestly instruction and oversight.

Exodus 23:10–19 is closely parallel in both form and content to Exodus 34:18–26, and some of its provisions are reflected in the catechetical passages of Exodus 13:3–16. The following table illustrates these parallels:

Subject	Exod. 23:10–19	Exod. 34:18–26	Exod. 13:3–16
Fallow year	10–11	————	
Sabbath	12	21	
Invocation of gods	13	————	
Three annual festivals	14/17	23 (+ 24)	
Unleavened bread	15	18	3–10
First fruits & Ingathering	16	22	
Leaven with sacrifice	18a	25a	
Fat overnight	18b	25b	
Duty of first fruits	19a	26a	
Boiling of kid in milk	19b	26b	
Firstborn	(22:29b–30)	19–20	11–16

There are some differences in coverage and treatment, and in general Exodus 34:18–26 is less coherent in order than 23:10–19. This discussion will focus on Exodus 23:10–19 and call attention to the others only when they supplement or differ from it.

"For six years you shall sow . . ." (23:10–13).

The first two laws are formulated on the pattern: work six _____ but do not work the seventh. The law prescribing the fallowing of cropland, vineyards, and orchards every seventh year lacks one critical detail: are all fields to be left fallow on the same year or in some pattern of rotation? The parallel in the Holiness Code (Lev. 25:2–7) and the related provision in Deuteronomy (15:1–18; also 31:10–13) presuppose the fallowing of the whole land in the same year, but this would be utterly impractical and Exodus 23:10–11 does not demand such an interpretation. Indeed, the rationale for the law ("that the poor of your people may eat; and what they leave the wild beasts may eat") is only sensible if the fallowing were staggered, leaving some volunteer crops in each district for the poor each year.

The commandment to abstain from work every seventh day (vs. 12) must be an early formulation of the sabbath commandment, though it lacks all reference to the religious meaning and rationale for observing it. The only reason given is that work animals and workers need a rest; not even the benefit to the addressee and his family is mentioned. Exodus 34:21 adds the point that even during those times of the year when farm work is most intense and speed is of the essence—planting and harvest—the provision is to be obeyed.

One of the most striking things about the fallow year and sabbath laws of the Book of the Covenant is their proximity to the laws protecting the rights of the weak (Exod. 22:21–27; 23:9). This is a strong indication that these two laws are an integral part of the lawbook and that social concerns were a primary force in the evolution of Israelite cultic practice and theology.

Verse 13 contains a homiletical remark encouraging obedience to the law and a rather distinctive, homiletical version of the first commandment, namely, forbidding the mention of other gods. The verse would make a fitting conclusion to the lawbook and might be taken to mean that the final unit is something of an appendix.

"Three times in the year . . ." (23:14–19).

The paragraph on the three annual festivals (vss. 14–17) exhibits careful craftsmanship. The first and last statements repeat a summary commandment in slightly different wording, and the central portion identifies the three festivals mentioned. The symmetry is partially broken by some explanations of the first festival. By "feast" is meant an assembly of all males at the same time "before the Lord Yahweh" (vs. 17), that is, at major shrines or (less likely) one central shrine. Since the assemblage of all Israelite men (and many women as well, according to 1 Sam. 1) would leave the countryside exposed to internal and external threats, Exodus 34:24 assures divine protection to festival-goers.

The three annual festivals were keyed to the phases of the agricultural year. Unleavened Bread (Mazzoth) came at the beginning and Harvest at the end of the grain harvest, and Ingathering came at the end of the grape, olive, and fruit harvest. The beginning of the grain harvest would have varied from year to year, so the celebration of

Mazzoth could be fixed no more precisely than the month of Abib (falling variously during April and May). The Harvest festival was computed, in later texts, in relation to the sabbath concluding Mazzoth and fell seven weeks and a day later, giving it the name "Weeks," or "Pentecost" in Greek. The fall festival, Ingathering, also seems to have had no fixed date but depended upon the time the fruit harvest was completed, which would have been sometime in August or September.

Verse 15 provides a few additional details regarding Mazzoth. Only the final day of the festival involved a pilgrimage to a sanctuary, where a sheaf of grain and animal sacrifices would have been presented. The warning that "none shall appear before me empty-handed" applies to this assemblage; everyone is expected to bring offerings. From the Sunday to the Friday before the assembly the people were under the stipulation not to eat any bread that had been raised (by means of sour dough) but to eat a type of cracker for bread. Although the ritual has an agricultural origin, the exodus from Egypt supplies the motive (Exod. 13:3–10) and etiology (12:34, "So the people took their dough before it was leavened. . .").

It is noteworthy that Passover is not mentioned in association with Mazzoth. Both Passover and Mazzoth were reminders of the Exodus, both were celebrated in the month of Abib, and later the two were combined, but at the time of the Book of the Covenant, Passover was not a pilgrimage festival but a family rite practiced at home. A lamb was to be slaughtered, its blood daubed on the doorframe of the house, and the animal cooked and consumed in the home in the course of the night (Exod. 12:21–27).

The final two verses of the passage (vss. 18–19) contain four commandments that are at least verbally associated with the festivals just summarized. The word translated "my feast" in verse 18 is the same as the word translated "feast" in verses 14–16, suggesting that the fat of any animal sacrifice of any festival was not to remain until the morning of the next day. Likewise, no festival sacrifice should be offered with leavened bread (vs. 18). Exodus 34:25, however, associates these rules specifically with Passover, which is there called a festival. Perhaps then 23:18 is not applicable to all festivals but only to Passover. The commandment to bring the "first of the first fruits" to the sanctuary may have the Harvest and/or Ingathering festival in mind.

The final prohibition (vs. 19b) is mysterious because it is so unmotivated and isolated; it is also the only provision specifically concerning goats (only goats were milked). It is now common to see in the prohibition the rejection of some type of Canaanite sacrifice, but why this one is mentioned and not others is not known.

This final division of the Book of the Covenant is quite important for the scholarly reconstruction of the social and cultic institutions of early Israel. Although it does not give a complete picture, it provides the basic lineaments of the cultus during the pre-monarchical era.

The unit is also important for understanding the lawbook itself. First, it points up the fundamental distinction between this corpus and the royal legal corpora of the ancient Near East—the latter were not formulated for a national community defined by religious loyalty, as biblical law was.

In addition, the section confirms the national context of the Book of the Covenant. From time to time scholars argue that C was not originally drawn up for the entire nation, but only by dismembering the lawbook is such a position possible. The festival calendar was clearly meant for the entire people of Yahweh. Indeed, it is probable that the lawgiver sought to reinforce the national consciousness by requiring nationwide observances as a part of divine law.

SUGGESTED READING

For the policy informing this selection, see the statement introducing the bibliography at the end of Chapter One. For the analysis of sources, forms of legal formulation, and history of tradition of the Book of the Covenant, consult the bibliography to Chapter Two. For commentaries on the book of Exodus and theological treatments of law, consult the bibliography to Chapter Three.

Monographs in English on the Book of the Covenant:

Morgenstern, Julian. "The Book of the Covenant," Parts 1–4, *Hebrew Union College Annual* 5 (1928), pp. 1–151; 7 (1930), pp. 19–258; 8–9 (1931–32), pp. 1–150; 33 (1962), pp. 59–105.

Paul, Shalom M. *Studies in the Book of the Covenant in the Light of Cuneiform and Biblical Law.* Vol. 18 of *Supplements to Vetus Testamentum.* Leiden: E. J. Brill, 1970.

See also the extensive treatment of the Book of the Covenant in:

Boecker, Hans Jochen. *Law and the Administration of Justice in the Old Testament and Ancient East.* Trans. Jeremy Moiser. Minneapolis: Augsburg Publishing House, 1980.

Major monographs in foreign languages on the Book of the Covenant:

Cazelles, Henri. *Etudes sur le code de l'alliance.* Paris: Letouzey et Ané, 1946.

Jepsen, Alfred. *Untersuchungen zum Bundesbuch.* Beiträge zur Wissenschaft vom Alten und Neuen Testament, 3d issue, no. 5. Stuttgart: W. Kohlhammer, 1927.

On the homiletical material in the Book of the Covenant:

Beyerlin, Walter. "Die Paränese im Bundesbuch und ihre Herkunft." In *Gottes Wort und Gottes Land,* ed. Henning Graf Reventlow, pp. 9–29. Göttingen: Vandenhoeck & Ruprecht, 1965.

Studies of the legal reasoning in the Book of the Covenant and elsewhere:

Buss, Martin J. "The Distinction between Civil and Criminal Law in Ancient Israel." In *Proceedings of the Sixth World Congress of Jewish Studies,* ed. A. Shinan, vol. 1, pp. 51–62. Jerusalem: World Union of Jewish Studies, 1977.

Daube, David. "Codes and Codas" and *"Lex Talionis."* In *Studies in Biblical Law,* pp. 74–101, 102–153. New York: Ktav Publishing House, 1969.

Greenberg, Moshe. "Some Postulates of Biblical Criminal Law." In *Yehezkel Kaufmann Jubilee Volume,* pp. 5–28. Jerusalem: Detus Goldberg, 1960.

Sauber, K. R. *Die Abstraktion im Israelitischen Recht.* Göttingen: Vandenhoeck & Ruprecht, 1953.

Wagner, Volker. "Zur Systematik in dem Codex Ex. 21:2—22:16," *Zeitschrift für die alttestamentliche Wissenschaft* 81 (1969), pp. 176–182.

Monographs on the sections of the Book of the Covenant governing the altar, sacrifices, and festivals:

Kraus, Hans-Joachim. *Worship in Israel: A Cultic History of the Old Testament.* Trans. Geoffrey Buswell. Oxford: Basil Blackwell, 1966.

Rowley, H. H. *Worship in Ancient Israel: Its Forms and Meaning.* Philadelphia: Fortress Press, 1967.

de Vaux, Roland. *Studies in Old Testament Sacrifice.* Cardiff: University of Wales Press, 1964.

A selection of studies of legal topics covered in the judgments and moral precepts of the Book of the Covenant:

Eichler, Barry L. *Indenture at Nuzi: The Personal Tidennūtu Contract and its Mesopotamian Analogues*. Yale Near Eastern Researches, 5. New Haven and London: Yale University Press, 1973.

Finkelstein, J. J. *The Ox That Gored*. Transactions of the American Philosophical Society, vol. 71, pt. 2. Philadelphia: The American Philosophical Society, 1981.

Gehman, Henry Snyder. "The Oath in the Old Testament: Its Vocabulary, Idiom, and Syntax; Its Semantics and Theology in the Masoretic Text and the Septuagint." In *Grace Upon Grace: Essays in Honor of Lester J. Kuyper*, ed. James I. Cook, pp. 51–63. Grand Rapids: Wm. B. Eerdmans Publishing Co., 1975.

Hanson, Paul D. "The Theological Significance of Contradiction within the Book of the Covenant." In *Canon and Authority: Essays in Old Testament Religion and Theology*, ed. George W. Coats and Burke O. Long, pp. 110–131. Philadelphia: Fortress Press, 1977.

Jackson, Bernard S. *Theft in Early Jewish Law*. Oxford: Oxford University Press, 1972.

––––––– . "The Problem of Exod. XXI 22–5 (*Ius talionis*)," *Vetus Testamentum* 23 (1973), pp. 273–304.

Loewenstamm, Samuel E. "Exodus XXI 22–25," *Vetus Testamentum* 27 (1977), pp. 352–360.

McKay, J. W. "Exodus XXIII 1–3, 6–8: A Decalogue for the Administration of Justice in the City Gate," *Vetus Testamentum* 21 (1971), pp. 311–325.

Mendelsohn, I. "The Conditional Sale into Slavery of Free-born Daughters in Nuzi and the Law of Ex. 21:7–11," *Journal of the American Oriental Society* 55 (1935), pp. 190–195.

Neufeld, Edward. "The Prohibitions Against Loans at Interest in Ancient Hebrew Laws," *Hebrew Union College Annual* 26 (1955), pp. 355–412.

A description of the institutions of ancient Israel:

de Vaux, Roland. *Ancient Israel: Its Life and Institutions*. Trans. John McHugh. London: Darton, Longman & Todd, 1961.

Studies by the author:

Patrick, Dale. "The Covenant Code Source," *Vetus Testamentum* 27 (1977), pp. 145–157.

––––––– . "I and Thou in the Covenant Code." In *Society of Biblical Literature Seminar Papers 1978*, pp. 71–86. Missoula: Scholars Press, 1978.

Chapter Five

THE DEUTERONOMIC LAW

The name "Deuteronomy" ("second law") originated with a mistranslation of Deuteronomy 17:18, but it is well suited to the book containing Moses' repetition or recapitulation of the law giving at Sinai. A new generation stands before Moses as he gives his last public address before ascending Mount Nebo to glimpse the promised land and die.

The reader might well wonder why I am treating this final address of Moses before concluding Sinaitic law. One reason is that critical scholars commonly date the authorship of Deuteronomy before the authorship of those portions of Exodus through Numbers that belong to the Priestly writer. Although this view is disputed today, even its opponents claim no more than that D and P are roughly contemporary. A second reason is that the code of Deuteronomy is a rather direct descendant of the Book of the Covenant; many of its provisions are restatements of C prototypes (consult the table below)

PARALLELS BETWEEN D AND C

Deut. 12:1–28	Exod. 20:24	Deut. 19:1–13	Exod. 21:12–14
Deut. 13:1–18	Exod. 22:20	Deut. 19:15–21 . . cf	Exod. 23:1–3
Deut. 14:21a	Exod. 22:31	Deut. 21:18–21 . . .	Exod. 21:15, 17
Deut. 14:21b	Exod. 23:19b	Deut. 22:1–4	Exod. 23:4–5
Deut. 15:1–11	Exod. 23:10–11	Deut. 22:28–29 . . .	Exod. 22:16–17
Deut. 15:12–18 . . .	Exod. 21:2–11	Deut. 23:19	Exod. 22:25
Deut. 15:19–23 . . .	Exod. 22:30	Deut. 24:6, 10–13 .	Exod. 22:26–27
Deut. 16:1–17	Exod. 23:14–17	Deut. 24:7	Exod. 21:16
Deut. 16:19–20 . . .	Exod. 23:6–8	Deut. 24:17–18 . . .	Exod. 22:21–24; 23:9
Deut. 17:2–7	Exod. 22:20	Deut. 24:19–21 . . cf	Exod. 23:10–11
Deut. 18:10b–11 . .	Exod. 22:18	Deut. 26:1–11 . . . cf	Exod. 22:29a; 23:19a

with a continuity of homiletical style. Hence, it seems reasonable to study the two codes in succession. Before beginning the commentary on the lawbook, however, it is necessary to review and continue the analysis of authorship, traditions, and speech forms.

Source Criticism

Almost all of the book of Deuteronomy is an address by Moses to the people of Israel, which can be outlined as follows:

  I. Homiletical Introduction (1–11)
 II. Deuteronomic Laws (12–26)
III. Pronouncement of Blessings and Curses (27–28)
 IV. A Covenant Homily (29–30)
  V. Final Acts and Words of Moses (31)
 VI. Poems: History of Israel, Tribal Blessing (32–33)
VII. Account of Moses' Departure (34)

Only the first thirty-one chapters center on the presentation of divine law, and within them are the contributions of several authors of the same school (language, style, concepts). For example, some of the chapters 1 to 11 are narratives reviewing events from Sinai to the present (chs. 1–3; 5; 9:8–10:11), while others are sermons on divine grace and human obedience (chs. 4; 6–9:7; 10:12–11:32). A popular scholarly thesis attributes the bulk of the latter to the author of the lawbook, and chapters 1–3, along with 29–31, to the historian known as the Deuteronomistic Historian (Dtr.) who compiled the account running through Joshua, Judges, First and Second Samuel, and First and Second Kings. Chapters 4; 5; and 9:8–10:11 seem to belong to yet another author or authors. The lawbook itself (chs. 12–26) may have some material from the Deuteronomistic Historian, but this is not sufficiently large or obtrusive to warrant being separated out in an introductory study.

The Deuteronomic Law (including introduction and conclusion) is probably to be identified with the Mosaic Law found in the Jerusalem temple in the eighteenth year of Josiah's reign (2 Kings 22:8–23:3). The law's intent is the elimination of foreign influences on Israel's religion, and Josiah purged his kingdom of heterodox practices and revitalized and reorganized other national institutions along lines suggested by the code. Moreover, the fear of impending doom evinced by Josiah's reading of the lawbook was a fitting response to the curses of Deuteronomy 28.

The History of Tradition

Critical scholars were once fond of calling this book a pious fraud composed during Josiah's reign to be "discovered" and made the basis of a reform. This position has been qualified in the course of the twentieth century by the study of D's traditions, and a majority of scholars would now say that the final text of the lawbook came into being in the century before its discovery and that its traditions derived from the centuries prior to that.

Within chapters 6–28 are fragments of covenant rituals linked to the northern city of Shechem (Deut. 11:26–32; 27:1–26) which constitute solid evidence that the original traditions behind the book were northern, indeed specifically Shechemite. The links to the Book of the Covenant also point in this direction, for C probably originated in the north. The northern traditions most likely were transferred to Judah when the Northern Kingdom fell in 721 B.C., and the Deuteronomic portion most likely was revised into its present form there.

The homiletical style of the book has also been taken as a clue to its oral background. The German scholar Gerhard von Rad argued forcefully that the book reflects a setting in which law was preached to the people of Israel. While the representation of these legal homilies as a Mosaic address is artificial, their style and phrasing indicate an oral, not a literary, mode of communication.

Von Rad was also struck by the peculiar combination of religious, military, and judicial traditions in the book. The speakers, he surmised, were the country Levites mentioned so often in the laws, spokesmen for a segment of the population (the "people of the land") who harbored the hope of a revival of the people's army and its traditions of holy war and who would be attracted to a strict, somewhat nationalistic Yahwism. In support of this identification is the account of Moses' handing the lawbook over to the Levites and commanding that it be read every seven years at the feast of Booths (Deut. 31:9–13, 24–26). In support of their rural location is the fact that the addressee of the law seems to be living in a town away from Jerusalem and has to adapt to the absence of a local altar.

The thesis that the Deuteronomic tradition originated in the north does not seem compatible with von Rad's thesis of Levitical preaching in rural Judah. Perhaps, however, the two can be brought into harmony. It is possible that the rural Levites responsible for the book were refugees from the defunct Northern Kingdom. When they escaped to the south, they would naturally have adapted their traditions to their new homeland and continued the practice of preaching the law as they had been accustomed to doing in the north. For fear of losing the tradition, they committed it to writing. Since they believed that they were passing on the law of Moses, it was natural to couch their presentation of law as a Mosaic address.

In Judah the refugees accepted the claim of the Jerusalem temple as the supreme shrine to Yahweh and developed this claim into the idea that it was the sole legitimate altar. This idea may already have been abroad during the reign of Hezekiah, who (according to 2 Kings 18:22 and Isa. 36:7) pursued a policy of destroying rural Judean altars. If so, the author did not so much invent the centralization of the cult as give sanction to an emerging Jerusalemite ideology.

D does not, however, adopt the Zion theology belonging to the temple (articulated in Pss. 46; 48; 78:67–72; 82; 125; 132). According to this theology, Yahweh actually *dwells* in the temple; the holy area therefore is off limits to common people and accessible only to ritually prepared priests. According to D, God dwells in heaven and only God's name dwells in the earthly sanctuary; consequently, the lawbook shows no concern for protecting the sanctuary from contact with laity. Moreover, Zion theology was integrated into Davidic royal theology (Ps. 132), but D subordinates the king to the people and the divine law.

The irony of the Deuteronomic centralization of the cult was that it thereby eliminated the sanctuaries at which Levites were based. Some scholars have denied the Levitical connection of Deuteronomy on the grounds that the Levites would not have put themselves out of business. The fact is, however, that D grants all Levites rights to perform their duties at the Jerusalem temple, possibly an attempt to open up opportunities for them. If the Levites who bore the Deuteronomic traditions were refugees, they would have had no sanctuary assignments in their adopted homes and no vested interest in maintaining rural Judean altars. In addition, the Deuteronomic author exhibits an idealistic and ideological flair that could well have made him oblivious to the politics of the situation.

This theory of the origins of Deuteronomy is by no means universally accepted. The major work to come out on Deuteronomy in the 1970s, Moshe Weinfeld's *Deuteronomy and the Deuteronomic School*, dismisses both the northern origin of the tradition and its roots in Levitical preaching. In his opinion, the author was a wise man and scribe who abstracted general principles from older covenant and legal traditions and adapted these to the Assyrian state treaty form. The language and tone distinctive to Deuteronomic address resembles, he believes, the teaching style of the wise man (e.g., Proverbs, Wisdom psalms, Job's friends). D's offer of rewards for obedience and threat of punishment for disobedience is the same as the Wisdom doctrine of retribution, and its stress on God's transcendence and its spiritualized view of the holy place and sacrifice fit the piety of the sophisticated, rationalistic wise man.

Weinfeld's study has yielded many insights into Deuteronomic literature, but his general thesis is unsatisfactory. The predominance of northern covenantal theology and absence of royal and Zion theology make it improbable that a professional scribe living in Jerusalem composed it. Deuteronomic theology and piety can be traced to northern tradition rather than to Wisdom. The language and thought shared by D and Wisdom literature may only show that both were disseminated throughout the intellectual classes. Uprooted Levitical refugees would have been quick to absorb the surface elements of their new intellectual environment. Finally, the homiletical style of Deuteronomic address cannot, in my opinion, be purely literary in origin.

Form Criticism

The distinctive homiletical style of Deuteronomic literature previously mentioned needs to be described more exactly. When one reads Deuteronomy 12–26, one is immediately struck by the difference in the style and form of legal formulations from any other collection or lawbook. If one searches diligently, the old forms of apodictic commandments, capital punishment, and casuistic law can be recognized, but they are substantially transformed by the Deuteronomic homiletical style. One might speak of a "homogenization" of the distinctive types of legal formulation.

Personal address pervades Deuteronomic legal formulations to a unique degree. In C, casuistic remedial law and the law governing capital crimes were impersonal. The lawgiver broke into personal address only sporadically in sections with these types of law. There is no such identifiable section of impersonal law in the Deuteronomic Law; even casuistic remedial law and those laws governing capital crimes are addressed.

The proportion of motive clauses to law proper is strikingly high in D—utterances motivating compliance make up more than half of the material. They are no longer limited to clauses attached to legal statements but include many independent sentences. Even the statements of law proper tend to lack technical precision because they are couched in homiletical language.

Another characteristic of D's legal formulations is the Mosaic speaker. All biblical law is portrayed as delivered by Moses, but Yahweh is the speaker in every collection and lawbook but Deuteronomy, where the "I" refers to Moses. Here the authority behind the law continues to be Yahweh, but a human interpreter has intervened to touch the heart of the people.

As in all biblical law, the addressee of Deuteronomic Law is the people of Israel, but D has *collectivized* a significant portion of its law. The "you" addressed is the people as a corporate entity:

> If a man is found stealing one of his brethren, the people of Israel, and if he treats him as a slave or sells him, then that thief shall die; so you shall purge the evil from the midst of you. (Deut. 24:7)

This law is identical in content to a provision in C ("Whoever steals a man ... shall be put to death," Exod. 21:16), but the Deuteronomic formulation adds a phrase ("If a man is found ... ") that reorients the law toward the community, the implied finder of the offender. The people are addressed directly in the attached motive clause ("so you shall purge the evil from the midst of you") which explains the collective orientation of the law: the community must assume collective responsibility for serious offenses that occur within it and execute the offender to remove the guilt attached to it. If it did not do so, the whole community would be subject to divine judgment.

Another motive clause, "And the rest shall hear, and fear, and shall never again commit any such evil among you" (19:20), looks to the social effect of strict enforcement of the law. This idea of deterrence sounds distinctively modern. It is D's idea that the community show their respect for God's law by treating violations with utmost seriousness; this respect is thereby instilled in the members.

A portion of Deuteronomic Law does not address the people collectively. Adjacent to laws equating "you" with Israel are laws addressing individual Israelites, namely, a "you" who is responsible for his or her own acts. The laws that are addressed distributively concern moral duties to one's neighbors, to the poor and needy, etc., and religious duties and practices related to sacrifice.

To summarize, the legal formulations of the Deuteronomic Law have been absorbed into a distinctive homiletical address. Characteristic of this homiletical address is personal address and a high proportion of motivational utterance. The speaker is Moses, and the addressee is the corporate community in cases of serious offenses and the individual members in cases of moral and religious duties.

COMMENTARY

The Deuteronomic code of laws is set off from the homiletical introduction by a superscription in 12:1, "These are the precepts and judgments which you shall take care to do in the land . . . " (author's translation). The terms *precepts* and *judgments* have lost any specific technical meaning they may once have had and have been assimilated to the homiletical style that characterizes all Deuteronomic prose. Hence, they do not aid in differentiating among parts of the code, as the term *judgments* did in the Book of the Covenant. The code does not exhibit formally homogenous units, so content must be relied upon to break it into sections.

In the following outline the code is broken into three sections and a conclusion. The sections on cult and religion and on offices and national institutions exhibit signs of conscious construction.

The third section appears to be a random assortment of relatively short paragraphs on religious, civil, and judicial matters. Chapter 26 seems to stand outside the three divisions as something of a conclusion.

OUTLINE OF THE DEUTERONOMIC LAW

I. Cult and Religion
    A. "The place which Yahweh your God will choose . . ." (12:2–31)
    B. "If he says, 'Let us go after other gods,' . . ." (13:1–18)
    C. "For you are a people holy to Yahweh your God" (14:1–21)
    D. "You shall tithe all the yield of your seed . . ." (14:22—15:23)
    E. "Three times a year . . ." (16:1–17)
    F. "You shall not plant . . . an Asherah . . ." (16:21–17:1)
II. Offices and Institutions
    A. "You shall appoint judges and officers in all your towns . . ." (16:18–17:13)
    B. "You may indeed set a king over you . . ." (17:14–20)
    C. "The Levitical priests . . . all the tribe of Levi . . ." (18:1–8)
    D. "Yahweh your God will raise up for you a prophet like me . . ." (18:9–22)
    E. "You shall set apart three cities . . . so that any manslayer can flee to them" (19:1–21)
    F. "When you go forth to war . . ." (20:1–20)
III. Miscellaneous Short Laws
    A. "If . . . any one is found slain . . ." (21:1–23)
    B. "You shall take [a lost ox or sheep] back to your brother" (22:1–12)
    C. "If a man . . . a young woman . . ." (22:13–30)
    D. "He . . . shall not enter the assembly of Yahweh" (23:1–14)
    E. "You shall not give up a slave to his master" (23:15–25)
    F. "When a man takes a wife . . ." (24:1–5)
    G. "No man shall take an upper millstone in pledge" (24:6–22)
    H. "Lest . . . your brother be degraded in your sight" (25:1–19)
IV. Rituals to Strengthen Israelite Identity (26:1–19)

A clause characterizing the passage to be discussed will be quoted at the head of the commentary, and the remainder is to be read from the Bible in hand.

Cult and Religion. By cult is meant the sanctuary and the rituals to be performed there. Chapters 12 and 16 fit this definition well. Chapter 13 has to do with the broader religious question of loyalty to Yahweh. Chapters 14 and 15 give rules for maintaining holiness and impose several cultic and social duties.

"The place which Yahweh your God will choose . . ." (12:2–31).

The Deuteronomic Law begins with the same subject as does C. Exodus 20:24 commands the making of altars wherever Yahweh has caused his "name to be remembered" and reviews the sacrifices to be made on them; Deuteronomy 12 commands the people to go to the place "which Yahweh your God will choose, to make his name dwell there" and lists the sacrifices to made there. The major difference is that Exodus 20:24 assumes a multiplicity of legitimate altars, whereas Deuteronomy 12 outlaws all but one.

Deuteronomy 12 seems rather repetitive and verbose. If it were reduced to statements with legal force, the unit beginning in verse 13 and ending in verse 19 would suffice. Verse 13 prohibits sacrifice at unauthorized altars, and verse 14 authorizes one unnamed site "in one of your tribes." Verses 15–16 allow for the slaughter of domesticated animals without an altar but retains the quasi-sacrificial practice of pouring out the blood. Verses 17–18 specify the sacrifices and offerings that cannot be done in the village but must be performed at the authorized sanctuary. Verse 19 calls for support of the country Levite. The following paragraph (vss. 20–28) repeats the same provisions with only slight variations.

Various features of the law reveal that it was in fact a new enactment after centuries of settled life. The provision for "secular" slaughter is a case in point. Prior to the centralization of the cult, every locality had an altar devoted to Yahweh. The slaughter of cattle, sheep, and goats for food was performed at the local altar, where the blood was thrown upon the altar and specified internal organs and fat were incinerated. With the elimination of the local altars, D had to provide an alternative method for slaughter, for the villagers could not be expected to go to the central sanctuary every time they wanted to eat meat. D therefore puts the slaughter of domesticated animals in the same class as the slaughter of wild animals, which was never sacrificial. Without an altar, the blood had to be poured out on the ground.

There remained, of course, the offerings which still required an altar. For these the addressee (who is depicted here and throughout D as a villager living away from the central sanctuary) had to make a journey to the legitimate altar. Even at the sanctuary it is the sacrificial meal, in D's theology, that constitutes the essence of communion with God; the whole household is to go together to "rejoice before Yahweh your God in all that you undertake" (vs. 18). Holocausts (RSV: "burnt offerings") are also mentioned (vs. 27), but they play no independent role in D's concept of sacrifice. For D, it is the inward attitudes of thanksgiving and social sharing that make sacrifice valid, and the sacrificial meal exemplifies these perfectly; D has no place for the objective efficacy (*ex opere operatum*) of the sacrificial rite itself, which is the doctrine behind the holocaust.

The concern for the local Levite also arises from the centralization of the cult. When the local altar was shut down, the person who officiated there lost his means of support. If he chose to live among the people rather than go up to the central shrine, he would become a ward of charity.

Why did the author of Deuteronomy undertake the radical alteration of the Israelite cult? The first portion of the chapter offers some explanations. Verses 2–7 contrast the one legitimate altar belonging to Yahweh to the multiplicity of Canaanite altars devoted to their gods. The Canaanite altars had, in particular, fertility associations (cf. e.g., Hos. 4:13) and should by all means be destroyed. Verses 8–12 contrast the laxity permitted in the wilderness to the more stringent rule of a central shrine. The central sanctuary thus was conceived as a measure to protect the Israelite cult and prevent it from adopting the ways of fertility religion and from developing irregularities within. A single sanctuary would be easier to regulate.

The final paragraph of the chapter (vss. 29–31) exhibits the same concern to maintain orthodoxy. It does not mention the central sanctuary, but it echoes verses 2–7 in warning against the adoption of Canaanite cultic practices after settlement, practices which were incompatible with the personality of Yahweh. The word translated "abominable thing" tends to mean an act that is morally repugnant to God. The burning of children—presumably child sacrifice, though some scholars have argued for something less horrifying—is mentioned as the most flagrant example of a Canaanite cultic abomination.

"If he says, 'Let us go after other gods,' . . ." (13:1–18).

The legal force of chapter 13 could be reduced to a single sentence: "Whoever says, 'Let us go and serve other gods,' shall be put to death." The prolix expansion of this basic sentence simply gives examples of the kinds of situations the addressee might encounter and exhorts him or her to remain loyal to Israel's God.

D probably composed this chapter with the law prescribing capital punishment for sacrificing to other deities (Exod. 22:20) as a prototype but changed the focus from an overt cultic act to the quasi-political act of *advocating* defection. The chapter is more concerned with the national religious crisis of loyalty as described by such prophets as Hosea and Isaiah than with the violation of cultic purity.

It has been aptly noted that D's condemnation of incitement to apostasy has parallels among provisions of Hittite and Assyrian treaties between emperors and their satellite kings. Satellite rulers were commanded to report and hand over anyone—diviners, lords, even family members—who advocated rebellion against the overlord. D may have modeled religious loyalty after such a political arrangement, thereby equating religious apostasy with political treason.

The interpreter should not overextend the analogy between treaty and covenant, however. Yahweh is not a supernatural emperor imposing his rule on a nation with its own internal structure and focus of loyalty. Loyalty to Yahweh, rather, unites the disparate elements of Israel into a people. The advocacy of apostasy threatens to destroy Israel's identity as the people of Yahweh and to fragment them into religious and political factions. The suppression of apostasy in Israel is an act of national self-preservation.

The first paragraph (vss. 1–5) deals with an apostate prophet. Since all authority in Israel derives from Yahweh, only one who speaks in Yahweh's name has a claim on Israelite obedience. To advocate apostasy is to appeal to authorities that are not recognized in Israel ("gods which you have not known"). Worse, he or she is inciting betrayal of the God who has bestowed divine grace on Israel and in relationship to whom Israel knows its identity. The cancer must be purged before it spreads and causes collective death.

The lawgiver is as concerned to maintain the loyalty of the addressee as to suppress apostates. The prophet's alleged revelation and power to perform signs have been granted by Yahweh to test the strength of Israel's allegiance. No matter how impressive the prophet's credentials, "you shall not listen to the words of that prophet . . . ; you shall walk after Yahweh your God . . ." (vss. 3–4). It is as if the lawgiver were saying, For goodness' sake, don't join this rebellion.

Loyalty to Yahweh is not only above symbols of authority, but it overrides the organic ties of family and friendship (vss. 6–11). Love of God is to take precedence over all human attachments. Not only is the addressee not to join the apostate out of personal affection, he or she is to inform on the guilty and take the lead in having the apostate executed. The method of execution, stoning, is apt because the community joins together in cutting off the malefactor, thereby exercising its resolve to defend its civilization. Throwing the first stone tests the accuser's conscience and implicates the accuser specifically in any miscarriage of justice.

The final case is the apostasy of an entire city (vss. 12–18). The point of view is a bit different from the others in that the addressee has not witnessed the incitement to apostasy but has heard a rumor. The rumor is to be investigated, and if it is confirmed, the city—not just the ringleaders—is to be destroyed according to the rules of the holy war (every living thing killed, buildings razed). D may have found precedent for this wording in Exodus 22:20, which speaks of "putting (an apostate) under the ban" (author's translation), but it is unique in applying the ban to Israelite political units. According to D, mass apostasy is an "abomination" of such monstrous proportions that it threatens to arouse Yahweh's wrath against the whole nation. Only by making the apostate city a "holocaust" can Israel turn his wrath aside.

Although the author undoubtedly composed these paragraphs in all seriousness, they have the ring of utopian theory. That Israelites would be willing to inform on family or friends or destroy a whole city is doubtful. No biblical narratives evidence such willingness. What the lawgiver succeeds in doing is instilling individual responsibility for loyalty to Yahweh (preparing the way for the survival of Yahwism after the dissolution of the nation) and conceptualizing religious defection in political terms. Thus, the chapter is a profound theological monument and a practical failure.

"For you are a people holy to Yahweh your God" (14:1–21).

The material in chapters 14 and 15 could be divided in several different ways. I have decided to set apart 14:1–21 because these verses are bounded by the same theological declaration (cited above) and have a similar style and subject matter. According to Deuteronomic theology, holiness is not a quality that Israel achieves by moral or ritual acts but a quality imputed to the people in their election by Yahweh. Israel is set apart from all other peoples for an intimate association with God, an association also described here as sonship (vs. 1a). As a holy people, Israel must not do things or consume things that are incompatible with Yahweh.

The first violation of holiness treated in this section (vs. 1b) is self-mutilation for the dead. Some scholars suggest that slashing oneself and shaving a portion of the head had something to do with honoring the "god" of death or communicating with ghosts. It is my opinion that these were simply customary funeral practices, ritualized expressions of grief and loss (cf. Jer. 16:6). An impulse toward masochism seems to be inherent to such moments in human experience. The lawgiver fights this impulse, even when permanent damage is not inflicted upon the body. His attempt is consistent with the general thrust of biblical law against masochistic behavior.

The second violation is the eating of an *abomination* (vs. 3). In the book of Deuteronomy, this word generally means something morally repugnant to Yahweh, but here and in 17:1 it refers to something neutral in itself but taboo by custom and sensibility. In verse 3 it is an animal that offends sensibility. All societies have dietary taboos—our own excludes dogs and cats, mice and rats, insects, and various internal organs of meat animals. A catalog of permitted and forbidden animals has been included. It begins with mammals (vss. 4–8), then proceeds to aquatic species (vss. 9–10), and concludes with birds and insects (vss. 11–20). There are some efforts at systematization, but it has an ex post facto appearance. Swine are singled out as particularly "unclean." (See the discussion of Leviticus 11 in Chapter Six.)

Verse 21 contains another dietary taboo concerning a carcass, that is, any animal that was not killed or slaughtered by human hand. The parallel law in Exodus 22:31 has the carcass thrown to the dogs, but here it can be given to a resident alien or sold to a foreigner. Deuteronomy has relaxed the law somewhat because it does not impose the rules of ritual holiness upon those who do not belong to the holy people.

The prohibition against boiling a kid in its mother's milk is preserved only because it is a traditional law. In Exodus 23:19 it seems to be understood as a prohibited sacrifice, but Deuteronomy has reclassified it as a dietary prohibition.

"You shall tithe all the yield of your seed . . ." (14:22—15:23).

A casual glance at the four topics covered between 14:22 and 15:23 might make one wonder how they could be considered parts of one section, but a closer examination reveals a degree of organization and design. The first and fourth paragraphs converge, while the second and third are associated by analogy:

A—Tithe (14:22–29)
B—Release from debt (15:1–11)
B—Release from slavery (15:12–18)
A—Firstborn (15:19–23)

The disparity between cultic and social duties is partially overcome when one realizes that the fallow year, the antecedent of the year of release, is classified as a cultic duty in the Book of the Covenant (Exod. 23:10–11).

The duties of tithing and of offering the firstborn of flock and herd belong together in the lawgiver's mind. This convergence is graphically demonstrated by 14:23:

> Before Yahweh your God, in the place which he will choose . . . you shall eat the tithe of your grain, of your wine, and of your oil, and the firstlings of your herd and flock.

Although the paragraph is devoted to the tithe, the firstborn are mentioned as well. To the author, both the tithe and the firstborn are portions of a farmer's agricultural production, both must be taken to the central sanctuary to be offered, and both are consumed by the pilgrims themselves.

The term translated "tithe" means "tenth," indicating the percentage of the crop under consideration. According to D, the tithe is not a donation to the sanctuary but food for the pilgrims' feast. Since the portion set aside is not considered sacred in itself, D permits conversion to money by those who live too far from the central shrine to transport it easily. Every third year the tithe is to be stored in the villages to support the local Levite and the destitute (14:28–29). It is not clear whether D's "year of tithing" (so 26:12) is the same for everyone or is distributed so as to provide a constant supply of food year by year.

In contrast to D, the Priestly Source prescribes an annual tithe of crops *and livestock* (Lev. 27:30–33) and grants these offerings entirely *to the Levites* (Num. 18:21–32). P may reflect an ancient tradition of presenting the tithe to the local priest. What D does, then, is grant the offerer the priest's portion two of every three years and the local Levite the rest. It was undoubtedly his desire to keep the priestly prebends from accruing to the clerical establishment of the central sanctuary.

Deuteronomy modifies the offering of the firstborn in much the same way (15:19–23). The firstborn is to be eaten at the sanctuary by the pilgrims themselves, which is a significant break with the original conception of this offering. Originally the animal belonged to Yahweh in principle, so it could not be retained by the owner as meat; either it had to be offered as a holocaust (probably Exod. 22:30) or given to the priests (Num. 18:17–20). Since D had no liking for holocausts and did not want the central sanctuary to get an increase in revenues, the offering of the firstborn was transformed into a species of sacrificial meal. Only the prohibition of working or shearing the animals to be offered recalls the idea of their intrinsic holiness. D does not mention the redemption of firstborn male children and non-offerable animals (contrast Exod. 22:29; 34:19–20). There is no need of redemption because the "opening of the womb" no longer has a numinous quality.

The provisions for the year of release (15:1–11) and for the release of indentured servants (15:12–18) seem to have been associated by analogy. Both are based upon a seven-year period, both are formulated for the benefit of the economically deprived, and the cancellation of debts resembles release from servitude. However, there is no attempt to go beyond this somewhat poetic association to integrate the two substantively.

The institution called the "year of release" derives its name from the Book of the Covenant, but its substance has been modified radically by the author of Deuteronomy. C prescribes the fallowing of cropland every seventh year to allow the destitute and wild animals to feed on the volunteer crop. D makes no mention of fallowing but prescribes the cancellation of debts throughout the land every seventh year. Any loan between Israelites that has not been repaid before the year of release is to be cancelled, which would extend emergency loans to the poor into a welfare measure to keep them from insolvency. There are ancient Near Eastern parallels in the occasional cancellation of debts by Mesopotamian rulers on ascension to the throne. Perhaps D sought to make an occasional, royal institution into a regular, religiously sponsored one.

The lawgiver foresees that the new provision might actually have a reverse effect. A potential creditor would be tempted to refuse to make a loan when it would most likely never be paid back (vs. 9). As no legal remedy exists for such hardheartedness, D threatens divine punishment (vs. 9b) and promises reward for compliance (vs. 10). There is also an appeal to the addressee's patriotism and social conscience. The well-to-do are stewards of God's blessing to the whole community and are under obligation to distribute it so that "there will be no poor among you" (vs. 4).

The law of indentured servitude (15:12–18) also derives from the Book of the Covenant, and its basic provisions remain the same. In both Exodus 21:2–6 and Deuteronomy, an Israelite ("Hebrew") who was sold or who sold himself or herself to another Israelite owed six years of service and was to be allowed to go free in the seventh. (Note that this "seventh year" has no relation to the year of release but is computed from the date of sale.) In both also there is a provision for renouncing the right to freedom in favor of lifelong servitude.

D, however, modifies the C prototype in several ways. (1) Now female slaves come under the same provision as males, suggesting that the purchase of a woman to become a wife has been discontinued. Indeed, Deuteronomy as a whole assumes that women have greater independence than the older traditions indicate. (2) There is no mention of the master's giving a wife to his slave or retaining her and their children after the slave is freed; probably the slave's marital status is no longer under the control of the master. (3) Without the master's ownership of a slave's wife and children, a primary motive for entering into lifelong servitude has been removed. (4) The ceremony for instituting lifelong servitude has been removed from the sacred sphere and has become a symbolic act of attachment to the household. (5) Overall, servitude has been reduced to ownership of a person's labor, not of the person.

As usual, the author of Deuteronomy has supplied motive clauses and extralegal prescriptions. The master is told to furnish the slave liberally when he or she leaves, obviously to aid the slave's establishment as a free person. The master should not begrudge his slave's freedom because he himself, as an Israelite, was once enslaved and given freedom by Yahweh. In addition, he should realize that his slave has cost him about half of a hired man's wages.

"Three times a year . . ." (16:1–17).

The calendar of pilgrimage festivals brings the cultic section of the Deuteronomic Law to a close. It is during these three festivals that the villager will make his trip to the central sanctuary and fulfill his sacred duties. The list of festivals directly reflects the older cultic calendar (in Exod. 23:14–17; 34:18–25), although some names have changed—Harvest to Weeks, Ingathering to Booths. Unleavened Bread (Mazzoth) has retained its name (see Deut. 16:16) but has been combined with Passover.

Much that is distinctive to Deuteronomy's festival calendar derives from the program of cultic centralization. The older requirement that all Israelite males appear before Yahweh now means a pilgrimage to the central sanctuary, and the Passover celebration no longer takes place in the home but at the one legitimate sacrificial altar. Moreover, the distinctive features associated elsewhere with each festival have given way to the trend toward Deuteronomy's favorite, all-purpose sacrifice—the sacrificial meal. At the festival times, D expects the pilgrim to deliver whatever dues and fulfill whatever duties and vows to which an individual has become obligated and in the process make a joyous celebration of it.

Chapter 16:1–8 mixes the regulations applicable to Passover and to Unleavened Bread (Passover: vss. 1–2, 4b–7; Unleavened Bread: vss. 3–4a, 8) in an effort to synthesize two independent festivals. Passover was always celebrated in the same month as Unleavened Bread (Abib), and the idea of combining them must have seemed a reasonable simplification. This would be doubly so since both festivals were reenactments of the exodus from Egypt. The dates, however, were calculated differently and would not have been easy to synchronize. D avoids the calculation formula and its difficulties, saying only that the seven days of Unleavened Bread begin after the celebration of Passover.

Prior to Deuteronomy, Passover was celebrated in private homes, while Unleavened Bread was a week-long eating rite concluded by a pilgrimage feast. When Deuteronomy made Passover a pilgrimage feast, the result was two pilgrimages a week apart. It is hard to believe that the author intended to put such a burden on villagers, but that is what the text says. The transfer from home to sanctuary was accompanied by significant modifications in the Passover ritual. According to Exodus 12:21–27 (the oldest Passover law), the victim was to be a lamb of one's choice, its blood was to be smeared upon the doorframe of one's house, the participants were to stay in the house all night, and the victim was to be consumed before morning or destroyed (Exod. 34:25b). Deuteronomy modifies the ritual in the direction of the sacrificial meal. Cattle as well as sheep can be slaughtered; gone is the daubing of blood on the doorframe, for one was no longer at home. Only the time of slaughter (evening), the eating during the night, and the disposal of leftovers are preserved from the older rite.

The second pilgrimage festival of the year, Weeks, is named by Deuteronomy for the dating formula, namely, seven weeks after the beginning of the grain harvest (perhaps seven weeks after the last day of Unleavened Bread). Various indications in other texts suggest that the original purpose of the festival was to celebrate the conclusion of the grain harvest with the offering of raised bread made of flour from the new crop. Deuteronomy does not mention this offering but speaks rather of making a "freewill offering"; here again D seems to be pushing all festivals toward a sacrificial meal performed out of gratitude and joy. Weeks is not linked specifically with any event of Israel's sacred history, but D links it indirectly with the Exodus (vs. 12) by commanding generosity—the offerer's household and the local Levites and the destitute are to enjoy the meal as well (vs. 11). As an Egyptian slave liberated by God, the addressee should be willing to imitate God by providing for dependents and the less fortunate.

The third pilgrimage festival of the year, Booths, is named by Deuteronomy for the distinctive ritual associated with the festival. It is to be celebrated sometime in the fall when all harvesting has been completed and food stocks are being stored away for winter. The text leaves the actual date open, perhaps indicating that the date varied from year to year according to the time crops ripened.

The name of the festival is not explained in the Deuteronomic description. According to the Holiness Code, the people are to construct "booths" of tree boughs and live in them for the duration of the festival (Lev. 23:33–43). Despite the lateness of the source, the practice must have antedated Deuteronomy and prompted the name given to it here.

D is silent regarding all offerings not consumed by the pilgrims themselves. If the celebrants remained at the central sanctuary for a full seven days (vs. 15), what would they have done during this time if they did not perform a host of sacrifices? According to Deuteronomic piety, however, rejoicing together in a fully inclusive fellowship is the heart and soul of this festival and indeed of all the festivals. The sacrificial meal embodies this spirit most closely, so D simply ignores the other sacrifices.

The summary of the festival calendar (vss. 16–17) repeats a statement from the Book of the Covenant, "Three times a year all your males shall appear before Yahweh your God. . . ." It is rather startling to have males singled out at this point. Until now women have been addressed along with men, as "your wife" is absent from the list of the people to join the addressee at the festival. Thus, this old phrase contradicts the tenor of the calendar. Perhaps the lawgiver understood Israelite males to be under strict obligation to attend, whereas females did so voluntarily.

I might say, in conclusion, that there is much that is not known about the dating, ritual, and evolution of Israelite festivals. These are the constant subjects of scholarly research, reconstruction, and debate. The Deuteronomist's studied vagueness and persistent reduction of the sacrificial system do not help in understanding these aspects.

"You shall not plant . . . an Asherah . . ." (16:21—17:1).

I have jumped over 16:18–20 to include under the topic of cult an isolated series of prohibitions governing the altar and sacrifice. Why this series is included in the Deuteronomic Law and is placed where it is defies explanation.

In subject matter these prohibitions belong with chapter 12, but the centralization of the cult made them all but unnecessary. When Israel had a multitude of altars, such directions were needed, but they would not be necessary when there was but one legitimate sanctuary under the authority of a well-schooled priesthood and the watchful eye of the entire nation. Perhaps they should be viewed not so much as useful directions for the sanctuary as an expression of the author's desire to purge Israelite religion of Canaanite influence. The post devoted to the goddess Asherah would clearly be out of place at a sanctuary devoted to Yahweh, as it violated both the first and second commandments. The stone pillars had sufficiently loose associations to have been accepted by orthodox Yahwists (read Gen. 28:18; 31:45, 51–54; Exod. 24:4; Josh. 24:26–27), but to the author of Deuteronomy they had the earmarks of idolatry and must be eliminated. With these two laws on the books, Josiah had one more reason to demolish the sanctuaries outside Jerusalem.

The prohibition against offering blemished animals as sacrifices is one of the few technical rules the author gives. Since he does not provide a catalog of blemishes (various sorts of birth defects and injuries), he may have expected the priests to oversee the observance of the rule. It must be realized that a blemish did not render the animal "unclean," for D specifically allows for the slaughter and consumption of such (15:22). Only when the blemished animal is a sacrificial victim does it cause Yahweh's repulsion. The assumption is that any animal brought into Yahweh's sphere, even if it were to be consumed by the offerer, should exemplify wholeness and perfection.

Offices and Institutions. Deuteronomy 16:18—21:20 shows evidence of conscious organization around four offices (judge, king, priest, prophet) and two national institutions (city of refuge, militia). To create these units, D drew together some older laws and composed some homilies to fill in for the absence of precedents. The result is a rough and ready mixture of principle, homily, and explanation by example.

"You shall appoint judges and officers in all your towns . . ." (16:18—17:13).

Deuteronomy 16:18—17:13 consists of three paragraphs devoted to the judiciary (16:18–20; 17:2–7, 8–13), interrupted by the cultic prohibitions just discussed (16:21—17:1). The initial paragraph (16:18–20) prescribes the appointment of judicial officials to serve in the places of residence. First the entire community is addressed (vs. 18), then the judges themselves (vss. 19–20). The shifting of addressee is intentional, for D seeks to identify the community and its judicial representatives. The community acts through its judges, and its fate depends upon their success in maintaining justice. The very fact that the community, not Moses (so Exod. 18:19–23; Deut. 1:9–18), appoints the judges constitutes a transfer of power and responsibility to the people.

The term translated "officers," or clerks, seems to mean persons with a scribal function, perhaps court recorders. It is possible that they were also legal scholars, who could advise the judges on legal concepts and principles. Some biblical scholars believe that these clerks were royal appointees rather than local officials.

The three prohibitions addressed to the judges reflect the very similar series in Exodus 23:6–8. Since these prohibitions are simple moral principles that everyone would know, the reason for uttering them must have been to give them greater authority and to instill the will for moral rectitude, stated positively in the emphatic conclusion, "Justice, and only justice, you shall follow. . . ."

The second paragraph (17:2–7) illustrates trial procedure by describing an instance of the capital offense of apostasy. The law is addressed to the judges of the court, who are to investigate rumors (vs. 4) and convict and execute the guilty (by stoning) only on the testimony of two or more witnesses (vss. 5–6). These rules actually apply to all capital crimes (see Deut. 19:15).

The designation of apostasy as "transgressing [God's] covenant" is the only example in biblical law in which an offense is so described. Since the covenant is between Yahweh and Israel, and the phrase "transgress [God's] covenant" typically has the people as its subject, it must be seen here as an example of the Deuteronomic collectivization of law. The acts of individuals bring guilt upon the entire people, and the guilty must be "purged" (vs. 7) to avoid collective punishment.

D has expanded the scope of apostasy to include acts of devotion to the sun, moon, and stars. This expansion was prompted by the encounter with Assyrian religion during the years of the Assyrian empire (read 2 Kings 23:5, 11), for the Assyrians were the first ancient Near Eastern people to practice astral worship.

The final paragraph (17:8–13) of the unit on the judicial office requires a system of judicial review. It should be noted that a case was brought to the superior court by the judges hearing the case, not by one of the disputants. When the members of the lower court decided that they lacked the legal sophistication to decide a case, they voluntarily submitted it to the court at the central sanctuary. Once it was submitted to the higher authorities, the lower court was duty-bound under threat of death to abide by their ruling.

The system of judicial review described here is clearly related to Exodus 18:19–23, but there are several significant differences. Jurisdiction is described differently: small versus greater matters (Exod. 18:22), simple versus difficult cases (Deut. 17:8). The composition of the superior court differs: Moses is replaced by a "judge," and a group of Levitical priests is added. The manner of deciding difficult cases is implicitly different: Moses is to seek divine revelation in the cases that come to him (Exod. 18:19), while D makes no mention of this resort and probably expected the legal authorities at the central shrine to arrive at their decisions by knowledge and reason. (D has an aversion to the use of the lot and oath; this is another example of his rationalism.)

It is uncertain whether D's system of judicial review reflects actual practice or derives from theorizing. Some scholars believe that it reflects the judicial reforms of Jehoshaphat reported in 2 Chronicles 19:5–11. In particular, Jehoshaphat's priestly court established in the temple could explain D's Levitical court. The office of "judge," on the other hand, seems like a revival of pre-monarchical traditions (perhaps maintained in the Northern Kingdom). Thus, D's superior court seems to be a synthesis of different institutions; whether it was instituted by Josiah is impossible to say.

"You may indeed set a king over you . . ." (17:14–20).

This is the only treatment of the office of king in biblical law. The author had no legal precedents to develop, so he worked various traditions preserved in the historical books (particularly 1 Sam. 8) into a set of principles and commandments governing the institution. The result is more a homily on kingship than a practical law.

Following D's typical temporal clause ("When you come to the land . . ."), he cites the people's declaration, "I will set a king over me, like all the nations that are round about me." Unlike the other three offices, the monarchy is not prescribed by the lawgiver; rather, it is requested by the people and allowed by God. This view is preserved in the anti-monarchical account in 1 Samuel 8 of the establishment of the kingship, where the desire to be "like all the nations" is considered blameworthy and puts the institution itself in the category of rebellion against God (1 Sam. 8:5–8). D is more reconciled to kingship and believes that the king can be kept from disturbing the theocratic constitution of Israel. Nevertheless, he shares with this source the view that the king was a concession to the people without any independent role or value.

It is noteworthy that D ignores those traditions in 1 Samuel 7–12 which depict the monarchy as instituted by God to deliver Israel from its enemies. D also ignores the theology that elevated the Davidic dynasty to a sacred status, covenanted with God and eternally under divine protection and sponsorship. Clearly, the Deuteronomist is not an apologist for the Davidic monarchy and an exponent of Judean tradition; he speaks, rather, for the theocratic-democratic north.

True to northern tradition, D assigns God the role of choosing a king. To relieve the people's uncertainty as to who this person would be, D assures them that the king will be one of their "brothers" (not a foreigner). As a "constitutional monarchy" under the rule of God, the king's freedom was limited by the divine will; hence, he was restricted in his exploitation of his office for personal gain or military and political power and glory.

Verses 18–20 seek to subordinate the king to the Mosaic Law. To counteract the danger that he will begin to think himself superior to his fellow Israelites and become a law unto himself, a copy of this very code is to be put in the custody of the Levites and read daily by the king. Submission to the law is the great equalizer, and only by accepting his equality can he retain his position among his brothers.

Nowhere does the Israelite legal tradition stand out from its environment more than on the question of kingship. The ancient Near Eastern codes were drawn up under the auspices of kings and were meant to present the king as the font of justice and right. By contrast, the only treatment of kings in Israelite law reduces them to a concession and subordinates them to the law imposed upon the entire people. This move was a signal contribution to the constitutional and legal traditions of Western civilization.

"The Levitical priests . . . all the tribe of Levi . . ." (18:1–8).

Chapter 18 covers the two offices that mediate between God and Israel—priest and prophet. In neither case do the people select the officeholders. In the case of the priest, the tribe has been chosen by God, and each member inherits the office by birthright; the other tribes have received shares of the land, but Levi has "inherited" Yahweh, and each member shares in this inheritance. That inheritance consists of the right and duty to "stand and minister in the name of Yahweh" (vs. 5) and to receive the priestly prebends (portions of sacrificial meals and all firstfruits).

The second paragraph of the unit (vss. 6–8) is occasioned by the centralization of the cult. With the closing of the local altars, the only place where Levites could exercise their tribal rights would be at the central sanctuary. Each Levite is here explicitly granted the right to go to the central altar at his own pleasure and to perform priestly duties and receive priestly prebends as an equal to those who are permanently assigned there.

A careful reader will notice a certain inconsistency between verses 3–5 and verses 6–8. According to verses 3–5, each Levite has the right to officiate at an altar and to receive support from the gifts of the altar. This may have been feasible when there were a multitude of local altars at which "the Levite(s) within your towns" officiated, but centralization cut off the means of support from all who did not locate at the central altar permanently. A Levite could not expect to earn a livelihood from occasional visits to the shrine. Those who remained in their towns would become wards of charity or have to take up secular occupations.

D was completely utopian in believing that the priesthood of the temple would allow the rural Levites to relocate there and continue to perform as priests or to perform a priestly function there at their pleasure. As is seen in the Priestly Source, the temple priesthood claimed sole priestly prerogatives, and the rest of the tribe of Levi was demoted to an auxiliary role. The irony of the Deuteronomic Law is that it heightens Levitical claims while undermining the system for supporting Levites; it asserts the equality of all Levites (there is no indication of a hierarchy) but institutes a cultic order that gave the temple priesthood supreme power and unique privilege.

"Yahweh your God will raise up for you a prophet like me . . ." (18:9–22).

The other mediator between Yahweh and his people is the prophet. D begins the section on the prophet with a condemnation of other modes of obtaining supernatural knowledge (vss. 9–14) and concludes with an offer of a better way—prophecy (vss. 15–22).

The inhabitants of the land which Yahweh is giving to Israel "give heed to soothsayers and to diviners" (vs. 14), but Israel must not do so because such modes of obtaining supernatural knowledge are "an abomination to Yahweh" and arouse him to wrath against the peoples who cultivate them (vs. 12). The people as a whole are responsible for keeping divination from being practiced among them. The list of kinds of divination (vss. 10–11) includes various modes of consulting the dead (who belong to a supernatural realm) and gaining knowledge of divine mysteries by technique (consulting lots, livers of sacrificial animals, astrology, etc.). Such practices cannot be dismissed as innocuous superstition because they represent to D a dangerous perversion of the proper commerce between God and God's creatures. Ancient Near Eastern civilization was permeated with divination and magic, so it was impossible for the author of Deuteronomy to regard them as impotent nonsense.

What was it about divination that made it incompatible with Yahweh's character? For one thing, divination involves discovering the meaning of cryptic and ambiguous signs, while Yahweh's will for his people is not mysterious (cf. Deut. 30:11–14). Further, divination and magic identify the supernatural as an impersonal "force," whereas Yahweh is known through personal communication as a person. Finally, the human who masters the technique of divination actually manipulates the divine, whereas Yahweh insists on revealing himself on his own initiative. The prophetic mode of communication, also known among Israel's neighbors, fitted Yahweh perfectly and by the time of Deuteronomy had attained supremacy in orthodox circles over competing modes of revelation.

The description of the prophetic office begins with a retrospect of Moses' election to be a mediator between the people and God. The prophet is to perform the same mediatory function after Moses dies. Yahweh will himself select the person and put his word in the prophet's mouth. Most interpreters construe this as a promise of a continuous succession of prophets—at least one in every generation.

The task of the prophet is simply to speak Yahweh's word. When he speaks in Yahweh's name, the people are duty-bound to heed it as Yahweh's own word. To disregard the prophetic word is tantamount to rebellion against the divine sovereign and therefore comes under divine sanction (but not judicial punishment: 18:19).

Verses 20–22 deal with the problem of false prophecy. Since a prophet trades on Yahweh's authority, it is obviously critical that he not arrogate that authority. By cynical deception or unconscious self-deception, a prophet can mislead the faithful by proclaiming an unauthorized word. In either case, he is guilty of presumption and should be condemned.

Although the lawgiver prescribes the death penalty for a presumptuous prophet, his real concern is not with punishing him as much as neutralizing his influence. How is one to know, he asks, what word is not authorized by Yahweh? If Israel can determine that, it need not be "afraid" of the prophet who uttered it; that is, the people would have no reason to become confused and uncertain as to the will of Yahweh when prophets disputed among themselves if they could separate the wheat from the chaff. For this purpose, the author enunciates two evidences of false prophecy: prophecy spoken in the name of some other deity, and prediction of events that do not come to pass. The first is self-evident; as to the second, D understands Yahweh to be the one who decides the course of human events, and therefore the one with power and moral consistency to confirm the message he has authorized and to disconfirm any word that misleads his people.

It is frequently noted that historical confirmation is rather impractical because the people needed to know which word was true before it came to pass. This criticism is cogent; it is doubtful that this or any other rule could be applied simply to decide between true and false prophecy. The sensitive believer, however, could look for historical confirmation as events were unfolding and evaluate past prophetic traditions according to their realism (cf. Jer. 28:1–11).

"You shall set apart three cities . . . so that any manslayer can flee to them" (19:1–21).

Chapters 19 and 20 shift from offices to institutions. Chapter 19 begins with the judicial institution of the cities of asylum and concludes with another example of judicial review. In the middle is an isolated verse (vs. 14) dealing with property markers.

The only legal treatment of homicide in the Deuteronomic Law looks at the crime from the point of view of the institution established to handle it. The people are told to set apart three cities of asylum and maintain a road network for easy access to them (vss. 1–3); three more cities are to be set aside after their territory expands (vss. 8–9). In this way the community gained some control over the self-help practice of blood vengeance.

It is uncertain whether the city of asylum was a Deuteronomic innovation or an established practice. (On Exodus 21:13–14, consult Chapter Four.) Several texts name the cities of asylum (Num. 35:9–28; Deut. 4:41–43; Josh. 20:1–6, 9). Probably, then, the institution was in existence before Deuteronomy.

According to the practice of blood vengeance, a male member of the family of a homicide victim was obligated to seek out and execute the killer. In D's law the killer could find asylum in one of the cities set apart as refuge. The avenger of the blood would pursue the killer to the city of asylum and request that the individual be handed over for execution, at which point the law becomes ambiguous. Perhaps the judges of the city of asylum convened an inquiry to determine whether the slayer would be granted long term asylum (the length of time is given in Num. 35:25, 28 but not in D) or would be delivered over for execution by the avenger of the blood. Alternatively, the judges of the city where the killing took place (note vs. 12, "the elders of *his* city") may have rendered a judgment and then notified those in charge of the city of asylum.

D does formulate rules for judging between accidental and intentional homicide (vss. 4–7, 10–13). D's definition and examples are clearer than the statements in the Book of the Covenant (Exod. 21:13–14). It is noteworthy that the lawgiver is as concerned to protect the accidental manslayer as to punish the murderer. If the community allows an accidental manslayer to be executed, it incurs the guilt of innocent blood (vs. 10), just as it does when the guilty go unpunished (vs. 13).

The prohibition against moving or removing (the Hebrew word can have either sense) a boundary marker is strangely isolated in the chapter (vs. 14). It has nothing to do with the institutions under discussion. The description of the marker as that "which the men of old have set" is also puzzling because it suggests that the reason for the prohibition is the preservation of tradition. One would think that moving such a marker was actually property theft, but this legal dimension of the forbidden act is not even alluded to. Some scholars believe that D dipped into proverbial tradition for this rule (cf. Prov. 22:28; 23:10); that thesis would go some way to explain the rule's peculiarities.

The final paragraph (19:15–21) of this chapter promulgates three related rules for judicial procedure. It begins by requiring the concurrence of two or more witnesses for conviction in criminal cases. This rule provides the occasion for prescribing a procedure of judicial review in cases of suspect testimony. Finally, a rule is laid down for the punishment of false witnesses. Why these rules are located here rather than, say, after 17:8–13, is unknown.

The Israelite trial depended heavily upon testimony; evidence played a much smaller role than it does in modern trial procedure. Consequently, trials were vulnerable to dissembling witnesses. The rule requiring the concurrence of multiple witnesses was devised to protect persons from malicious and fabricated charges, but the remedy is imperfect. Some crimes are, obviously, witnessed by only one person and would go unpunished under this rule, as would crimes without any witnesses but with substantial evidence. On the other side, two or three persons could conspire to concur in false testimony (read 1 Kings 21). Perhaps testimony and character witnesses in favor of the defendant could neutralize such machinations (I detect evidence of this in Exodus 23:1–3; Amos 5:10).

The remainder of the paragraph is devoted to the procedure for handling a "malicious witness." The wording suggests that any time a single witness persisted in his charges, both accuser and accused were to be brought before the court of review at the central sanctuary, described here somewhat differently than in 17:8–13. The judges may also have exercised judgment when two or more witnesses gave suspect (conflicting, vacillating, prejudiced) testimony.

Prior to Deuteronomy, it may have been customary to have disputing parties appear in a sanctuary to take oaths and perhaps have the case resolved by lot. If so, D has changed the mode of resolving the conflicting testimony from a sacred to a judicial procedure—a diligent inquiry involving cross-examination and review of the evidence. Such a change would fit D's general preference for rational deliberation.

The witness who is found guilty of making false charges is to suffer the punishment with which the accused was threatened—an application of the *lex talionis* (vs. 21). The idea of applying *lex talionis* to false witnesses entered into ancient Near Eastern law first in the

Code of Hammurabi, before which time they were punished by a civil penalty (a fine).

"When you go forth to war . . ." (20:1–20).

Deuteronomy is the only biblical legal code to include military law, though narratives do preserve some laws of this kind (e.g., Num. 31; 1 Sam. 30:24–25). Presumably such traditions were preserved within the militia, and D has taken them into the legal tradition in an effort to bring all institutions under the concept of *the people*. The militia might now be said to be the people organized militarily.

The rules of war enunciated in this passage are associated with the citizen army levied according to clan and tribe. Before the establishment of the monarchy, this was the only mode of military organization known in Israel. When a crisis arose, the adult males of the affected territory (clan, tribe, or several tribes) were expected to fight in the *army of Yahweh*, and the action was known as a *war of Yahweh*. The soldiers had to be ritually sanctified before battle. The human commander was frequently possessed by the "spirit of Yahweh" before and/or during battle, and Yahweh himself was the decisive combatant on Israel's side. To acknowledge that the victory was to be credited to Yahweh, captives and booty were killed or destroyed (called the *ban*) rather than enslaved or appropriated as the victor's spoils. These practices fell into disuse in the monarchical period, when wars were fought by professional soldiers in the king's employ and the citizen army was used only as an auxiliary force. By enunciating the rules of the war of Yahweh and addressing the people as an army, D seems to be endeavoring to revive the spirit and institutions that animated early Israel.

The opening nine verses of the chapter prescribe a ritual to be performed in preparation for battle. First, a priest addresses the troops in a mini-sermon encouraging bravery. The soldiers were expected to go into battle in the confidence that God would give them victory. (Hosea and Isaiah were to draw quasi-pacifist conclusions from the same ideas; cf. Hos. 14:3; Isa. 30:16; 31:1–9.) There follows a declaration of exemptions by the "officers" (probably royal officials in charge of mustering and numbering the citizen army) which are based upon the idea that someone who has initiated an action should be allowed to enjoy the fruits. In addition to exemptions, fearful persons are allowed to return home to avoid affecting others' morale.

The second paragraph (vss. 10–18) enumerates rules of war. Three different cases are outlined, of which the first two are a pair: surrender without fighting, defeat of a foreign city, and defeat of a Canaanite city. Before battle is joined, the enemy city is to be offered terms of peace. If they accept, they are to be put to forced labor (exactly what is meant in this context is obscure). If they refuse and are defeated in battle, the adult males are to be killed, and the women, youths, and possessions will become Israelite property. The third case belongs to the era of the conquest of Canaan. Actually, it expresses D's ideal of the Conquest, according to which all Israel was to act in concert to gain control of the entire land and was to practice mass extermination so that nothing would remain to lead Israel astray.

The barbarism of these rules is shocking. They violate modern standards for the treatment of prisoners and the vanquished, but for D, wars prosecuted in the name of God and with the participation of the entire people of God demanded extreme measures. This is an example of religion's compounding the ferocity of war with a demonic passion prompted by unconditional faith in the cause of righteousness and truth. When one believes that an unconditional good is at stake in a conflict, the enemy quickly loses the protections belonging to our common humanity.

The author of Deuteronomy, it must be remembered, devised these rules centuries after the Conquest. His real concern was the faithfulness and righteousness of the Israel of his own day. God's judgment upon the Canaanites, executed by the Israelites, was a warning to Israel itself that a similar fate awaited them if they repeated the Canaanite abominations.

The chapter concludes with a humanitarian measure. Fruit trees, as noncombatants, should not be destroyed to construct siegeworks. Since nonfood-bearing trees are not protected, it is likely that D wants to leave sources of food for survivors of the war, a measure in stark contrast to the above.

Miscellaneous Short Laws.   Chapters 21–25 cannot be described as a systematic order or even loose pattern. Every scheme proposed by scholars is too complex to be credible. One can notice some grouping at times, but the overall impression is of a haphazard compilation of relatively short paragraphs. I will simply break down this material into chapters, heading each with a clause from the first law.

"If . . . any one is found slain . . ." (21).

The first paragraph (vss. 1–9) in this chapter lays out a ritual to be performed for an unsolved murder. When a murder victim is found in open country and there is neither witness nor evidence to identify the murderer, the nearest town must perform a ritual in place of a trial. It is assumed that guilt will accrue to the community if it is not pinned on the culpable party, and the ritual is meant to neutralize the harmful effect of such guilt. There is a nonverbal rite accompanied by formal declarations. The slaughter of the unused heifer on an uncultivated plot of land seems to reflect the scapegoat concept; perhaps the divine wrath was "drawn off" from the community to the animal. Accompanying this obscure rite is the very reasonable dissociation of the elders from the crime. In reshaping an older ritual to conform to his concepts and principles, D has added to the elders' declaration of innocence a prayer requesting forgiveness, changing the rite from a quasi-magical act to a picturesque way of eliciting divine mercy. This conforms to the rationalistic tendency of the book. D has also collectivized the law; the ritual obviously expiates the guilt of the town near the body, but the prayer requests forgiveness of the people of Israel. The concluding motive clause makes the performance of the ritual a purgation of guilt from Israel's midst.

The next two paragraphs (vss. 10–14, 15–17) share a concern to protect the rights of vulnerable members of the family unit. The first protects the marital rights of a foreign woman taken captive in war and claimed by an Israelite as his wife. When claimed, she has the right to mourn one month according to her own customs for the loss of contact with her parents; the fact that no husband is mentioned suggests that only unmarried women were considered marriageable. After she has sexual intercourse with the Israelite, she gains the status of a free woman. If the man ceases to love her, she cannot be sold but goes free. The motive clause, "since you have humiliated her," could refer either to having had sexual intercourse or to having spurned her afterward.

The second paragraph (vss. 15–17) protects the rights of the first-born son against arbitrary infringement. The ruling assumes the principle of primogeniture—that a man's firstborn male child receives a double portion of his inheritance—and an odd bit of biological theory is used to justify this principle. The law simply insists that the principle cannot be arbitrarily abrogated by a man who prefers another wife to the mother of the firstborn.

Verses 18–21 also treat a family matter. A child, presumably an adolescent still living in the home, who seriously misbehaves and cannot be corrected can be executed at the request of both of his parents and the agreement of the court of the town. The precedents in C (Exod. 21:15, 17) may permit summary execution by a parent; if so, D is instituting safeguards against the unlimited authority of parents over their children by requiring a court hearing and communal execution. Furthermore, by introducing motive clauses that depict the execution as purging the people of evil and inspiring respect for the law (vs. 21), what begins as a family conflict becomes a collective act of preserving the social order.

The thought of executing a rebellious child may have brought to mind the burial of executed persons. The ruling assumes the practice of displaying the body of a malefactor by hanging it on a tree. Though the evidence for such a practice is weak (only 2 Sam. 4:12 is evidence for it; foreign captives are so treated in Josh. 8:29; 10:26–27), it would fit well with Deuteronomy's desire to inspire fear of the law. The body is to be buried before nightfall to avoid "defiling" the land of Israel. The explanatory clause "a hanged man is accursed by God" is opaque; it could mean that being a public spectacle makes the body itself a bearer of divine wrath, or that the execution exhibits the operation of the divine curse on malefactors. In any case, the body seems to have the capacity to harm the environment if left through the night. Since D is not generally attracted to ideas of cultic holiness and defilement, it might not be too farfetched to surmise that he is guarding against the fouling of the land by the odor of the putrifying body. Bad odors signified the numinous for ancient Israelites (cf. Amos 4:10).

"You shall take [a lost ox or sheep] back to your brother" (22:1–12).

The first twelve verses of this chapter are a random selection of duties and customs, while the remainder are a homogenous unit on sexual offenses. The first paragraph (vss. 1–4), imposing duties of assistance, is a restatement of the casuistic primary laws of Exodus 23:4–5 as commandments in phrasing that is a rather awkward negative expression of a positive duty. Loose animals are to be captured and either returned or kept until claimed. Although it is not mentioned, the finder is surely expected to spread word that the animal has been found; otherwise, the finder might be subject to a charge of theft. Verse 3 extends the duty to cover any lost animal or article. Verse 4 requires assistance for a person with a down beast of burden.

Verse 5 prohibits transvestism. Some scholars believe that the designation of the practice as an "abomination to Yahweh" identifies the prohibition as a polemic against a foreign cultic practice, but the law is quite understandable as a rejection of actions exhibiting confusion of sexual identity.

Verses 6–7 urge a policy of conserving wildlife. A mother bird should be spared for future reproduction, while her eggs or young can be taken for food. Such concern for wildlife puts the lie to allegations that biblical religion encourages the rape of nature.

In the Middle East, where the roofs of houses were flat and used as porches, it was advisable to build a railing or parapet (vs. 8). A person who fell off and died would bring "guilt" upon the house. What legal consequences this might have remain unsaid; perhaps the house would have to be destroyed. If one took Exodus 21:28–31 as an analogy, the owner himself would be subject to execution or ransom.

Verses 9–11 forbid mixing kinds. It is unclear whether verse 9 forbids mixing different varieties of grapes or grapes and other crops, and the penalty given is equally unclear. Does "become holy" mean forfeiture to the sanctuary or removal from use? The import of the other two prohibitions is clear, but their motivation is not. What is wrong with mixing species of work animals, cloth fibers, or kinds of seed? Scholars have generally assumed that these are archaic taboos whose original motivation had long been forgotten.

The next practice mentioned (vs. 12) is equally unmotivated. Perhaps making tassels on the corners of one's cloak was simply a custom which progressively took on an aura of religious significance. Numbers 15:37–41 extends the significance by explaining the tassels as reminders of the commandments. The custom is preserved to this day in the Jewish prayer shawl.

"If a man . . . a young woman . . ." (22:13–30).

Verse 13 introduces a homogenous unit devoted to sexual offenses. The first paragraph (vss. 13–21) sketches in narrative rather than legal form the procedure for dealing with a charge of premarital unchastity. On the wedding night, the bridegroom finds no blood on the sheet from the bride's broken hymen and charges her with not entering the marriage a virgin. To clear her name, her parents take the sheet to the court. If the bridegroom is proven false, he is punished, fined, and forbidden to divorce her; if proven true, the woman is stoned in front of her home, because she brought a bad name on the family and "wrought folly in Israel." This language suggests that her offense was not against her future husband (viz., depriving him of sole rights to sexual access) but against the social order. Unchastity is, to use modern terms, a sign of a lack of moral discipline and sense of honor.

Verses 22–29 make up a rather closely connected group of casuistic laws governing illicit sexual intimacy. The fundamental principle is that a woman should have intercourse only with her husband, and from this principle all the rulings follow. A married or betrothed woman who consents to intercourse with any man but her husband involves both of them in adultery, and both are executed if detected; if she is seized and forced to have intercourse, the man is guilty of a capital crime. If the woman is unattached, the rape or seduction precipitates a process leading to the marriage of the couple. These laws do not indicate how the act of adultery or rape is detected. The initial law (vs. 22) seems to require that they be caught in the act, but it probably covers other means of detection. In fact, the phrase "If there is found someone who. . ." (author's translation) is a regu-

lar Deuteronomic formula for apprehension and could include preg-
nancy, indirect evidence, and in the case of rape the woman's report.

In verses 23–27, the author offers a rough and ready rule for
differentiating adultery and rape. Rape will be accompanied by the
woman's scream for help, which in a populated area will be heard
and answered. Hence, if the scene of the act was a populated area and
there was no scream, it is assumed that the woman is complicit. If the
scene was the open country, a scream might not be heard, so the case
is classified as rape (giving the woman the benefit of doubt). Most
likely this rule was not applied automatically, for the woman raped
in a populated area could claim her life was threatened, that her
scream went undetected, or similar conditions.

The interests of the community are brought to the fore in motive
clauses in cases of adultery (vss. 22, 24). The parties of a liaison are
categorized with apostates, murderers, and kidnappers as dangerous
to the community and must be purged from Israel to expiate the
guilt in the midst of the community.

The last verse of the chapter (22:30 [Hebrew: 23:1]) prohibits
sexual intercourse between a man and any wife of his father. This
was formulated for a society in which polygamy was practiced. A
much more complete set of incest prohibitions is found in Leviticus
18:6–18.

"He . . . shall not enter the assembly of Yahweh" (23).

The chapter begins with a group of related rules governing admission to the religious assembly (vss. 1–8), followed by a group
covering camp cleanness (vss. 9–14); the remainder of the chapter
(vss. 15–25) is miscellaneous in the extreme.

The assembly, or congregation, of Yahweh appears to be the
gathering of the community for corporate worship and political deliberation. Possibly this body also acted in war. In all probability
only adult males were counted as members of the assembly, and the
rules governing admission assume that all Israelite men were admitted unless they had some defect. The first verse of the unit states a
physical defect—mutilated sex organs—that would exclude admission,
perhaps because such a person was not fully "male." The most likely
candidate for this exclusion would have been a eunuch. The other

defect mentioned, bastardy, might be considered a genealogical defect. Such a person could not claim proper family identity for membership in the community. The Old Testament contains the account of one bastard who rose to the status of judge of Israel—Jephthah son of Gilead, born to a prostitute—thus demonstrating greater flexibility than this rule suggests.

The remainder of the unit concerns persons of foreign extraction. Ammonites and Moabites who live within Israelite territory may never become naturalized citizens of Israel, but Edomites and Egyptians may do so after three generations have lived in Israel. These exclusions and admissions are justified by historical reference, but the justifications are rather artificial, and the real reasons may never be known.

The rites for keeping the military camp "clean" are enunciated under the heading of avoiding "every evil thing." A man who has a nocturnal emission must remove himself from camp for a day and then bathe (vss. 10–11); elimination must be done outside the camp and covered up (vss. 12–13). These rules give a religious aura to what would be considered matters of hygiene. The camp has the quality of a holy place, for Yahweh is present. It must be kept in a state of ritual compatibility with the holy God, or God will leave. Consult Chapter Six for more on the concept of clean and unclean.

In verses 15–16, the lawgiver requires the harboring of escaped slaves on the assumption that any slave who endeavors to escape has been mistreated by his or her master. The author desires a slave system so benign that a slave would serve the master of his or her own free will. Obviously such an institution is utopian. For slavery to operate, a slave must be compelled to work and not allowed to break the relationship at will.

The view of some scholars that this ruling applied to slaves escaping from foreign countries is not attested in the text. It is based upon the assumption that the author of Deuteronomy would not be so utopian as to propose discretionary slavery. Utopian passages, however, are found in all biblical lawbooks, and Deuteronomy is more given to them than any other.

Verses 17–18 prohibit any form of cultic prostitution in Israel. By cultic prostitution is meant the practice of prostitution at sanctuaries and the performance of sexual intercourse by a lay person (apart from the sanctuary) for money to pay to the sanctuary in performance of a vow. Both forms of prostitution, by either males or females, is prohibited in these verses. Israel was tempted by their neighbors to take up these practices. In a religious system in which the deities were closely associated with the power of fertility and productivity, the sacralization of the sex act was quite logical. To Yahweh, who was not a sexual being, the sacralization of sex and the associated divorcing of sexual intercourse from marriage were anathema.

Verses 19–20 prohibit charging interest on loans among Israelites (compare Exod. 22:25; Lev. 25:35–37), specifically loans to persons in financial straits. To charge interest in such circumstances would be to make a profit off the distress of others. Unfortunately, the author makes no provision for business loans among Israelites, although he permits them to foreigners.

Verses 21–23 is one of the few paragraphs in this section of the book devoted to cultic practice. Actually, these verses are not so much law as exhortation. A vow was a promise, voluntarily made, to perform a cultic act (usually a sacrifice) to move God to act on one's request or to thank God for acting. Obviously, one should keep one's promises, so the passage is simply a reminder.

The final paragraph of the chapter (23:24–25) provides a rule of thumb for distinguishing between innocent snacking in a vineyard or field and crop theft. Its leniency marks it as more humanitarian legislation.

"When a man takes a wife . . ." (24).

This chapter begins with a pair of rulings involving marriage (vss. 1–5), and the balance is devoted largely to the protection of the rights and welfare of the disadvantaged.

Biblical law everywhere assumes the theory and practice of divorce but nowhere states the grounds and procedures for it. Deuteronomy 24:1–4 comes closest to such a statement, although its explicit concern is much narrower. Verses 1–2 outline the procedure for divorce. According to this law and other indications in biblical law, only a man could initiate divorce, though a woman could leave and thereby force a situation (cf. Judg. 19:2–30). The grounds for divorce are vaguely stated: "if then she finds no favor in his eyes because he has found some indecency in her." Since the husband was not required to obtain a court decision, the operative phrase is "finds no favor"; he could divorce her, in principle, for any reason. The suggestion that she was "indecent" lacks legal force. As adultery had more serious consequences than divorce, "indecency" should be understood to cover any quality of personality that made for an unhappy marriage. The statement contains significant lacunae; there is no mention of custody of children, division of property, or obligation to pay alimony.

The explicit concern of the paragraph is remarriage. The divorced woman has the right to remarry, but if her second husband divorces her or dies, she cannot marry her first husband again. Here sexual intimacy with her second is said to defile her in relation to her first husband, but she may marry a third man without stigma. There really is no explanation for this peculiar sort of defilement; the statement "that is an abomination before Yahweh" simply renews the mystery. My suspicion is that the author is opposing wife swapping, a pattern of moral behavior that would indeed be repugnant to Yahweh and threaten the moral health of the community.

Verse 5 allows a newlywed to be released from military and civilian obligations for a year to enjoy an extended honeymoon. This is even more lenient than the exemption provided in Deuteronomy 20:7 (the right to consumate a marriage).

Verses 6, 10–13, 14–15, 17–18 and 19–22 are prime examples of Deuteronomy's famous humanitarian provisions for the poor and disadvantaged. Scholars over the years were wont to interpret the term translated "pledge" as a *pawn* held by the creditor from the time of lending until repayment. Recently, however, it has been forcefully argued that the "pledge" was an item distrained by the creditor when the loan came due to force repayment. There is no indication that it could be sold to recoup loss. Verse 6 forbids distraining the wherewithal to grind flour for the daily meal on the assumption that the tool was necessary for life. Verses 10–11 demand that courtesy be shown a debtor, and if the distrained chattel is an article of clothing needed for sleeping, it must be returned every night for the borrower's comfort (vss. 12–13).

Verses 14–15 protect hired labor from ill-treatment. The first verse is a general maxim explicitly extended to non-Israelite as well as Israelite workers. The second verse gives a specific example of mistreatment—withholding wages at the end of the day, which the employer would be tempted to do to assure the return of the laborer the following day and to simplify accounting. The author assumes that day labor is taken up out of dire necessity, so the worker needs the wages for a meal that night.

Verses 17–18 protect the legal rights of persons who cannot defend their rights in judicial proceedings—the sojourner, or resident alien, who was not a citizen, and the widow and her minor children, who lacked an adult male to stand up for them. These people had to rely upon the help of the righteous men in the community (see Job 29:12–17). The motive clause recalling Israel's enslavement in Egypt is prompted by the mention of the sojourner (cf. Exod. 23:9).

The concluding paragraph of the chapter (vss. 19–22) adds another provision for the sojourner, orphan, and widow. The fields, vineyards, and orchards of the land are not to be gleaned, so that those who are on the edge of starvation may glean them. Verse 19 is a bit odd, for it is based upon the unlikely prospect that sheaves will accidentally be left in the grainfield; perhaps the author means to speak of stray, loose stalks. Leviticus 19:9 calls for leaving the borders of the field unharvested.

Deuteronomy's humanitarian laws are more on the order of moral instruction than enforceable law. Their reliance on divine promises (24:13) and threats (24:15) indicates their unenforceable nature. The law reaches beyond the scope of courts to cover the quality of life throughout the community. While relying on the consciences of those who have enough wealth and power to protect and provide for the poor and powerless, D knows that the cumulative effect of their actions will determine the fate of the nation as much as the enforcement of the criminal law.

Verse 7 interjects into the section a capital offense—the crime of kidnapping into slavery—which was already treated in the Book of the Covenant (Exod. 21:16). Deuteronomy accentuates the community's role and stake in the apprehension and execution of one so depraved as to "steal one of his brethren." Execution will avert the communication of the offender's guilt to the community.

Although the author is not inclined to enunciate technical cultic law, he does recognize the need to alert the community to its existence (vs. 8). The law has no interest in the medical aspects of the variety of unrelated skin diseases known by the term translated "leprosy," but it does provide for quarantine. In Leviticus 13–14, which contains the procedures the priests would follow, the reason for quarantine is religious, namely, keeping the camp holy. Physical deformity, filth, and contact with the unclean constitute a large proportion of the conditions classified as ritually unclean.

Verse 16 introduces an underlying legal principle of biblical law: no one is to be executed for the offense of a family member. This prohibition limits the extent of corporate responsibility of the family for the acts of members. It is noteworthy that D changes the liturgical phrase "visiting the iniquity of the fathers upon the children to the third and the fourth generation of those who hate me" (Exod. 20:5) to "requites to their face those who hate him" (Deut. 7:10), reinforcing the idea that only the guilty are to be punished.

There are examples in biblical narrative of the execution of whole families for the acts of some members (Josh. 7:24–26; 2 Sam. 21:1–9; 1 Kings 21:13/2 Kings 9:26). Although this is not quite the issue of Deuteronomy 24:16, it could be construed as coming under the same rubric. The elimination of potential rivals to the throne (1 Kings 15:29; probably 2 Sam. 21:1–9) is comprehensible in political terms and can hardly be classed as a judicial execution. Execution as a divine curse (Josh. 7:24–26; 2 Sam. 21:1–9; cf. 2 Sam. 3:9) comes under the rubric of God's visiting the sins of the fathers on the children for generations (Exod. 34:7). Legal justice is to be more discriminating. Only 1 Kings 21:13/2 Kings 9:26 reports a judicial act involving several generations, and the text understands it to be an outrage of justice.

Why was the judicial system expected to adhere to a justice more discriminate than that to which God adhered? The justice of God operates not only through judicial means but through the course of human events. An evil deed sets in motion consequences which do not cease within one generation but continue for generations. God promises to channel these consequences in such a way as to ensnare the family that benefited from the evil. Only God has the authority and wisdom to judge this larger dimension of guilt; the community must accept its own restricted powers.

"Lest . . . your brother be degraded in your sight" (25).

This last chapter of the legal code proper is loosely knit together by the theme of shame. The first paragraph (vss. 1–3) limits punishment by lashing to avoid shaming the guilty person unduly. The employment of lashing as a penalty is nowhere mentioned in any of the codes, so coming across a law that assumes it to be a regular practice is somewhat surprising and points up the degree of our ignorance of Israelite judicial procedure. Lashing functions not only to inflict pain but to make a spectacle of the guilty. By limiting the number with the stated purpose of guarding the offender's dignity, the lawgiver acknowledges the humanity of the offender and facilitates his regaining social respectability. This notice stands in tension with Deuteronomy's oft-stated desire to instill fear of the law.

Verse 4 expresses sympathy for the ox drawing a threshing sledge. Although allowing it to eat to its heart's desire sounds humanitarian, it might actually be harmful to the ox.

Verses 5–10 sketch the institution known as levirate marriage, which was designed to serve the principle that a man's "name" and inheritance should be preserved in Israel by descendants. If a man dies childless, his widow is to bear a son by his brother to perpetuate his name. If the brother refuses to do his duty, the deceased man's wife is told to institute a procedure which will either shame him into performing it or stigmatize him and his descendants. One reason the brother might not be willing to impregnate his brother's wife is that he and his children are in line for inheriting the deceased man's estate (according to Num. 27:9). If the lawgiver had wanted to put legal force behind the practice of levirate marriage, he could have declared the humiliated brother ineligible to inherit.

The next paragraph (vss. 11–12) also turns on the idea of shame. The woman who grabs the genitals of her husband's opponent in a scuffle has acted shamefully, and it is the shamefulness of her act, not the harm done (which is negligible), that calls forth the harsh punishment. This is the only biblical law that prescribes corporal mutilation.

Verses 13–16 might be called an ethical code for merchants. Weights (literally *stones*) were used in commerce to weigh valuable metals; before coinage it was according to weight that copper, gold, and silver were used as a medium of exchange. A crooked merchant might keep several weights, one set lighter and one heavier than standard, to underpay and overcharge unsuspecting customers. The term translated "measure" is *ephah*, a standard dry measure (probably a bit smaller than a bushel). A crooked merchant might receive produce in a large ephah and sell in a small one. False liquid measures could be used in the same way. Of course, false weights and measures do not exhaust the dishonest and unfair practices of merchants but represent the whole range. The dishonest merchant falls under the same condemnation—an abomination to Yahweh—as the most heinous offenders against divine law. The future of the people of Yahweh depends upon the maintenance of justice in commerce.

The chapter closes with a command to exterminate the Amalekites (vss. 17–19). This is not really a law but a historical tradition that looks back to the Exodus and forward to the Conquest and even to the monarchy. Why Deuteronomy, which comes from the centuries following the disappearance of these desert marauders, should conclude the code with an unnecessary exhortation in such a distastefully vindictive spirit is a mystery. It probably does not actually belong to the original Deuteronomic Law but to the Deuteronomistic Historian, who used the tradition to give the code historical setting. Despite its vindictive spirit, the passage serves an important purpose as a reminder that national existence requires the assertion of a national will against all groups and forces opposing its success. The same force of will that establishes and maintains a law against violation within must be shown toward those whose interest it is to weaken or pirate it from without.

Rituals to Strengthen Israelite Identity. Chapter 26 concludes the presentation of law with rituals designed to integrate individual Israelites into the symbolic life of the community and to inculcate the dominant values of the author. While each has materials drawn from older traditions, in their present form they are Deuteronomic creations.

The first is the rubrics and liturgy for the presentation of the firstfruits (vss. 1–11). A symbolic portion of the farmers' grain is to be brought to the sanctuary as an offering of thanksgiving to God. Although the name of the festival is not given, the fact that the farmer is expected to go on pilgrimage to the central shrine strongly suggests one of the three annual festivals. One might argue that the rite could be performed at any of the three (according to the crop), or that it was reserved specifically for the one known as First Fruits (Exod. 23:16), or Weeks (Exod. 34:22; Deut. 16:10).

The unit is repetitious, as verses 3–4 are a brief form of verses 5–10, with a slightly altered rubric. According to verses 3–4, the farmer delivers the offering to the priest, who sets it at the altar, while in verses 5–10 the farmer himself sets the offering before God. Perhaps verses 3–4 are a later addition to fit the rite to temple procedure.

The liturgical recitation in verses 5–10 has played a premier role in modern biblical scholarship. It was identified by Gerhard von Rad as an example of what he called *a historical credo*, a speech form which compressed Israel's story of salvation into a brief compass for liturgical purposes. It was his opinion that this historical summary antedated the narrative sources and provided them with the outline for their narratives. Other scholars have noted its correspondence to the pattern of the recounting praise (or thanksgiving) psalm: distress, cry for help, deliverance.

The author of Deuteronomy has made this ancient recitation a profound expression of his own spirituality. The individual Israelite integrates himself into Israel's story in a most delicate way. He presents his offering in acknowledgment of Yahweh's gift of the land, which is the last act of the story beginning with the fathers. The recitation switches to first person plural with the Exodus, so that the worshiper identifies himself as a part of the group which experienced Egyptian bondage and deliverance. When he steps forward with his offering, he expresses the gratitude all Israel has for the beneficence of Yahweh. The presentation of the firstfruits ends with a banquet for the family, to which the Levites and sojourners are to be invited. Thus, the whole community can share Yahweh's bounty.

The second ritual (vss. 12–15) adapts old traditions to Deuteronomy's newly invented triennial tithe for the Levite and the needy. With the elimination of local sanctuaries, the Levites of the countryside would lose their means of support, so Deuteronomy offers this tithe as a substitute. Deuteronomy changes the tithe for two out of three years from a donation to the sanctuary to a sacrificial meal (see Deut. 14:22–27); every third year it was a donation to the Levite, but now it is a dole to which other needy persons are also entitled (Deut. 14:28–29).

When the tithe is delivered, it is to be accompanied by a statement swearing that the tithe has been treated properly:

> I have removed the sacred portion out of my house . . . I have not eaten of the tithe while I was mourning, or removed any of it while I was unclean, or offered any of it to the dead.   (vss. 13, 14)

These statements antedate Deuteronomy's revision of tithing. They are assurances that the donations are in a state of purity, a necessary condition if they are donated to the sanctuary but not if they are distributed to the needy. To this older language the author adds statements of his own:

> I have given it to the Levite, the sojourner, the fatherless, and the widow, according to all thy commandment, . . . I have not transgressed any of thy commandments, . . . I have obeyed the voice of Yahweh my God.

These statements soar high above issues of cultic purity to sweeping assertions of moral and religious righteousness. Being in conformity with God's will, the worshiper can ask God's blessing on Israel and its land (vs. 15). The act of providing for the Levite and the poor has become the occasion for declaring allegiance to the law and procuring a continuation of divine beneficence.

The chapter concludes with a hortatory reminder of covenant declarations made by Israel and Yahweh. The text says that they were made "this day," though there is no narrative of such a ceremony. Some scholars see here a report of an actual liturgical performance, perhaps even the one performed by Josiah and the people in the covenant ceremony recounted in 2 Kings 23:1–3. Alternatively, it could be the echo of a ritual that had ceased to be performed. For an exposition of the content of the ritual, see Chapter Eight on Law and Covenant.

SUGGESTED READING

For the policy informing this selection, see the statement introducing the bibliography at the end of Chapter One. For the source, form, and traditio-historical criticism of Deuteronomy, consult the bibliography of Chapter Two as well as the works listed below.

Among the commentaries on Deuteronomy in English, the following are satisfactory:

von Rad, Gerhard. *Deuteronomy, A Commentary*. Trans. Dorothea Barton. Old Testament Library. Philadelphia: Westminster Press, 1966.

Wright, G. Ernest. "The Book of Deuteronomy." In *The Interpreter's Bible*, 12 vols., ed. George Arthur Buttrick, vol. 2. New York and Nashville: Abingdon Press, 1953.

The argument for the breakdown of Deuteronomic literature into the work of the Deuteronomist and that of the Deuteronomistic Historian is advanced in the following works:

Cross, Frank Moore. "The Themes of the Book of Kings and the Structure of the Deuteronomistic History." In *Canaanite Myth and Hebrew Epic: Essays in the History of the Religion of Israel*, pp. 274–289. Cambridge and London: Harvard University Press, 1973.

Minette de Tillesse, Georges. "Sections 'tu' et Sections 'vous' dans le Deutéronome," *Vetus Testamentum* 12 (1962), pp. 29–87.

Noth, Martin. *Überlieferungsgeschichtliche Studien*. Tübingen: Max Niemeyer Verlag, 1957. Pp. 1–110.

Major monographs in English on Deuteronomy and its traditions:

Nicholson, Ernest W. *Deuteronomy and Tradition*. Philadelphia: Fortress Press, 1967.

von Rad, Gerhard. *Studies in Deuteronomy*. Trans. David Stalker. Studies in Biblical Theology, vol. 9. London: SCM Press, 1953.

Weinfeld, Moshe. *Deuteronomy and the Deuteronomic School*. Oxford: Oxford University Press, 1972.

A sample of the literature arguing that Deuteronomy reflects the structure of suzerain-vassal treaties:

Kline, Meredith G. *Treaty of the Great King: The Covenant Structure of Deuteronomy: Studies and Commentary*. Grand Rapids: Wm. B. Eerdmans Publishing Co., 1963.

McCarthy, Dennis J. *Treaty and Covenant: A Study in Form in the Ancient Oriental Documents and in the Old Testament*. Analecta Biblica, vol. 21. Rome: Pontifical Biblical Institute, 1963.

Specific connections between Deuteronomy and Assyrian treaties:

Frankena, R. "The Vassal-Treaties of Esarhaddon and the Dating of Deuterono-my." In *Oudtestamentische Studiën*, vol. 14, pp. 122–154. Leiden: E. J. Brill, 1965.
Weinfeld, M. "Traces of Assyrian Treaty Formulae in Deuteronomy," *Biblica* 46 (1965), pp. 417–427.

A selection of studies of various themes and passages of Deuteronomy:

Abba, Raymond. "Priests and Levites in Deuteronomy," *Vetus Testamentum* 27 (1977), pp. 257–267.
Bee, Ronald E. "A Study of Deuteronomy Based on Statistical Properties of the Text," *Vetus Testamentum* 29 (1977), pp. 1–22.
Bellefontaine, Elizabeth. "Deuteronomy 21:18–21: Reviewing the Case of the Re-bellious Son," *Journal for the Study of the Old Testament* 13 (1979), pp. 13–31.
Brueggemann, Walter. *The Land*. Overtures to Biblical Theology, vol. 1. Philadel-phia: Fortress Press, 1977. Pp. 45–70 in particular.
Carmichael, Calum M. "A Ceremonial Crux: Removing a Man's Sandal as a Fe-male Gesture of Contempt," *Journal of Biblical Literature* 96 (1977), pp. 321–336.
———. "A Common Element in Five Supposedly Disparate Laws," *Vetus Testa-mentum* 29 (1979), pp. 129–142.
DeVries, Simon J. "Deuteronomy: Exemplar of a Non-Sacerdotal Appropriation of Sacred History." In *Grace Upon Grace: Essays in Honor of Lester J. Kuyper*, ed. James I. Cook, pp. 95–105. Grand Rapids: Wm. B. Eerdmans Publishing Co., 1975.
Frymer-Kensky, Tikva. "Tit for Tat: The Principle of Equal Retribution in Near Eastern and Biblical Law," *Biblical Archaeologist* 43 (1980), pp. 230–234.
Gammie, John G. "The Theology of Retribution in the Book of Deuteronomy," *Catholic Biblical Quarterly* 32 (1970), pp. 1–12.
Gitlin, Emmanuel. "The Tithe in Deuteronomy," *Religion in Life* 32 (1962–63), pp. 574–585.
Gottwald, Norman K. " 'Holy War' in Deuteronomy: Analysis and Critique," *Re-view and Expositor* 61 (1964), pp. 296–310.
Harvey, Dorothea Ward. " 'Rejoice Not, O Israel!' " In *Israel's Prophetic Heritage: Essays in Honor of James Muilenburg*, ed. Bernhard W. Anderson and Walter Harrelson, pp. 116–127. New York: Harper & Brothers, 1962.
Kaufman, Stephen A. "The Structure of the Deuteronomic Law," MAARAV 1 (1979), pp. 105–158.
Kooy, Vernon H. "The Fear and Love of God in Deuteronomy." In *Grace Upon Grace: Essays in Honor of Lester J. Kuyper*, ed. James I. Cook, pp. 106–116. Grand Rapids: Wm. B. Eerdmans Publishing Co., 1975.
Kuyper, Lester J. "The Book of Deuteronomy," *Interpretation* 6 (1952), pp. 321–340.
Lind, Millard C. *Yahweh Is a Warrior: The Theology of Warfare in Ancient Israel*. Scottdale: Herald Press, 1980.
Lohfink, Norbert. *Das Hauptgebot: Eine Untersuchung literarischer Einleitungsfragen zu Dtn 5–11*. Rome: Pontifical Biblical Institute, 1963.

————. "Culture Shock and Theology," *Biblical Theology Bulletin* 7 (1977), pp. 12–21.

Milgrom, Jacob. "Profane Slaughter and a Formulaic Key to the Composition of Deuteronomy," *Hebrew Union College Annual* 47 (1976), pp. 1–17.

Moran, William. "The Ancient Near Eastern Background of the Love of God in Deuteronomy," *Catholic Biblical Quarterly* 25 (1963), pp. 77–87.

Myers, Jacob M. "The Requisites for Response: On the Theology of Deuteronomy," *Interpretation* 15 (1961), pp. 14–31.

Nicholson, Ernest. "The Centralisation of the Cult in Deuteronomy," *Vetus Testamentum* 13 (1963), pp. 380–389.

Phillips, Anthony. "Uncovering the Father's Skirt," *Vetus Testamentum* 30 (1980), pp. 38–43.

Preiser, W. "Vergeltung und Sühne im altisraelitischen Strafrecht." In *Festschrift für Eberhard Schmid*, pp. 7–38. Göttingen: Vandenhoeck & Ruprecht, 1961.

von Rad, Gerhard. "The Promised Land and Yahweh's Land in the Hexateuch" and "There Remains Still a Rest for the People of God: An Investigation of a Biblical Conception." In *The Problem of the Hexateuch and Other Essays*, trans. E. W. Trueman Dicken, pp. 79–93, 94–102. Edinburgh and London: Oliver & Boyd, 1966.

Smend, Rudolf. *Die Bundesformel*. Theologische Studiën, no. 68. Zurich: EVZ-Verlag, 1963.

Toombs, Lawrence E. "Love and Justice in Deuteronomy: A Third Approach to the Law," *Interpretation* 19 (1965), pp. 399–411.

Wenham G. J. "The Restoration of Marriage Reconsidered," *Journal of Jewish Studies* 30 (1979), pp. 36–40.

Wenham, G. J., and J. G. McConville. "Drafting Techniques in Some Deuteronomic Laws," *Vetus Testamentum* 30 (1980), pp. 248–252.

Westermann, Claus. *Blessing in the Bible and the Life of the Church*. Trans. Keith R. Crim. Overtures to Biblical Theology. Philadelphia: Fortress Press, 1978. Pp. 46–49 in particular.

Special treatment of Deuteronomy in several biblical theologies:

Eichrodt, Walther. *Theology of the Old Testament*. 2 vols. Trans. J. A. Baker. Old Testament Library. London: SCM Press, 1961. Vol 1, pp. 72f, 90–96.

von Rad, Gerhard. *Old Testament Theology*. 2 vols. Trans. D. M. G. Stalker. Edinburgh and London: Oliver & Boyd, 1962–65. Vol. 1, pp. 219–231.

A study by the author:

Patrick, Dale. "Collective Address in Deuteronomic Law." In *American Academy of Religion Biblical Literature: 1974*, comp. Fred O. Francis, pp. 1–13. Missoula: American Academy of Religion, 1974.

Chapter Six

THE HOLINESS CODE AND PRIESTLY LAW

The sheer volume of legal material in the Priestly Source is staggering. By far the largest portion of the Sinaitic account belongs to this source (Exod. 25–31; 35–40; Lev. 1–27; Num. 1–10), the bulk of which is legal or quasi-legal. Yahweh reveals to Moses the pattern of the wilderness sanctuary, known as the *tabernacle*, and its paraphernalia. Once the tabernacle is constructed, the sacrificial ritual for the sanctuary is given, the priesthood is installed, the procedures for keeping the tabernacle and camp ritually clean are dictated, the camp structure is set up, and the Levites are given their duties. Then the people of Israel depart from Sinai.

Within this mass of legal material, Leviticus 17–26 stands out as an independent corpus of laws. This corpus has been named the "Holiness Code" because of its stress on maintaining holiness through obedience to the law of the holy God. Like C and D, H contains laws and exhortation on a wide range of religious, communal, and economic topics. As part of the Priestly Source, it fills the need for a law governing the total life of the community. Without it, Priestly Law would be too narrowly focused on the sanctuary and ritual.

In this chapter, my approach will be to expound the text of the Holiness Code and insert commentary on related P texts at relevant points. It is impossible to provide commentary on every Priestly legal text within the limited scope of an introduction. As the Holiness Code is most like the other biblical lawbooks in form and content, it is the logical subject within the Priestly work on which to concentrate. I might add that H is more immediately relevant to the contemporary reader than the rest of P, for it covers matters of personal and social morality, while the remaining Priestly legislation governs an institution that no longer exists. The law of the sanctuary is of historical interest, but the law of the Holiness Code continues to instruct all those who recognize the biblical God as God indeed. The Priestly understanding of the institutional and ritual structure of the people of Israel deserves some separate consideration, however. Before introducing the Holiness Code, I will give a general impression of P's depiction of the people of Israel.

The Religious Community Envisaged by Priestly Law

The classical formulation of the Pentateuchal hypothesis dated the Priestly writer to the Exile or afterward, that is, between 587 and 450 B.C. He wrote from the point of view of the Jerusalem temple priesthood deported to Babylon, who hoped to return to Jerusalem, reconstruct the temple, and revive the sacrificial ritual at the heart of temple worship. The Priestly Source was written to preserve the memory of the structure, paraphernalia, and ritual of the first temple in order to duplicate it in the revival. Since the traditions of the first temple were believed to be of divine origin, P traced them back to divine revelation; since it was assumed that all of God's law derived from Sinai, with Moses as the mediator, temple traditions were naturally traced to the same event; since the actual temple was built centuries later at an entirely different site, P transformed an old tradition about a "tent of meeting" (a place to receive oracles) into a surrogate temple for the wilderness period. According to this account of the matter, P's retrospect was simultaneously a prospectus. Like Ezekiel 40–48 it was a program for reconstruction, incorporating new ideas and rituals that had arisen from the experience of the Exile and reflection on its causes. The result of P's fusion of old and new is a program for reconstructing the people not as a political kingdom but as a religious community centered around the temple and ruled by a religious hierarchy. Symbolic of the political shift was the appropriation of the royal installation rite of anointment by the high priest (Lev. 8:12).

The classical formulation has always had some opponents, and in recent years this opposition has become formidable. Led by the research of the Israeli scholar Y. Kaufmann, a company of noted savants have argued for a pre-exilic dating of the Priestly Source. Many provisions of the Holiness Code and Priestly Law seem best suited to a pre-exilic situation, and various words and phrases characteristic of these writings diverge from the common expressions of the late pre-exilic and exilic eras, suggesting that they were coined prior to that time. P's conception of holiness and the ritual pattern for maintaining it have been shown to be of great antiquity in the ancient Near East, making it probable that the substance of Priestly theology existed in Israel's early days. Finally, the evidence alleged to require an exilic or post-exilic dating can just as well be fitted into a pre-exilic situation.

Although I admit the cogency of these arguments for pre-exilic dating, I am still inclined toward the exilic period. The community envisaged by the Priestly Source is not a political entity but a religious one. This image of Israel would be fitting for exiles designing a restoration of the people but not for the clergy of the Judean royal sanctuary in Jerusalem.

The Priestly Source presents the establishment of the institutions and practices of the people of Israel in stages. The covenant between God and Abraham inaugurates the people's history. Abraham and his descendants are promised an everlasting relationship with God and the land of Canaan as a permanent possession (Gen. 17:7–8). The sign of this covenant is the circumcision of males, and those without this brand in the flesh are "cut off" from the covenant community (Gen. 17:10–14). The importance of this sign for P reflects the new conditions under which the people live—they are no longer a political entity defined by territory and political institutions but a somewhat voluntary society dispersed among non-Israelites. Circumcision enabled a family to consciously affirm its membership in Israel and set off the members of this community from their milieu.

The exodus from Egypt is the next step in the establishment of Israel. The divine name "Yahweh" is revealed for the first time, and Moses is selected as Yahweh's spokesman and Aaron as Yahweh's priest (Exod. 6:2–13, 26–27). Yahweh reveals his glory in the plagues and deliverance at the Sea of Reeds for all later generations to behold. The dual festival of Passover and Unleavened Bread is instituted to recall this revelation (Exod. 12:1–20, 43–49). Again, there is a sign marking membership in the people: blood smeared around the door of the Israelite house on the eve of Passover (vs. 13).

The formation of Israel culminates in the revelation at Sinai. Yahweh establishes a place for himself in the midst of the people, the tabernacle, which is to be a dwelling place for God. P is strikingly objective in its view of the divine presence in the sanctuary: Yahweh sits enthroned above the ark and mercy seat, flanked by cherubim, in the holy of holies. His presence made this space qualitatively different from all other space, where holiness gradually decreased until one came to the outside of the camp. Holiness was a quality that could

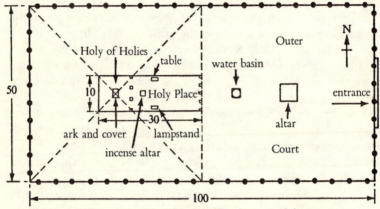

FIGURE 6–1. Diagram of the tabernacle area. (Reprinted, by permission, from Menahem Haran, *Temples and Temple Service in Ancient Israel: An Inquiry into the Character of Cult Phenomena and the Historical Setting of the Priestly School*, Oxford: Oxford University Press, 1978, p. 152.)

not come into contact with the profane without adverse consequences. Hence, the closer one came to the holy of holies, the more preparation (or desecularization) was necessary. Only the high priest was allowed to enter the holy of holies, and then only once a year (the Day of Atonement) after putting on vestments belonging to this sphere and creating a shield of incense. Only ritually clean and properly attired priests could enter the holy place and handle its paraphernalia. Levites were stationed in front of the tabernacle to prevent any Levite or layperson from entering it. In the outer court stood the altar, which was off limits to all but the priests. The Levites and laity were allowed in the outer court if they were ritually clean.

The arrangement of the camp also reflected the principle of graduated holiness. Around the tabernacle area lived the tribe of Levi as a
sort of protective wall between the holy area and the secular community, which fanned out from it in all directions. The camp

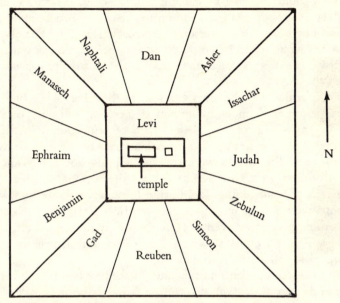

FIGURE 6–2. Diagram of the Israelite camp (see Num. 2).

itself was sufficiently holy to require separation from extreme degrees
of uncleanness. Things that had become unclean and needed to be
destroyed were taken outside the camp for destruction (Lev. 8:17;
9:11). Persons who were unclean because of "leprosy" had to reside
outside the camp until they were healed (Lev. 13:46).

The priests were critical for the life of the community because
they had been selected (as a family by God) to maintain a special
degree of ritual holiness so that they could enter the most holy areas
of the sanctuary. They had to perform the rites that took place within the tabernacle: burning lamps and incense, keeping bread upon the
table, and smearing and sprinkling blood on the incense altar, the veil

covering the inner sanctum, and the ark cover. They also had to perform all the rites that took place upon the altar in the courtyard: smearing and sprinkling blood on the altar, and incinerating the meat and vegetable offerings in the altar fire.

The rest of the tribe of Levi, according to P, was non-priestly. They could not enter the tabernacle nor ascend the altar. Their chief duty was to serve as guards to protect the holy areas from encroachment by unauthorized persons. If encroachment did occur, the divine wrath would be absorbed by the tribe rather than break out into the people. Levites also performed menial labor for the priests and assisted the laity.

Sacrifice was the heart and soul of the tabernacle ritual. Every layperson was under obligation to perform offerings of various sorts, assessed according to a variety of principles. Some, like the offering of the firstborn and firstfruits, acknowledged God as the source of life, others were to express praise for deliverance, and still others were to purge or expiate the personal and communal effects of wrongdoing. In addition to obligatory offerings, laypersons were encouraged to make sacrifices freely to celebrate and commemorate the events of life. Not only individual citizens but also the community as a whole, its rulers, and its priesthood were under sacrificial obligations.

Yahweh's presence in the midst of the people was both beneficial and dangerous. It gave the people a sacred value and made Yahweh accessible to the community for personal and social needs. However, his holiness could "break out" and destroy persons who profaned the sanctuary by ritual improprieties (e.g., Lev. 10) or anyone who sinned flagrantly (e.g., Num. 16). "In anyone approaching me I will show myself holy, and before all the people I will be glorified" (Lev. 10:3, author's translation). An opposite danger was that physical or moral impurity would drive Yahweh from the community. P understands sin to generate an impurity that gravitates toward the sanctuary, where it must be removed before it drives Yahweh away. The more serious the sin, the further it penetrates. Many rites are devoted to removing the impurity that has become physically attached to the altar, the holy place, and the holy of holies. Blood, in particular, was smeared on holy things to purge them of contamination or sprinkled on them to symbolize the reparations of the one responsible.

In summary, the Priestly conception of Israel centers on the dwelling of God in the midst of the people. God's presence created spheres of extreme holiness and a holiness which declined gradually from its epicenter. Segments of the community had to be set off as areas of commerce with the most holy areas and as a buffer between these areas and the secular community. A ritual pattern facilitated interaction between the divine center of the community and its human members and preserved it from catastrophic breakdown. God was able to promise Abraham and his seed an everlasting covenant and perpetual possession of Canaan because God had provided a priesthood and ritual that assured maintenance of a holy community.

Introduction to the Holiness Code

Although there is no title or superscription setting off Leviticus 17—26 from the rest of the book, there is a subscription that would fit just as well at the beginning: "These are the statutes and ordinances and laws which Yahweh made between him and the people of Israel on Mount Sinai by Moses" (Lev. 26:46). Like the Deuteronomic Law, this lawbook concludes with an assurance of blessings for obedience and a threat of curses for disobedience (Lev. 26:3–45). Like both the Covenant and Deuteronomic Codes, it begins with instruction for the place of sacrifice (Lev. 17:1–9). In between, it covers the same broad range of social, civil, and religious topics as the other biblical lawbooks.

It is common among scholars to differentiate between the portions of Leviticus 17—26 that belong to P and those that belong to the original code. Various passages exhibit clear evidence of Priestly origin or reworking. All references to the tabernacle, for example, can be ascribed to P, and it is likely that the chapters devoted to the priesthood (Lev. 21—22) and the annual cycle of festivals (Lev. 23) are Priestly creations. This material integrates H into P's conception of the religious community. The assemblage of laws and exhortation that remains after the Priestly layer has been removed can be called the "original" Holiness Code, exhibiting a basic homogeneity of language and concepts. Its spirit is summed up in the exhortation that gave the code its name: "You shall be holy; for I, Yahweh your God, am holy" (19:2).

The date of the composition of the Holiness Code has generally been fixed by reference to the exilic prophet Ezekiel. The many parallels of content and language between H and Ezekiel suggest that H either was in existence by the Exile or was being compiled out of older traditions at about the same time that Ezekiel was ministering to his exiled compatriots. The Exile is only the date of the finished product, however. Most scholars concur that many of the traditions of the book are centuries older, and a number have attempted to trace the stages of its growth. Some take the many doublets and erratic ordering of the material as clues. It would seem that the recurrence of the same law in two or three places would indicate independent collections, and interruptions would evidence clumsy editorial reworking. Unfortunately, no explanation based on such phenomena has compelled general acceptance.

Another approach has been to trace the growth of homogenous sections such as the commandments outlining incest (Lev. 18:6–18) and the chapter describing the sabbatical and Jubilee years (Lev. 25). Such analyses are premised upon the conviction that biblical legal texts grew by increments. It is quite possible, however, that they were the conscious creations of an author, and the evidence used to reconstruct the evolution of the text should be explained by reference to the aesthetic principles under which the author was working. Whatever the decision on this question, I believe one is justified in interpreting the final form of the text as exhibiting intellectual and artistic design, within which even the Priestly layer can be included.

The author of the Holiness Code does not achieve aesthetic unity in the same way as the author of the Deuteronomic Law. Rather than assimilating the laws proper into hortatory address, he juxtaposes clusters of law and exhortation. Each cluster inclines toward a recognizable type (commandment, capital punishment, etc.) with stylistic consistency and symmetry. There is a pronounced drive toward assembling clusters of law around single subjects. Several sections are actually constructed to describe an institution systematically.

Most of the classical types of legal formulation can be discerned in H. The classical *prohibition form* is predominant in chapter 19. This chapter, in fact, has much in common in subject matter and scope with the Ten Commandments and apodictic series in C and D. This large series is constructed of smaller units (of two, three, or four members) governing the same or related topics. The prohibition form also predominates in chapter 18 but with an inverted word order. All the remedial law to be found within H conforms to a slightly altered formulation of the *capital punishment type* or to a variant of this type sentencing the violator to divine punishment. Chapter 20 consists of these two types, and a few more appear in 24:10–23. The absence of *casuistic remedial law* is quite striking. The day-to-day decisions of the judges seem to have been removed from the purview of the divine law. There is a generous sampling of *primary law*. The description of the Jubilee Year (25:8–17, 23–55), in particular, presents the rights and duties of property and slave ownership with uncommon thoroughness and order.

A large portion of the Holiness Code is devoted to cultic subjects, which can be subsumed under the category of *priestly torah*, though it bears a considerable degree of stylistic variation. Like the other law-books, H contains rules on the place and procedures for sacrifice (Lev. 17) and a festival calendar (Lev. 23). Other cultic duties of the laity are scattered through the code. Unlike any other biblical lawbook, H contains sections on the priesthood (Lev. 21; 22). Both chapters are addressed to the priests rather than the people (21:1, 16; 22:1; 22:17 includes laity), suggesting that in fact these rules are out of place in a lawbook designed for the publication of the divine law to the community.

This introduces one of the stylistic features of H derived from P. Each chapter has a commission from Yahweh to Moses designating the addressee: in chapter 17 it is both the priests and the general populace; in chapters 18, 19, 20, 23, 24, 25 it is the general populace alone; in chapters 21, 22 it is the priesthood alone. The same procedure of designating the addressee recurs throughout P. Although this differentiation should not be necessary in a legal code which by its very nature is intended for the community at large, it is needed because of the technical quality of P's provisions. P has merely assimilated H to its presentation of cultic tradition and integrated some description of the nature and duties of the "new rulers" of the community.

Before leaving this discussion of speech forms, one should take note of the address format and hortatory sections of the code. As in C rather than D, H is cast as an address of Yahweh to his people (and priests). Wherever the speaker refers to himself as "I," the reference is to Yahweh. This divine "I" recurs frequently, particularly in the hortatory sections and in the unique motive clause attached to series of laws: "I am Yahweh (your God)." This motive clause reinforces the law by recalling the authority behind it and dramatizes the I–thou relationship established by legal address.

The hortatory sections within the code (18:1–5, 24–30; 19:1–2, 19a, 37; 20:22–26; 22:31–33; 25:17–18, 38 [42, 55]) call Israel to obey the law to distinguish themselves from the Canaanites by their ethical holiness and to recall their redemption from Egypt in their dealings with one another. One exhortation within the code (18:24–30) warns the people that they will be "vomited out" of the land as were the Canaanites if they defile themselves by imitating the Canaanites. Chapter 26 underlines this motive by dramatizing the punishment Israel will suffer if they persist in disobeying the divine law. A host of blessings is the prospect for an obedient people (26:3–13), but if they disobey, God will expose them to divine wrath (vss. 14–20); if they do not take heed and obey, they will suffer more (vss. 21–26); if repeated punishment cannot turn them around, they will be expelled from the land (vss. 27–39); yet even then there will be an opportunity to repent and start again (vss. 40–45). Encapsulated in this warning is a history of the action that led to exile and a challenge to the exilic generation to redeem the time.

COMMENTARY

The Holiness Code is organized along the lines of chapter divisions. With a few exceptions, each chapter is independent of the others and relatively homogenous. Some can be grouped for exegesis, as has been done with chapters 18–20 and 21–22 in the following outline. Chapters 18 and 20 and chapters 21 and 22 will be dealt with as exegetical units.

OUTLINE OF THE HOLINESS CODE

I. The Place of Sacrifice and Subsidiary Rules (17).
II. The Holiness Required of Israel (18–20).
  A. Prohibited Sexual Intercourse (18).
— B. Commandments Exemplifying the Holiness of God (19).
  C. Penalties for Violation of Religious and Sexual Prohibitions (20).
III. Qualifications for Priests and Rules for Offerings (21–22).
  A. Physical and Social Qualifications of Priests (21).
  B. Encroachment upon Offerings, etc. (22).
— IV. Calendar of Annual Festivals and Daily Ritual (23:1–24:9).
  A. Cycle of Festivals (23).
  B. Oil and Bread for the Holy Place (24:1–9).
V. Remedial Law for Blasphemy and Homicide (24:10–23).
— VI. The Sabbatical and Jubilee Years (25).
VII. Appendix: Desacralization of Sanctuary Donations (27).

In the exegesis of certain chapters, I will include discussions of other relevant passages in P: (1) within chapter 20, ritual for woman accused of adultery (Num. 5:11–31); (2) at the end of chapters 18/20, catalog of clean and unclean animals (Lev. 11:1–47); (3) at the end of chapter 21, various texts treating priests and Levites; (4) within chapter 22, types of sacrifices (Lev. 1–7; Num. 18); (5) within chapter 23, ritual of the Day of Atonement (Lev. 16); (6) at the end of chapter 24, cities of asylum (Num. 35).

The Place of Sacrifice and Subsidiary Rules (Lev. 17). The basic provision of this chapter is stated in verses 8–9:

> Any man of the house of Israel, or of the strangers that sojourn among them, who offers a burnt offering or sacrifice, and does not bring it to the door of the tent of meeting, to sacrifice it to Yahweh; that man shall be cut off from his people.

Around this central provision are specific applications, procedures, and explanations. The chief concern of the chapter is to apply the rule to the slaughter of animals for meat (vss. 3–7). Any domestic animal that an Israelite would slaughter for food (ox, sheep, goat) falls under this provision (vs. 3). The text of verses 3–4 can be read as allowing the actual slaughter of the animal to occur in or outside the camp, requiring only that the victim and its blood be brought to the sanctuary, but it is more likely that the lawgiver is requiring that the animal be slaughtered at the entrance to the sanctuary, its blood be drained and dashed upon the altar, and the fat from around the entrails (see Lev. 3:3–4) be burned on the altar as a "pleasing odor" to Yahweh (Lev. 17:4–6).

The concept of the blood plays a pivotal role in the ruling. The eating of the blood of any animal, domestic or wild, is strictly prohibited (vss. 10, 12, 13–14), in that the blood contains the life-force (vss. 11, 14) and must be allowed to "return" to its source. When a wild animal is killed as game, its blood is to be poured out on the ground and covered (vs. 13). When a domestic animal is slaughtered, its blood is to be splashed on the altar (vs. 6). In the latter case, the blood *expiates* (makes amends by repayment) for the slaughter. The killing of an animal incurs guilt, but the blood has been provided as a means to expiate this guilt (vs. 11; cf. Gen. 9:3–5). If someone slaughters an animal and does not have the blood splashed upon the altar, that person must bear the guilt (vs. 4), with the result of being "cut off from among his people." This common P formula sounds like formal excommunication, but there is good reason to believe that it is solely a divine sanction—God will cause premature death and/or the cessation of the family line.

The provision that all slaughter be treated as sacrifice reflects pre-Deuteronomic practice. As mentioned earlier, D allows for secular slaughter because D eliminates all local altars, and it would be unfeasible to require all Israelites to go to Jerusalem every time they wanted to eat meat. Leviticus 17 contradicts D's provision in specifying that even the slaughter of animals for meat must be treated as a sacrifice. This would have been feasible when all Israel was encamped about the shrine. It would not have been when Israelites were dispersed in the land and the Jerusalem temple was the only legitimate altar.

Leviticus 17:7 supports this provision in stating that it is instituted to keep the people from offering sacrifices to "satyrs" or goat-demons. Whatever these are, they seem to be associated with wild and desolate places (cf. Isa. 13:21; 34:14). P apparently reasons that if slaughter is not maintained as a sacrifice to Yahweh, the people will make it a sacrifice to other supernatural beings. The author of Deuteronomy was, perhaps, idealistic in thinking that slaughter could be completely secularized.

To round off the discussion of meat eating, the chapter concludes with a provision for eating dead or torn animals. It assumes that Israelites as well as resident aliens were permitted to eat such meat (contrast Exod. 22:31; Deut. 14:21). Those who do so incur a minor level of uncleanness and must wash themselves and their clothing and wait until evening (the beginning of the next day) before having commerce with holy things. Anyone who does not perform the ritual remains unclean and incurs guilt when coming in contact with holy things. It was thought that physical ailments would result.

Prohibited Sexual Intercourse and Penalties for Violation of Religious and Sexual Prohibitions (Lev. 18; 20).   Chapters 18 and 20 overlap in subject matter and act as complementary units. Chapter 18 lays down the prohibitions, and chapter 20 states the punishments for violating them.

The first section of laws (18:6–18) forbids sexual intercourse with next of kin. Verse 6 serves as a superscription: "None of you shall approach any one near of kin to him to uncover nakedness." The key expression *uncover nakedness* means "have sexual intercourse with." When the text describes a person's mother as the "nakedness of your father" (vs. 7), it means that the father has exclusive rights to sexual intimacy with her. This principle continues to operate within the family even after a husband dies, though the woman may remarry outside the family.

Other prohibitions in the series are based on the principle of consanguinity and familial intimacy. They are addressed to an adult male and begin with the most immediate family: the addressee's mother (vs. 7) or another wife of his father (vs. 8) and his sister or half sister (vs. 9). Unrelated sisters by marriage are also included (vs. 11). Spliced in here is a prohibition against sexual intercourse with grandchildren (vs. 10). Verses 12–14 cover aunts by blood or marriage. The prohibitions based upon consanguinity conclude by forbidding intercourse with a daughter-in-law (vs. 15) or sister-in-law (vs. 16).

The final two verses of this section are based upon the principle that closely related women—mother-daughter, mother-grand-daughter (vs. 17), and sisters (vs. 18)—should not be the wives or sexual partners of one man. The prohibition against marrying sisters has a humanitarian-social explanation and therefore is in force only as long as both are alive.

Chapter 20 (vss. 11–12, 14, 17–21) prescribes punishments of graduated severity for violating these prohibitions. The death penalty is imposed upon both parties in the union of a man and his father's wife, a man and his daughter-in-law, and a man and his wife and her mother (all three are to be burnt). Sexual intercourse with an aunt (20:19, 20), sister-in-law (vs. 21), or half sister (vs. 17) is sub-ject to divine sanction—being "cut off" from the people or dying childless. Some prohibitions of chapter 18 are not covered in chapter 20, but one can guess that they were subject to divine sanctions.

This series might be said to define *incest* within Israelite society. All societies attempt to draw a circle around a kinship unit within which intermarriage or extramarital sexual intercourse is forbidden, and the series does precisely that. It is predicated upon polygamous marriage. It also realistically assumes that some men will engage in sexual liaisons outside the marriage bond. Although such liaisons were morally suspect in the Old Testament, only intercourse within the circle of kin and with a married woman other than a man's wife are strictly prohibited.

The incest series is followed, in chapter 18, by a series of other sexual prohibitions. Verse 19 concerns a case of ritual impurity: sexu-al intercourse with a woman (wife) during menstruation. As in much of biblical law, physical uncleanness involves ritual impurity as well (see Lev. 15:19–23). In chapter 20, the punishment for violating this taboo is limited to divine sanction (vs. 18). P allows for ritual purification (Lev. 15:24).

Verses 20, 22, 23 treat more serious sexual offenses. Sexual inter-course with a married woman is adultery (vs. 20), an intervention in the one-flesh unity of the married couple breaking up the funda-mental unit of society. The man and woman who commit adultery *defile* themselves, which in this case must be more than a temporary state of uncleanness; they acquire an irremovable impurity that makes them "marked persons" before God. If the couple is caught, the death penalty is imposed on both of them (20:10).

Numbers 5:11–31 deals with a case of suspected adultery. If a husband rightly or wrongly believes that his wife has had sexual liaisons with other men (vss. 11–14), he can force her to submit to what is best called an oath ritual (vss. 15–28). The woman must enter the presence of Yahweh with an offering meant to prompt God to bring out the truth (vss. 15–18), take an oath that calls down divine sanctions upon her if she is guilty (vss. 19–22), and drink ritually prepared water (containing dust from the floor and ink of the curse) which will communicate the curse to her body (vss. 23–26). In theory, the accused woman will suffer a fallen womb if guilty but remain healthy and fertile if innocent (vss. 27–28). Her husband will not be punished, even if his jealousy is proven to be unfounded (vs. 31).

Leviticus 18:22 forbids male homosexual intercourse (the Old Testament does not seem aware of lesbianism). The only explanation given is that it is an "abomination," that is, something abhorrent or repulsive to God. Perhaps it was believed that the sexual drive was meant to unite man and woman (so Gen. 2:23, 24), and any other expression of it violated its purpose. Alternatively, it was condemned as a confusion of sexual identity. Leviticus 20:13 prescribes the death penalty for the offense. The formula "their blood [bloodguilt] is upon them" means that the community which executes them is not guilty of murder because their offense is itself the cause of death.

Leviticus 18 concludes the catalog of sexual prohibitions with bestiality, that is, sexual intercourse with an animal. Both men (the addressees) and women are included. The only explanation given is that it is a "perversion." It diminishes the human to be united with a beast. Both the human and the animal shall be put to death (Lev. 20:15–16), for although the dumb creature is not morally responsible, it has been irredeemably defiled by the perverse union.

The series is interrupted in Leviticus 18:21 by a prohibition of offering children to Molech. Perhaps this topic made its way into the chapter through the association of sexual intercourse and "seed." It is also treated in Leviticus 20, where the offense is placed under the death penalty. Interpreters long took it for granted that "giving a child (lit., seed) to Molech" was equivalent to Deuteronomy's "make pass through fire," but recently a number of scholars have suggested that the offense named here was only a dedication of a child to a deity, an act of apostasy but not child sacrifice. I personally find the older interpretation more compelling, for the other uses of the expression in the Old Testament (2 Kings 23:10; Jer. 7:31; 32:35) are best interpreted as child sacrifice. The word "Molech" has occasioned extensive scholarly discussion. Whatever the original meaning, the author of H uses it as the name of a deity competing with Yahweh for Israel's loyalty (Lev. 20:5). Thus, the offense is a compound of murder and apostasy. Leviticus 20:2–5 prescribes the death penalty by stoning (vs. 2) and threatens divine sanctions as well (vs. 3). Apparently the offense was tolerated by "the people of the land," so Yahweh will "set his face" (an emphatic expression of divine punishment) against the perpetrator and all who follow in his or her apostasy (vss. 4–5). There is a hint of collective punishment in the inclusion of the family in verse 5, perhaps due to the interfamily character of the offense.

Leviticus 20:6 prescribes the penalty for violating a prohibition enunciated in 19:31. Translations differ, reading "mediums and wizards" (RSV) or "ghosts and familiar spirits" (JPS), but the difference is more apparent than real, for one consulted ghosts and spirits by means of human mediums. In any case, H concurs with D that divination is incompatible with Yahweh and subject to severe divine sanctions (20:6b). The medium or wizard himself or herself is under the death sentence according to a law at the end of the chapter (20:27).

Leviticus 18 and 20 contain the largest hortatory sections in the Holiness Code. Chapters 18:1–5, 24–30, and 20:22–24a are variations on the same theme: Israel should not imitate the practices and laws of Egypt or the peoples of Canaan. The latter are being dispossessed precisely because they defiled themselves by doing the things prohibited in the laws Yahweh is giving Israel. If Israel imitates the peoples of Canaan rather than obeying Yahweh, they will defile the land, and the land will vomit them out, just as it did the previous inhabitants. There is no question of arbitrary favor for Israel. They will suffer the same fate as their predecessors if they act the same way.

The divine law itself, however, is a special gift to Israel. By obeying it and thus avoiding defilement, Israel can possess the land forever (20:22–24a). Yahweh has already set Israel apart as a holy people by making them his own (20:24b, 26b). As the Holy One, Yahweh communicates holiness to all with whom he chooses to associate. The law provides the means by which he embodies his holiness in Israel, and obedience to its provisions protects the community from defilement.

Inserted into the homily concluding chapter 20 is a reminder of an entirely different kind of holiness—the observance of the distinction between clean and unclean animals. This reminder, seeming to come from left field, may have once introduced a catalog of clean and unclean animals. There are, in fact, verbal similarities between H and the catalog in Leviticus 11 (compare, in particular, 11:44–45), suggesting that chapter 11 once belonged to the Holiness Code. The catalog given there is organized according to a fourfold division of the animal kingdom: land animals (mammals), birds, aquatic animals, and "swarming creatures" (reptiles and insects) (Lev. 11:46). The chapter is concerned with identifying what species in each category can and cannot be eaten (vss. 2–23, 41–45) and with describing the uncleanness incurred by contact with carcasses (vss. 24–40). Among land animals, species that have cloven hooves and chew the cud are deemed edible, but species without these traits are not (vss. 2–7). Aquatic animals with fins and scales are edible, but others are not (vss. 9–12). Only a list of unclean birds is given without classification, and they are birds of prey plus others (vss. 13–19). A few winged insects are clean (vss. 20–22); otherwise, insects and reptiles are not (vss. 41–43).

Contact with the carcass of an unclean animal makes the person unclean and requires ritual cleansing (vss. 24–31). Inanimate objects also become unclean by such contact (vss. 32–33, 35); some objects "absorb" the uncleanness and must be destroyed, while others do not and can be restored. Any liquid which is present communicates contamination to food it touches and renders it unclean (vss. 34, 37–38), but a spring or cistern does not (vs. 36).

There is something of an analogy between maintaining separation from the abhorrent practices of the nations dispossessed by Israel and from the unclean animals enumerated in this list (so Lev. 20:25

in the context of 20:22–26). *Holiness*, one should remember, means "set apart" from the profane as well as the exemplification of the moral perfection of God.

Commandments Exemplifying the Holiness of God (Lev. 19).   The heading for this chapter comes from the introductory exhortation (vs. 2), which can be translated either as an imperative, "You shall be holy; for I, Yahweh your God, am holy," or as an indicative, "You are holy. . . ." Both are appropriate, for Israel is called to be what it already is by virtue of Yahweh's election. Israel is to imitate or exemplify the holiness of the God who confers holiness upon them.

When the lawgiver seeks to summarize this mode of life, he articulates the famous love commandment, "You shall love your neighbor as yourself" (vs. 18). However, the demands of neighborly love are so sweeping and inexhaustible that one despairs of enumerating the specifics. The strategy of the lawgiver, then, is to prohibit untoward behavior. It is rather paradoxical to exemplify the positive by refraining from the negative, but such a paradox is typical of law and morality. Healthy relationships are the fabric of communal life, and law and morality are focused on preventing and repairing tears.

At the heart of the chapter are the commandments that parallel the Decalogue:

I	monotheism	vs. 4a
II	idolatry	vs. 4
III	abuse of name	vs. 12
IV	sabbath	vss. 3b, 30
V	parents	vs. 3a, cf. vs. 32
VI	murder	cf. vss. 17–18
VII	adultery	ch. 18
VIII	theft	vss. 11, 13, cf. vss. 35–36
IX	false witness	vs. 16
X	coveting	———

These give the chapter a broad scope of basic principles. Other subjects seem to have been drawn to the chapter like iron to a magnet. The profound and the trivial were included to give a comprehensive picture of the life of holiness, and the result is a somewhat uneven and disorderly text. My procedure will be to expound the material seriatim.

(1) Verses 3–4, 30; 26:1–2. Verse 3 states the fourth and fifth commandments in reverse order. Both are expressed as positive duties. Reverence of parents has a sacred quality about it, for parents mediate both the divine action of creation and nurture and the community's life and tradition. To revere parents is to acknowledge God and show gratitude for being included in God's people. The keeping of the sabbath acknowledges the Lord of time and distinguishes sacred time from profane time. In 19:30 and 26:2 keeping the sabbath parallels revering the sanctuary, so that sacred time and sacred space are delineated together. (On the meaning and importance of the fourth and fifth commandments, consult Chapter Three.)

Verse 4 parallels the first and second commandments. The first part of the verse, translated literally, reads, "You shall not turn to *nothings*." This word is used in the Old Testament both for idols and for the deities they represent, so I would interpret the verse as forbidding both the recognition of other gods and the manufacture of images of other gods (*molten statue* is but one type). Leviticus 26:1 repeats the prohibition of images with the variant purpose of preventing the construction of images of Yahweh or the erection of imageless pillars and stones for Yahwistic worship (compare Deut. 16:22). (On the meaning and importance of the first and second commandments, consult Chapter Three.)

(2) Verses 5–8; 22:30. These verses remind the lay Israelite to perform the sacrificial meal ("peace offerings") properly. The meat of this sacrifice was to be eaten by the laity, probably away from the sanctuary and therefore without priestly supervision. They should take care to eat it within two days and burn any remaining by the third day. Evidently the meat became ritually unclean on the third day, which had the retroactive effect of nullifying the sacrifice. Moreover, profaning the holy by omission brought guilt upon the violators which would, if reparations were not made, produce divine sanctions. The thanksgiving offering, which was a species of sacrificial meal, was under an even more restrictive time limit for consumption (Lev. 22:30).

(3) Verses 9–10; 23:22. These provisions, as an element in Israel's welfare system, specify that gleanings of grain and grapes are to be

left by farmers for the needy (both the Israelite and resident alien). The same provision is repeated in the festival calendar as if it were to be performed as a ritual duty (23:22). (Consult Chapter Four on C's sabbatical year and Chapter Five on D's humanitarian laws.)

(4) Verses 11–13, 35–36. I have drawn together series on similar topics. Beginning with verse 11 is the prohibition of one kind of stealing, theft by stealth, followed by prohibitions of dissembling and the concluding prohibition (vs. 12) of false oaths. The proscriptions against dissembling would appear to extend theft by stealth to shady dealing having the same effect as overt theft. The oath comes into the picture because charges of theft were settled by oath when testimony and evidence were inconclusive. If the accused were guilty but swore innocence to avoid prosecution, he or she profaned the holy name, compounding the civil offense with a religious one.

The Priestly Law allows for a reparation offering by one who has appropriated others' property, lied under oath, and then felt guilty (Lev. 6:1–7 [Hebrew: 5:20–26]). This provision departs from the Priestly principle that intentional violations of divine prohibitions are not subject to sacrificial expiation (Num. 15:30–31). It may be that this exception was intended to encourage admission of wrong and restitution in a case where the crime would otherwise go unsolved. A severe punishment for turning oneself in would discourage such an act of moral integrity, so the lawgiver creates what amounts to a legal fiction—treating a confessed crime as an unintentional violation of the sacred—to induce the desired behavior.

Verse 13a forbids transactions in which a stronger party exploits or overpowers a weaker one—both overt robbery and oppressive action having the form of legality. An example of the latter, deferring payment of wages for work performed, is given in 13b. An employer would be tempted to do this to force the worker to return to work the next day. The lawgiver seems to want to protect the worker from such coercion and provide him or her with the wages needed for the evening meal.

Verses 35–36 cover fraud in the marketplace. In a monetary system based upon a coin's weight rather than its face value, weights that deviated from the standard (heavier to receive payment, lighter to give it) could be used to overcharge or underpay. Deviant bulk measures could be used in a similar fashion.

(5) Verse 14. The prohibition of insulting the deaf and tripping the blind appears to be directed against pranks. The aggrieved are defenseless against such capricious assaults and must depend on God.

(6) Verses 15–16. These verses deal with aspects of the judicial system. All judgments should be rendered on the intrinsic merits of the parties' causes, not on who the parties are. The judge should favor neither the lowly out of sympathy nor the great out of deference. The translation of the key clauses in verse 16 is uncertain. The first clause probably concerns slander or the spreading of rumors, which is analogous to false witness. The second clause "You shall not stand on the blood of your neighbor" (author's translation) may have to do with judicial murder, that is, taking the life of an innocent person on the basis of trumped-up charges, perhaps for personal gain (cf. Exod. 23:7). (On the meaning of the ninth commandment, consult Chapter Three; also consult Chapters Four and Five on the rules governing judicial behavior.)

(7) Verses 17–18. In this series are found the most famous utterances of the Holiness Code, the epitome of the first half of the chapter. In all dealings between Israelites, the rule should be love (vs. 18b), not hate (vs. 17). One should value others as highly as oneself and seek their good with the same intensity that one seeks one's own. This obligation assumes that the worth of every person is determined by God, who shows no partiality.

It is sometimes objected that one cannot be commanded to love, for love is spontaneous. The love in this verse, however, is not an emotional attraction but a deliberate attending to the good of another. Moreover, the commandment seeks not to coerce the conscience but to prompt recognition of the claims of others on one's concern. One is already aware that a neighbor deserves the same consideration one gives oneself, so the commandment is a reminder.

Two specific examples are given of comportment in trying situations (vss. 17b, 18a). The first advises admonishing a neighbor (who provokes to anger) but doing nothing to bring guilt upon oneself (or upon the neighbor; the Hebrew phrasing is ambiguous). The second warns against retaliation for personal hurt. Even when put to the test, love must govern a person's response.

(8) Verse 19. The verse begins with a general admonition to conform to Yahweh's teaching. I believe this signals a division of the chapter into two equal parts. Most of the parallels to the Ten Commandments occur in the first half, while the second half lacks the same broad sweep of fundamental postulates. The remainder of verse 19 contains three taboo mixtures: crossbreeding of livestock, mixing of crops, and mixing of materials in a fabric. No reason is given. Linen and wool were combined in the fabrics of the tabernacle (e.g., Exod. 26:31; 36:35); perhaps this mixture was reserved for the most holy use. The reason for the other two prohibitions, or even how they were applied, is obscure. It is known that Israel crossed horses and asses to produce mules (2 Sam. 13:29); no other crossbreeding is biologically possible.

(9) Verses 20–22. Here is a ruling that begins as a casuistic law but ends with a cultic duty. Sexual intercourse with a betrothed slave woman is not to be treated as a case of adultery. The implied reasoning, I believe, is that such a woman was not free to resist the advances of her master or of another man of similar social standing. If she is not subject to the law of adultery, her male partner cannot be so treated. Indeed, he would probably be exempt from judicial punishment even for rape, given the lack of legal standing of the slave. Nevertheless, adultery has occurred and a divine commandment has been violated. The free person has to make amends before God to satisfy the majesty of the law. The sacrifice required to obtain forgiveness is termed a *reparation offering*, and here again a reparation offering is specified for an intentional offense (see the discussion of Lev. 19:11–13; cf. 6:1–7, above). Perhaps the lawgiver chose this category of sacrifice because it would provide forgiveness for the offender, though it does not otherwise fit the crime.

(10) Verses 23–25. Fruit-bearing trees have a distinctive life cycle and therefore come under special rules. During the first three years, a new tree is not to be harvested; it is to be regarded as "uncircumcised," possibly because the crop is negligible. In the fourth year, the crop is to be set aside as holy as a praise offering to Yahweh. This probably means that the fruit is to be picked and devoted to the

sanctuary. The dedication of the fruit to Yahweh is recognition (praise) of his bountiful goodness. From the fifth year onward, the crop belongs to the owner for food or trade, and God promises to compensate the grower for the loss of fruit by an added yield.

(11) Verses 26–31. These three small series forbid religious practices which were common in Israel's cultural milieu but which were deemed incompatible with Yahweh. Similar prohibitions are found in the Deuteronomic Law. They are significant examples of the revolution wrought by Yahweh in the religious practice of the ancient Near East. The whole range of practices that can be subsumed under the term *divination* (consult Chapter Five for a more specific description) is banned (vss. 26b, 31). Consulting any deity or supernatural being (including ghosts) other than Yahweh was excluded by the first commandment, nor was Yahweh himself subject to manipulation by word or gesture. Yahwistic practice retained vestiges of divination for some time (e.g., the sacred lots), but the grip it had on the ancient mind was broken decisively.

Customs symbolizing sorrow for the loss of loved ones were severely restricted by Yahwism. Verses 27–28 prohibit self-laceration and even cutting the hair or beard. Self-mutilation was incompatible with Yahweh.

Ancient Near Eastern religion ritualized the sex act as a part of the fertility cult. Yahweh, too, was a source of fertility but could not be manipulated by any sacred rite. Not only was sacred prostitution not encouraged, it was vehemently opposed. Verse 29 forbids Israelites to devote their daughters to such practices and warns against the moral corruption of the land in the guise of religion. (Consult the discussion of Lev. 17 on the ban against eating blood, of Lev. 19:3–4 on the sabbath and sanctuary.)

(12) Verse 32. The attitude of a society toward the elderly is an important clue to its sense of cohesion and identity. If the elderly are honored in gesture and respected in their expression of their views, the younger members of the community will more likely maintain the tradition that makes the community a cohesive entity enduring in time. The elderly represent the living presence of the past, and honoring the one is honoring the other. If individuals want to be respected in old age and have their values and accom-

plishments preserved by their children, they must do the same for their ancestors.

(13) Verses 33–34. The love commandment returns to bring the second half of chapter 19 to its height. The commandment to love the alien as oneself binds all members of the community together in a mutuality that overrides social distinctions. It supports the admonition to treat the alien the same as the citizen. The Holiness Code and Priestly Law go farther than any other biblical legal tradition toward incorporating the alien into the legal community. With respect to criminal law, the rule "You shall have one law for the sojourner and for the native" (Lev. 24:22) seems to have obtained. Serious violations of the social order, it should be remembered, brought impurity to the land and the sanctuary whether the perpetrator was a citizen or an alien, so the same law applied to both. With respect to cultic obligations, the alien was not bound by sacred duty to Yahweh and the cultic regimen but was permitted to participate voluntarily, beginning with submission to circumcision (Exod. 12:48–49). When he did participate, he was bound by the same rules as the full citizen (e.g., Lev. 17:8–9, 12–13, 15).

The chapter concludes by recalling that the divine lawgiver brought Israel out of Egypt (vs. 36b) and admonishing the recipients of grace to obey God's will (vs. 37). (On vss. 35–36a, consult the discussion of Lev. 19:11–12.)

Qualifications for Priests and Rules for Offerings (Lev. 21; 22). These two chapters protect the sacral order of Israel. The priesthood must be kept in a condition of holiness so that it can perform its duties (21), and the offerings must be treated properly and offered correctly (22). To explain the provisions here, other Priestly texts that treat the priesthood and sacrificial system will need to be considered.

Leviticus 21:1 addresses the chapter to Aaron and his sons. According to the Priestly Source, only the family of Aaron enjoyed priestly prerogatives. According to Exodus 6:16–25, Aaron and Moses were sons of Amram, son of Kohath, the Kohathites being one of three Levitical clans. By an irony of history, this one family took exclusive possession of a tribal prerogative, and the rest of the tribe was demoted to servants of the sanctuary.

According to the tribal blessing of Moses, the entire tribe of Levi had been chosen by Yahweh to serve at his altar:

> [The Levites] shall teach Jacob thy ordinances,
>   and Israel thy law;
> they shall put incense before thee,
>   and whole burnt offering upon thy altar. (Deut. 33:10)

Old Testament narrative reflects this status of Levites. Occasionally non-Levites were installed as priests (Judg. 17:5; 1 Kings 12:31, 32), but a priest from the tribe of Levi enjoyed greater prestige (Judg. 17:7–13), and non-Levitical priests came to be regarded as illegitimate (1 Kings 12:31).

The Deuteronomic Law regards the entire membership of the tribe of Levi as possessing the right to perform priestly duties and be supported by offerings (Deut. 18:1–5; also 31:9–13). It specifically states that Levites could exercise priestly duties at the sole legitimate altar (Deut. 18:6–8), though it foresees that a goodly number will not (above all, Deut. 26:12–13).

There are intimations in the account of Josiah's reform (2 Kings 23:4–20, above all vs. 9) that the Levites were not permitted to officiate at Jerusalem. One can imagine that the Zadokites were jealous of their exclusive privileges within the Jerusalem temple. The entire Priestly account legitimates the claims of this family, which traced its lineage to Aaron, and demotes all other Levites to the status of servants of the sanctuary (Num. 16:8–11). If any Levite sought to challenge this arrangement, he was reminded of the demise of Korah and his party, who insisted on their equality with Aaron (Num. 16:1a, 2b–11, 16–24, 32b, 35).

Leviticus 21 falls into three parts: purity of priests (vss. 1–9), purity of the high priest (vss. 10–15), and physical disqualifications in priests (vss. 16–23). To understand the defilement of priests, one must recall that priests had to keep themselves in a state of ritual holiness which allowed them to enter into the sphere of the holy. Contact with dead bodies made any person unclean seven days and required ritual washing on the third and seventh days (Num.

19:11–13, 14–22). The priest is to avoid contact with the dead so that he can perform his duties, although the deaths of closest family members are an exception (Lev. 21:1–4). When he mourns, he like all Israelites, must not mutilate himself (vs. 5). The sexual contact of the priest and his family is restricted. A priest may not marry a prostitute, violated woman, or divorcee (vs. 7). Evidently having sexual contact with another man made such a woman unfit for sexual contact with one who would enter the most holy precincts. A daughter who had illicit sexual intercourse profaned her priestly father and had to be executed (vs. 9). This may simply be a case of moral profanation, hence a special case of the law laid down for all Israelites in Deuteronomy 22:20–21. It may, however, be a provision to protect the priest from contact with someone who has been contaminated.

The people also have a duty to treat the priests as holy (vs. 8). The priests were set apart from the people to enter the sphere of the holy God and perform sacrifices, and it was incumbent upon the laity not to jeopardize the lives of those who approached the holy God in their behalf.

Among the priests one was supreme (Lev. 21:10). This office was hereditary (from Aaron to his oldest living son, Eleazar, etc.). Narrative texts show that the high priest was a deputy of the king and chief administrator of the sanctuary, but the Priestly Source only alludes to his political and institutional roles (e.g., Num. 3:5–10; 4:1–33) because it is concerned with his ritual role. Of the priests only the high priest was anointed on the head with oil during installation (vs. 10, see Lev. 8:12), and he alone wore the vestments for the performance of communal sacrificial rituals and for entering the inner sanctum (vs. 10; see Lev. 8:7–9; 16:4). The anointment seems to have made him permanently holy, so that he could not participate in rites of mourning, even for his parents (vss. 10–11). The text actually says that he was not to leave the precincts of the sanctuary (vs. 12), but this probably should be construed as referring to funerals; otherwise, the high priest would be a prisoner of the sanctuary. When the high priest selected a wife, he had to choose a virgin of priestly descent ("of his own people," vs. 14); here concern for the purity of the high priestly line is added to the general considerations of sexual purity.

The chapter concludes with a prohibition of physically defective persons from serving in any priestly capacity. Evidently any of the assortment of disabilities and deformities named marked a person as incapable of bearing the holiness required to officiate at sacrifices ("to offer the bread of his God," a vividly anthropomorphic description) or go into the holy place. There is an analogy, perhaps, with the exclusion of blemished animals from sacrifice. Nevertheless, he is allowed to eat of the priests' portion, even the most holy offerings (those consumed in the tabernacle precincts solely by the priests; see Num. 18:10).

Leviticus 22:1–16 concerns the handling of sacred donations, that is, animals and produce dedicated to Yahweh to be consumed by the priests and their families. Verse 2 states the fundamental rubric: the priests are to be scrupulous about the sacred donations that the Israelite populace consecrate to Yahweh, lest they profane his holy name. Verses 3–9 and 10–16 give two examples of the exercise of care. The first section deals with a priest who is not in the proper ritual condition to partake of sacrificial food, whose state of uncleanness may have been caused by things coming from his body or coming to his body by touch (vss. 4–5). Before he can eat a sacred thing, he must return to a state of cleanness. If his uncleanness is temporary, he must wash himself and await sundown (the beginning of another day). The unclean priest could undoubtedly satisfy his hunger by procuring non-sacrificial food, but the eating of flesh that caused uncleanness was forbidden (vs. 8; cf. Lev. 17:15–16 for the laity). Any violation of these provisions would provoke divine sanctions (vss. 3, 9).

The second section (vss. 10–16) identifies the persons other than the priests who may eat sacrificial food; these are the priest's dependents—his wife, children, and slaves (vs. 11). A daughter married to a layman may not (as she belongs to the family of her husband), but if she returns to the household she may eat it (vss. 12–13a). No layperson (including workers hired by a priest) may eat it (vss. 10, 13b), and if one does so inadvertently, he must replace it and add a fifth (vs. 14). The priest, however, should not let such mistakes occur (vss. 15–16).

Numbers 18:8–20 provides a catalog of the sacred donations under consideration. The catalog begins in verse 9 with "most holy offerings," flesh and bread that must be consumed within the tabernacle compound by the priests alone—the cereal, purgation, and reparation offerings. The cereal offering is evidently a poor person's substitute for a holocaust (see below). It consists of unbaked flour or baked cakes of unleavened flour mixed with oil and sprinkled with frankincense (Lev. 2:1–10). A portion is incinerated on the altar, and the rest goes to the priests.

The two other sacrifices whose flesh must be eaten in the sanctuary proper are expiatory in nature. The purgation offering (RSV: "sin offering") purges the sanctuary of pollution accumulated by ritual or moral violations of divine law (Lev. 4:1–5:13). The understanding is that every untoward act of the community, both by individuals and by the people as a whole, gives off "impurity" which gravitates to the sanctuary. This pollution has the potential of forcing Yahweh to depart from the holy place. The blood of the purgation offering has been provided to act as a cleansing agent, absorbing the impurity from the contaminated object and removing it.

There are grades of impurity according to the seriousness of the offense. When an individual violates a prescription unintentionally or contracts impurity through contact, the impurity gravitates to the outer altar; the blood of the purgation sacrifice offered by the offender is daubed on the horns of the altar to decontaminate it. The flesh of the sacrificial victim is eaten by the priests. When the community or a priest violates a prescription unintentionally, the impurity penetrates deeper, into the holy place; the blood of the purgation sacrifice is daubed on the horns of the inner (incense) altar and sprinkled before the veil. The flesh of the victim has become so infused with impurity that it cannot be eaten but must be incinerated outside the camp. Finally, deliberate sins of individuals and the people as a whole penetrate all the way into the holy of holies. The violators cannot have these sins purged; however, on the Day of Atonement a purgation sacrifice is performed which cleanses the holy of holies by sprinkling blood before and upon the ark, removing the collective consequences of these serious offenses. The value of the victim is calculated by social position: a bull for the high priest and community, a billy goat for a secular leader, and a nanny goat for a common citizen. In certain cases specified in Leviticus 5:5–13, the victim is scaled according to ability to pay all the way down to birds and even flour.

The reparation offering (RSV: "guilt offering") obtains forgiveness for a person who has unintentionally desecrated holy things (Lev. 5:14–6:7). By "holy thing" is meant an animal or inanimate object that belongs to the sanctuary; desecration occurs by treating the animal or object as though it belonged to the offender. The offender must restore the value of the desecrated thing, pay a one-fifth fine, and bring a ram or its monetary equivalent as a reparation offering. The repayment and fine went into the sanctuary treasury, and the victim was eaten by the priests in the sanctuary.

The same offering was extended to cover cases of suspected trespass and desecration of the divine name. In cases of physical ailment (e.g., leprosy in Lev. 14:10–32) or misfortune, a suspected trespass could be repaired by a reparation offering without repayment or fine (Lev. 5:17–19). The breaking of a Nazirite vow was to be repaired by a reparation offering, along with a purgation and holocaust for atonement (Num. 6:1–12). When one committed fraud and lied under oath to avoid prosecution but later confessed the sin, repayment plus a one-fifth fine was to be given the defrauded party and a reparation offering made to obtain divine forgiveness for desecrating the divine name in a false oath (Lev. 6:1–7). Here, voluntary confession has reduced the deliberate sin to an unintentional trespass (see above on Lev. 19:11–13).

Numbers 18:11–20 lists the sacred donations that are to be eaten outside the tabernacle compound by the priest and his dependents. These offerings are dedicated to the sanctuary either before they are brought or upon presentation at the sanctuary (in a *ritual of elevation*) (vs. 11). The particulars surveyed in verses 12–18 are all "first things." When a person began to harvest a crop, a portion was set aside for the sanctuary (cf. Lev. 19:24–25 discussed above), and later a portion of the first processing of crops (oil, wine, grain, fruit syrup, bread dough) was also due. Analogously, the first offspring of every mother belonged to Yahweh (vss. 14–18). The offerable animals were offered according to the ritual of the sacrificial meal (peace offering), but the meat went to the priests (vss. 17–18). A human or an animal not for sacrifice was redeemed by a monetary payment (consult chapters Four and Five for the parallels in C and D). The catalog concludes with a justification for the support of the priests by holy offerings—Yahweh is the priests' portion in Israel. In Deuteronomy 18:1–2 this rationale is applied to the entire tribe of Levi.

The non-priestly Levites could not partake of the sacred donations just listed. They were to receive the tithe (tenth) of the people for the service they rendered the sanctuary and laity (Num. 18:21–24). The tithe is also called an "offering to Yahweh," but it is not presented at the altar; one could call it an income tax in kind. Numbers 18:25–32 mentions only vegetable offerings—wine, flour, seed, and fruit—whereas Leviticus 27:30–33 includes both vegetable offerings (limited to seed and fruit) and herd and flock animals selected at random. The latter may be an innovation to increase Levitical income. Since the tithe was Levitical revenue, a tithe of the tithe was owed the priests (Num. 18:25–32).

Leviticus 22:17–25 instructs the priests and people alike respecting the condition of animals for holocaust and the sacrificial meal. The name *holocaust*, or whole burnt offering, is descriptive, as the entire victim was incinerated (Lev. 1:2–13; in Lev. 7:8 the hide was saved and given to the officiating priest as an honorarium). The victim had to be a male ox, sheep, or goat (Lev. 1:14–17 allows birds) without physical defect. The holocaust was obligatory in most public rituals but voluntary for private citizens, who performed it to fulfill a vow or simply to petition or celebrate. It carried general expiatory value, too (Lev. 1:4).

The slaughter of an animal for meat was to be done sacrificially (consult the discussion of Lev. 17). The blood was drained and thrown upon the altar, specified internal organs and fats were incinerated on the altar, and the rest was sanctified thereby for human consumption. The flesh belonged to the offerer, but he owed the breast and right thigh to the priests (as an honorarium?); the rest could be consumed by family and guests wherever they pleased. The victim could be male or female, but major physical defects were unacceptable (Lev. 22:22–24; minor defects were allowable for a "free-will offering," which was not obligatory or votive). This kind of sacrifice was not obligatory for the laity but was done to fulfill a vow, express thanksgiving (under further restrictions; vss. 29–30), or simply to enjoy meat.

Leviticus 22:26–30 is an addendum to the chapter. Verses 27–28 give age restrictions and prohibit sacrifice of a mother and her off-spring, implying a humanitarian outlook.

Calendar of Annual Festivals and Daily Ritual (Lev. 23:1–24:9). Like the other lawbooks, H has a calendar of national feasts to be celebrated in the course of the year. It parallels the others but contains more detail, adds some festivals, and fixes exact dates for celebration. While there is probably a pre-Priestly substratum, this chapter is now integrated into the Priestly Source and can be correlated with and supplemented by other P texts.

(1) The sabbath (Lev. 23:3) was not an annual festival requiring attendance at the central shrine but a weekly observance without positive ritual duties for the laity. The only requirement was negative: to refrain from work. According to Exodus 31:12–17 (P), the day was set apart as a sign that Yahweh has sanctified Israel; it was to be respected as a covenant, witnessing to the fact that Israel's God created the world in six days and rested on the seventh. The public sacrifices performed at the tabernacle were to be increased on this day. According to the catalog of tabernacle sacrifices given in Numbers 28–29, every morning and evening there was to be a whole burnt offering of a ram lamb, accompanied by an offering of flour kneaded with oil and a libation of wine (28:3–8); on the sabbath, the same sacrifices were to be doubled (vss. 9–10). At the beginning of each month (the new moon), a male goat was to be offered as a purgation offering to remove any pollution that would threaten the efficacy of the other offerings of the month; and two bulls, one ram, and seven ram lambs, again accompanied by cereal and drink offerings, were to be added to the daily holocausts (28:11–15).

(2) Passover and Unleavened Bread (Lev. 23:4–8) were combined to form the first festival of the year. The numbering of the months was based upon a year beginning in the spring (variously in

March and April). On the fourteenth day (full moon) of the first
month, the passover sacrifice was to be performed in the evening. A
yearling buck (sheep or goat) was to be slaughtered, its blood
smeared around the doorframe of the offerer's house, and its flesh
roasted and eaten with unleavened bread and bitter herbs during the
night by the household and guests. Any meat left over was to be
burnt (Exod. 12:3–13). On the following day, the feast of Unleavened Bread began and continued for seven days (vss. 6–8). Old
leavened bread was to be destroyed and unleavened bread eaten
throughout the week, and on the first and seventh days, the people
were to refrain from work and gather for religious services (Exod.
12:14–20). The same purgatory offering, holocausts, cereal offerings,
and libations that were required for new moon were required for
each of the seven days of Unleavened Bread (Num. 28:16–25).

(3) The First Sheaf and Feast of Weeks (Lev. 23:9–21) are related by date calculations and content. Both are associated with the
grain harvest and hence are not applicable until settlement. At the
beginning of the harvest season, the first sheaf of grain cut was to be
presented to the sanctuary, and at the end (fifty days later) two
loaves of bread from the grain harvested were to be presented. The
offering of the sheaf released the new crop for regular use (vs. 14).
Both offerings were presented in a ritual of elevation (vss. 11, 17)
and were to be consumed by the priests and their families (so Num.
18:11).

The description of First Sheaf is cryptic. Verse 11 says that the
priest was to elevate it on the day after the sabbath. Was the "sabbath" the first after the beginning of the harvest, varying year by
year, or the sabbath falling within or at the end of the week of Unleavened Bread? Was each farmer's sheaf elevated separately, or were
all dedicated together? Was the required whole burnt offering of a
yearling lamb a donation of the entire community or of the individual celebrant?

The Feast of Weeks, named for the calculation formula (a week
of weeks plus a day from First Sheaf, also called Pentecost for the
fifty days), could not be given a fixed day of the month because First
Sheaf varied. H describes a communal convocation at the sanctuary
with public sacrifices accompanying the dedication of loaves. The

sacrifices required (vss. 18–19) are the same as those at the new moon, but verse 20 appears to require the slaughter of two additional animals for a sacrificial meal for the priests. On all days of communal convocations H forbids work (so vs. 21). (On vs. 22 see the discussion of Lev. 19:9.)

(4) The seventh month (falling variously in September and October) was the highpoint of the festival year, the first day of which had become a festival in its own right. The trumpets (*shopharoth*) were blown, the community was gathered for a convocation (according to Num. 29:1), and a multiplicity of offerings were made— daily and new moon holocausts and an extra bull, ram, and seven yearling rams, all accompanied by cereal and drink offerings and preceded by a goat for purgation. In post-Old Testament times this festival evolved into New Year's.

(5) The Day of Atonement (Lev. 23:26–32) is the great contribution of the Priestly Source to the festival cycle. On the tenth day of the seventh month, all members of the community were to humble themselves, probably by fasting, as a sign of contrition. Violating the day by working or failing to humble oneself would lead to severe divine sanctions.

Although Leviticus 23:26–32 does not explicitly mention a communal convocation at the sanctuary, Leviticus 16 describes an elaborate public ritual. On this day the high priest, properly washed, attired, and screened by incense, was to slaughter a bull, take its blood into the holy of holies, and sprinkle the blood on the mercy seat to purge it of pollution caused by priestly uncleanness and sin (16:14). Later, blood from the bull was to be rubbed upon the horns of the altar and sprinkled about it for the same purpose (16:18–19). For the people, two he-goats were brought to the entrance of the tent of meeting, where one was chosen by lot for Yahweh and one for "Azazel" (a demon haunting the wild). The goat for Yahweh was slaughtered and its blood sprinkled like that of the bull (vss. 16–19) to purge the sanctuary and altar of the pollution of all forms of the people's sin and impurity.

After the purgation of the sanctuary and altar, the high priest laid his hands upon the live goat and transferred to it the guilt and impurity of the community, after which the animal was led into the wilderness and released (vss. 20–22). The idea seems to be that the goat could siphon off the guilt of the community and with it God's wrath upon evil. This removed not the guilt of perpetrators but the collective guilt contracted by association with them. Once the atonement rites were concluded, the high priest removed his special vestments, washed, put on other vestments, and offered a burnt offering for himself and one for the people (vss. 23–25). All the leftovers from the purgation offerings were burnt outside the camp (vss. 27–28).

(6) The Feast of Booths (Lev. 23:34–36, 39–43), the final festival of the cycle, lasted seven days, beginning on the fifteenth of the month. A communal convocation was to be held on the first day and on the day following the week-long festival. The only ritual mentioned in verses 34–36 is sacrifice, and the number required of the community is staggering: thirteen bulls, two rams, fourteen yearling male lambs as holocausts, a goat purgation offering, and the daily holocausts—on the first day! One less bull is required on each succeeding day (Num. 29:12–34). In something of an appendix (Lev. 23:39–43), the ritual that gives the festival its name is described. Actually two rituals are involved; the boughs of an assortment of trees are to be cut and carried in procession about the sanctuary (vs. 40), and "booths" (huts) are to be constructed, probably of boughs, and lived in for the seven days of the feast (vs. 42). Although the text is silent as to their location, it is assumed to be the settlements where the people normally lived. The custom is to remind the people of the tents used in the wilderness (vs. 43).

(7) The first nine verses of chapter 24 do not belong to the festival calendar, but they do concern the ritual of the tabernacle and therefore can be treated with the festival rituals. The addressee of the section shifts in midstream: from Moses in verses 1–4, who is to oversee the supplying of the lamps with oil, to the priests in all probability in verses 5–7. It would be members of the priesthood, not Moses or the laity, who would bake the bread, set it on the table, and burn incense. Verses 8–9 confuse the matter further by speaking of the priests in the third person, as if verses 5–7 were addressed to Moses.

Leviticus 24:2–4 imposes on the general populace the duty of providing olive oil for the lamps of the golden menorah set on the south side of the holy place (cf. Exod. 25:31–40; 27:20-21). The lamps were lit only at night, and at the lighting and the extinguishing of the lamps, incense was burned on the altar of incense before the veil of the holy of holies (Exod. 30:1–10). On the north side of the holy place stood a table (wood overlaid with gold, Exod. 25:23–30) on which a dozen loaves of bread always rested in two piles of six. These were replaced weekly, the stale bread being eaten by the priests when it was removed (Lev. 24:5–9). The incense on the bread would probably have been burnt when the bread was set out; libations would have been poured out as well (cf. Exod. 25:29).

Remedial Law for Blasphemy and Homicide (Lev. 24:10–23). This little section is an abrupt move from the divine address of the code to the life of the legal community in order to recount a precedent for holding aliens within Israel to the divine law. This provides the occasion for enunciating the remedies for blasphemy, murder, animal slaughter, and assault. I will begin with the precedent, relate it to other precedents in P, and then consider the rules for blasphemy, murder, and violent assault. P's law of asylum (Num. 35) will be examined in conjunction with the law for murder.

The narrative (vss. 10–14, 23) concerns a man with an Egyptian father who uses the name of Yahweh profanely during a dispute. Though his mother was an Israelite, he seems to have been counted an alien. The onlookers seize him and seek a ruling from Moses. Yahweh tells Moses to have him executed by stoning after those who had heard him place their hands on his head. Analogous to the ritual of the Day of Atonement, the gesture of placing hands on the offender's head could mean a transfer of guilt or impurity. Perhaps the very hearing of blasphemy communicated impurity, which had to be returned to its source.

The use of narratives recounting Mosaic precedents for difficult cases recurs several times in P. The reliance on precedent was not characteristic of Israelite law, so these examples must be viewed as a special development of the more general idea that the divine law was revealed to Israel for all time through Moses. Numbers 15:32–36 recounts the case of an Israelite found gathering fuel on the sabbath. The penalty for this offense was not established until Yahweh imposed death by stoning. Numbers 27:1–11 recounts the request of Zelophehad's daughters to receive the inheritance of their sonless father. Yahweh rules in their favor and outlines a lateral line of inheritance: if no sons, the inheritance falls to the deceased man's daughters, then to his brothers, then his uncles, then his closest kinsman. The daughters, who became members of the families into which they married, had to be restricted to husbands from the same tribe to avoid the loss of tribal land to other tribes (Num. 36:1–12).

The case of the alien's blasphemy is subsumed under rules of law for Israelites (Lev. 24:15–16) which are of graduated seriousness. If someone profanes God without using the name "Yahweh," he or she is left to divine punishment ("bear his sin," vs. 15); if the name "Yahweh" has been uttered, the death penalty by stoning is to be imposed by the community. (Consult Chapter Three on the third commandment.) In the rulings following the case of blasphemy (vss. 17–22), the alien is again subsumed under the law for Israel, because anyone who lives in the community and enjoys its privileges must share its burdens.

The rulings for murder, animal slaughter, and assault all exemplify the *lex talionis*. The murderer is to be executed, and the person who slaughters another's animal must replace it (presumably with compensation). These are unexceptional judgments, but the ruling on assault is another matter. Anyone guilty of assaulting and maiming another is to be subjected to the same treatment (eye for eye, etc.). This deviates from my understanding of biblical *lex talionis* as a poetic expression of equivalence applied literally for murder but figuratively for injury. In examples of bodily injury, the guilty party is to render payment (e.g., Exod. 21:18–19, 26–27). There is no example which stipulates bodily mutilation according to the principle of *lex talionis*. Thus, it is my belief that the author of this passage misunderstood the poetic nature of the *lex talionis* and thereby introduced the alien practice of mutilation into the law.

Relevant to the law of murder in P is the provision for cities of asylum (Num. 35:9–34). According to the practice of blood vengeance, a member of the family of a slain person was obligated to pursue and kill the slayer. The problem was that the slayer might not be guilty of murder and in any case deserved the right to be judged by a neutral party. Cities of asylum—three in Canaan, three in Transjordan—were to be set aside as places to which a slayer could flee for temporary safety (vss. 9–15). When the avenger of the blood sought the slayer at the city of asylum, an unspecified judicial body (Num. 35:25 says only "the congregation," raising a question as to whether the judges were from the city of asylum or the city where the killing occurred) would decide whether the slayer was guilty of murder and undeserving of asylum or was guilty of accidental homicide and deserving of asylum.

Numbers 35:16–18, 20–21, 22–23 describe cases of intentional and unintentional homicide. Whenever a weapon or tool with lethal potentiality was used and there was evidence of enmity or deliberation, the slayer was adjudged a murderer. If a weapon or tool of lethal potentiality caused death but there was no evidence of enmity, deliberation, or desire to harm, the slayer was innocent and therefore had a right to asylum. According to verse 30, two or more witnesses were required to establish guilt. How witnesses were to be summoned from the city of the slaying and who were valid witnesses (those who had seen the killing or those who could testify to prior enmity) are not specified.

The person adjudged innocent of murder had to remain in the city of asylum until the death of the high priest of the central shrine (vs. 25). The slayer who left the city was no longer legally protected (vss. 26–27). Payment to be allowed to leave before the death of the high priest was prohibited (vs. 32), as was any ransom for the life of a convicted murderer (vs. 31). The death of the high priest may have been thought to purge the pollution of the land caused by unintentional homicide, just as the death of the deliberate killer was necessary to purge the pollution caused by his deed (vs. 33).

The Sabbatical and Jubilee Years (Lev. 25).   The basic stock of the Holiness Code concludes with one of the great chapters of biblical law. Provisions for the sabbatical year in C and D have already been mentioned, and H devotes only a few verses to it. Most of the chapter describes the Year of Jubilee, an institution found nowhere else in biblical law. Whether it was an ancient practice revived or a new creation of H is hard to say. Within H it has the character of a program for maintaining traditional principles of landownership and citizenship.

(1) The sabbatical year (vss. 3–7, 20–22) requires farmers to abstain from planting grain and pruning vineyards every seventh year. The theological reason is that the land is to enjoy a periodic rest, as the people do weekly. The underlying idea may be that the land should be periodically restored to its divine owner (compare vs. 23) by being removed from human use.

The text assumes that all farmland within Israel will be fallowed during the same year. The provision in C (Exod. 23:10–11) could be interpreted either way. H's view creates obvious economic problems which the lawgiver attempts to solve by modifying the older ordinance, according to which the owner is not to reap the volunteer crop (vs. 5). In the very next verse, H allows the owner to eat whatever the land during its sabbath will produce. Verses 20–22 return to the problem and provide yet another answer: God will provide a double yield in the sixth year so that the farmer will have food until the harvest of the eighth year's planting (which would be the ninth year according to a spring calendar).

(2) The Year of Jubilee (vss. 8–17, 23–24) is the sabbath year of sabbath years (7 × 7). In the fall of the forty-ninth year (reckoned on a spring calendar) on the Day of Atonement, a trumpet is to be sounded to begin the Jubilee. This trumpet blast seems to be the origin of the festival's name (*yobel* = "ram's horn"). According to verses 11–12 it is a sabbath year, that is, a suspension of farming, as well as a "liberation." There must be some trick of computation that makes this fiftieth year the same as the forty-ninth of a sabbath of sabbaths—say, counting the previous Jubilee plus the forty-nine years to equal the fiftieth year.

The year grants "liberty" (or release) to the inhabitants of the land (vs. 10). Scholars have compared this to the remission of debts and invalidation of contracts that often was granted at the accession of Mesopotamian kings. This law does not mention such provisions but rather provides for the return of the people to their own families and holdings (vs. 10), a kind of family reunion.

This reunion was not, however, simply to be a temporary social gathering but was to be a repossession of landholdings by the families who had received them from God. According to biblical tradition, each tribe was granted territory by lot, and this territory was subdivided into clan and then family holdings (Num. 34; Josh. 13–19). The family holding was a share in Israel (a basis of citizenship) and an inheritance to be passed on from generation to generation in perpetuity. Unfortunately, holdings might have to be sold due to bankruptcy or other reasons. The purpose of H's Year of Jubilee was to return families to their divinely ordained holdings. Yahweh, according to verse 23, is the real owner of the land, and each Israelite is a "temporary resident" who cannot buy or sell the land in perpetuity. This theological principle means in fact that the family has been granted a right of usage in perpetuity (like a fief-holding according to feudal law) and can only alienate it temporarily.

The principle application of this theory of landholding is found in verses 13–16. Family inheritances revert to the grantee in the Year of Jubilee. Hence, any sale is for the years remaining from the date of sale to Jubilee, somewhat comparable to a long-term lease. The price to be paid is to be calculated on the years of use. The purchaser is not allowed to penalize the seller for the temporary duration of the transaction, nor the seller to charge more than the value of the remaining harvests.

The following paragraphs (vss. 25–34) cover ancillary aspects of this institution. The primary reason for selling a family inheritance would be economic destitution; an individual would sell to pay off debts. The next of kin (vs. 25) are morally obligated to buy the land and return it to the seller. If the seller lacks relatives in a financial position to perform this duty (in effect, to subsidize the seller), the land is to be sold according to the above provisions (vs. 28). The seller, however, has the right to redeem the land when he or she accumulates the capital to pay for the years remaining to Jubilee (vss. 26–27).

Some houses fall under the category of inheritances but others do not. A house in an unwalled village is counted as if it were on the land (vs. 31); a house in a walled town or city does not revert to the family in the Year of Jubilee, so any sale is permanent when a year in which it is subject to redemption has elapsed (vss. 29–30).

The houses of Levites within Levitical cities constitute an exception to the alienability of houses in walled cities. These houses revert to their original owners in the Year of Jubilee and are redeemable at any time (vss. 32–33), because the Levites were granted not land but "cities" and the surrounding pasturage as their share in Israel (vss. 33b–34). These cities (listed in Josh. 21; see also Num. 35:1–8) were not occupied solely by Levites nor under their rule; indeed, what set them apart as Levitical is difficult to say and a matter of much scholarly discussion. What can be said on the basis of the text is that the houses within these Levitical cities were categorized as family inheritances, and their "commons" were inalienable Levitical possessions. Elsewhere Levites would not have enjoyed these privileges.

The remainder of the chapter (vss. 35–55) follows the degradation of the man who has sold his inheritance. He must make a living by a trade, commerce, or day labor. His status is reduced to that of a resident alien (vs. 35). He may need to borrow, and when he does, the creditor should not charge interest on either money or food (vss. 36–37; consult Chapters Four and Five for parallels in C and D). The objective is for the substantial members of the community to help him maintain solvency to avoid slavery.

If community support fails to maintain him, he will be forced to sell his children or himself into slavery (vs. 39a). As an Israelite, he shall not be treated as a slave but as a day laborer (vss. 39b–40a). He and his family become free in the Year of Jubilee and can return to the family inheritance (vss. 40b–41). An Israelite cannot be a slave of a human, for he or she has been freed forever by Yahweh to be his slaves (vs. 42). Surprisingly, the text does not take cognizance of the duty to emancipate a Hebrew slave after six years of labor (see Exod. 21:1–6; Deut. 15:12–18). One can only guess that slave owners were not abiding by this older law and that H was attempting to work out a compromise.

Verses 44–46 allow for the perpetual enslavement of persons from foreign countries or of resident aliens. Unfortunately, here in the Holiness Code is the only discrimination against the resident alien. In the reverse situation, when an Israelite is enslaved to a resident alien, the lawgiver is especially sensitive to the rights of the Israelite. The Israelite is not to be treated as a slave (vs. 53) and is subject to redemption at any time (vss. 48–49). If not redeemed, the slave becomes free in the Year of Jubilee (vs. 54). Hence, the price of redemption is to be computed according to the purchase price divided by the years between date of purchase and Jubilee multiplied by the years remaining (vss. 50–52); in other words, the years of service are to be counted as partial payment (vs. 50b).

There is serious question whether the provisions of the Year of Jubilee were enforced during the pre-exilic period or afterward. Most scholars believe it to be utopian. However that may be, it is a valuable expression of the theory of landholding and Israelite citizenship. Yahweh alone owns the land and grants a share in perpetuity to each family; he has redeemed every member of this people, and they can be slaves only of him. These theological principles far outweigh the rather quixotic institution meant to preserve them.

On Leviticus 26:1–2, consult the discussion of Leviticus 19.

Appendix: Desacralization of Sanctuary Donations (Lev. 27). This chapter stipulates which donations can and cannot be redeemed and at what cost. The first portion of the chapter (vss. 1–13) treats votive offerings (or vows, see Num. 30:1–15), the second (vss. 14–25) treats either votive or voluntary dedications of real property, and the remainder (vss. 26–34) deals with persons, animals, and produce belonging to Yahweh as a matter of principle.

The chapter's fundamental law is that offerable animals cannot be redeemed but must be sacrificed (vs. 9), whereas donations not offered to Yahweh are redeemable. The dedication of humans to Yahweh is solely for their redeemable value, which is calculated according to age and sex (vss. 3–7). Animals which cannot be offered are assigned a value by the priest, and the owner can redeem them by paying their price plus a fifth for desacralization (vss. 11–13, 27). If the animal is not redeemed, it can be sold to anyone but the owner at its assessed value. Houses (vss. 14–15) fall under the same provisions, and fields (vss. 16–25) differ only slightly, being complicated by the reversion principle of the Year of Jubilee.

Anything that already belonged to Yahweh could not, obviously, be given as a voluntary offering as well (vs. 26). If one replaces an animal that belongs to Yahweh with another, the penalty is forfeiture of the original animal and its replacement (vss. 10, 33). If one sells land that was already dedicated or simply fails to redeem dedicated land, it becomes the permanent possession of the sanctuary (vss. 20–21).

Verses 28–29 include the "devoted things" (*ḥerem*) in the category of sacred donation. The practice of devoting captives and booty to Yahweh, resulting in killing or destruction, originally belonged to the war of Yahweh (see the discussion of Deut. 20). By the time the Holiness Code was written, the war of Yahweh was dead, so either the law is archaic theory or the practice has been transferred to some other institution. The text gives no clue as to how or why a person, animal, or field might be devoted.

SUGGESTED READING

For the policy informing this selection, see the statement introducing the bibliography at the end of Chapter One. For the source, form, and traditio-historical criticism of the Holiness Code and Priestly Law, consult the bibliography to Chapter Two as well as the works listed below.

Among the commentaries in English on Leviticus and Numbers, the following are satisfactory:

Noth, Martin. *Leviticus: A Commentary*. Trans. J. E. Anderson. Old Testament Library. Philadelphia: Westminster Press, 1965.
————. *Numbers: A Commentary*. Trans. James D. Martin. Old Testament Library. Philadelphia: Westminster Press, 1968.
Wenham, Gordon J. *The Book of Leviticus*. New International Commentary on the Old Testament, vol. 3. Grand Rapids: Wm. B. Eerdmans Publishing Co., 1979.

A selection of studies of the form and content of passages in the Holiness Code:

Bigger, Stephen F. "The Family Laws of Leviticus 18 in Their Setting," *Journal of Biblical Literature* 98 (1979), pp. 187–203.
Gabel, J. B., and C. B. Wheeler. "The Redactor's Hand in the Blasphemy Pericope of Leviticus XXIV," *Vetus Testamentum* 30 (1980), pp. 227–229.
Muraoka, T. "A Syntactic Problem in Lev. XIX 18b," *Journal of Semitic Studies* 23 (1978), pp. 291–297.
von Rad, Gerhard. "Form-Criticism of the Holiness Code." In *Studies in Deuterono-*

my, trans. David Stalker, pp. 25–36. Studies in Biblical Theology, no. 9. London: SCM Press, 1953.

Research into the Holiness Code and Priestly Law by Jacob Milgrom:

Milgrom, Jacob. *Cult and Conscience: The Asham and the Priestly Doctrine of Repentance.* Ed. J. Neusner. Studies in Judaism in Late Antiquity, vol. 18. Leiden: E. J. Brill, 1976.

————. *Studies in Levitical Terminology, I: The Encroacher and the Levite; The Term 'Aboda.* University of California Publications, Near Eastern Studies, vol. 14. Berkeley: University of California Press, 1970.

————. "Atonement in the OT," pp. 78–82; "Day of Atonement," pp. 82–83; "Encroachment," pp. 264–265; "First-Born," pp. 337–338; "First Fruits, OT," p. 337; "Heave Offering," pp. 391–392; "Leviticus," pp. 541–545; "Repentance in the OT," pp. 736–738; "Sacrifices and Offerings, OT," pp. 763–771; "Wave Offering," pp. 944–946. In *The Interpreter's Dictionary of the Bible Supplementary Volume*, ed. Keith Crim. Nashville: Abingdon Press, 1976.

————. "The Betrothed Slave-Girl, Lev. 19:20–22," *Zeitschrift für die alttestamentliche Wissenschaft* 89 (1977), pp. 43–50.

————. "The Biblical Diet Laws as an Ethical System," *Interpretation* 17 (1963), pp. 288–301.

————. "A Prolegomenon to Leviticus 17:11," *Journal of Biblical Literature* 90 (1971), pp. 149–156.

————. "Two Kinds of Ḥaṭṭā' t," *Vetus Testamentum* 26 (1976), pp. 333–337.

Other studies of the Priestly Law and cultic system:

Buttrick, George Arthur, and Keith Crim (eds.). *The Interpreter's Dictionary of the Bible.* 5 vols. Nashville and New York: Abingdon Press, 1962–76. May be consulted for a wide variety of subjects in addition to those cited above.

Feldman, Emanuel. *Biblical and Post-Biblical Defilement and Mourning: Law as Theology.* New York: Ktav Publishing House, 1977.

Haran, Menahem. *Temples and Temple Service in Ancient Israel: An Inquiry into the Character of Cult Phenomena and the Historical Setting of the Priestly School.* Oxford: Oxford University Press, 1978.

Levine, Baruch A. *In the Presence of the Lord: A Study of Cult and Some Cultic Terms in Ancient Israel.* Studies in Judaism in Late Antiquity, vol. 5. Leiden: E. J. Brill, 1974.

————. "Book of Numbers" and "Priestly Writers." In *The Interpreter's Dictionary of the Bible Supplementary Volume*, ed. Keith Crim, pp. 631–635, 683–687. Nashville: Abingdon Press, 1976.

Wilkinson, John. "Leprosy and Leviticus: The Problem of Description and Identification," *Scottish Journal of Theology* 30 (1977), pp. 153–169.

————. "Leprosy and Leviticus: A Problem of Semantics and Translation," *Scottish Journal of Theology* 31 (1978), pp. 153–166.

On the topic of cultic holiness:

Douglas, Mary. *Purity and Danger: An Analysis of Concepts of Pollution and Taboo.* New York: Praeger Publishers, 1966. An anthropological view worth consulting.

General studies of the conception of the sanctuary and sacrifices in biblical literature:

Brichto, Herbert Chanan. "On Slaughter and Sacrifice, Blood and Atonement," *Hebrew Union College Annual* 47 (1976), pp. 19–55.

Clements, R. E. *God and Temple.* Oxford: Basil Blackwell, 1965.

Daly, Robert J. *The Origins of the Christian Doctrine of Sacrifice.* Philadelphia: Fortress Press, 1978.

Davies, Douglas. "An Interpretation of Sacrifice in Leviticus," *Zeitschrift für die alttestamentliche Wissenschaft* 89 (1977), pp. 387–399.

de Vaux, Roland. *Studies in Old Testament Sacrifice.* Cardiff: University of Wales Press, 1964.

Studies of the Priestly response to the Exile:

Cross, Frank M. "The Priestly Work." In *Canaanite Myth and Hebrew Epic*, pp. 293–325. Cambridge and London: Harvard University Press, 1973.

Klein, Ralph W. *Israel in Exile: A Theological Interpretation.* Overtures to Biblical Theology, vol. 6. Philadelphia: Fortress Press, 1979. Pp. 125–148.

Koch, Klaus. "Sühne und Sündenvergebung um die Wende von der exilischen zur nachexilischen Zeit," *Evangelische Theologie* 26 (1966), pp. 217–239.

Special treatment of the Holiness Code and Priestly Law in biblical theologies:

Eichrodt, Walther. *Theology of the Old Testament.* 2 vols. Trans. J. A. Baker. Old Testament Library. London: SCM Press, 1961. Vol. 1, pp. 96–97.

von Rad, Gerhard. *Old Testament Theology.* 2 vols. Trans. D. M. G. Stalker. Edinburgh and London: Oliver & Boyd, 1962–65. Vol. 1, pp. 232–279.

Chapter Seven

THE WRITTEN AND UNWRITTEN LAW

In the course of setting up the Israelite judicial system, the Deuteronomic Moses admonishes the judges of the future:

> Justice, and only justice, you shall follow, that you may live and inherit the land which Yahweh your God gives you. (Deut. 16:20)

The noun translated "justice" here could just as well be rendered "right." The question in this chapter, however, is not the proper translation of the word but the substance it denotes. What was involved in the pursuit of right judgment? Was it a matter of enforcing the letter of the lawbooks or the spirit of the Law? Were the people of Israel held accountable to the rules of divine law or to the sense of justice and right that informed these rules?

It is frequently alleged that a fatal defect of divine law is its giving timeless and unqualified authority to time-bound and provisional rules of law. If conditions change or the moral sensibility of a community evolves, the law should change as well. The natural and healthy adaptation and evolution of law is, it is said, retarded by legal formulations ascribed to the eternal God and accorded the unconditional validity appropriate to God's word.

Does biblical law suffer from this alleged defect? Were the formulations of divine law accorded the honor of timeless truth? Were the codes examined here considered to be an exhaustive, comprehensive revelation of God's will for the people? To these questions I propose a negative answer. I contend that, for the period during which the legal tradition was in formation, the law of God was an unwritten Law. It was the sense of justice and right shared by the legal community and sharpened by lawgivers and judges. According to this theory, the precepts and judgments of the codes were not prescriptions with statutory force but testimony to God's just and righteous will.

In the first part of this chapter, I will endeavor to elaborate and support this theory of biblical law, beginning with codes of judicial ethics. These addresses directed to judges and disputants call for substantive justice but are silent regarding adherence to rules of law. Second, I will review a number of narratives depicting judicial deliberation. These accounts show that judges and disputants argued from principles and concepts of justice and right, not from written or oral rules of law. Third, I will take another look at the precepts and judgments found in the series and codes of the Torah with the intent to show that these documents were created to inculcate the values, principles, concepts, and procedures of Israel's legal tradition, not to decree specific rulings for specific cases. Finally, I will note a change of theory toward the identification of divine law with the rules of law given through Moses. This change is to be attributed, I believe, to the adoption of the Deuteronomic Law as the basis of King Josiah's reform.

The portion of the law governing the sanctuary, sacrifice, festivals, and other religious rituals will not be included, as this type is not rooted in the sense of justice and right but in the sense of holiness and supernatural reality. It is probable that a similar relation of rules to substance could be established for this law as well, but I do not want to complicate the argument.

In the second part of the chapter I will extend the thesis to include the New Testament. It is my contention that Jesus, followed by most New Testament authors, revived the idea that God's law is an unwritten Law. The epitome of this unwritten Law is the commandment to love God and one's neighbor, which both fulfills and surpasses the sense of justice and right forming the basis of Old Testament divine law.

Substantive Justice and the Rules of Law

The task now is to reconstruct the theory of law either stated or assumed by the authors of legal texts and narratives, a difficult task because people customarily take such underlying conceptions for granted. It is as important to note what the authors do not say as what they do say. Moreover, it is often easier to establish that a given theory is absent from a text than to identify what theory is present. Hopefully the difficulties and uncertainties inherent in this project will be overcome for the achievement of a thorough understanding of divine law.

Judicial Ethics.   The most sensitive task of Israelite judges was to hear the diputants in a case and decide who was in the right and who was guilty of wrongdoing (Deut. 25:1). The word used in the Deuteronomic verse for rendering justice to the innocent means "to set right," which can be taken as an indication of the mindset of Israelite jurisprudence. Their objective was to restore the community to health by recognizing the righteous party and imposing on the guilty a penalty proportionate to the wrong. How the judges were expected to realize this ideal can be pursued by consulting those biblical texts which indicate how a responsible judge was expected to act.

The Book of the Covenant has a series of prohibitions (Exod. 23:1–3, 6–9) directed to judges and witnesses, such as:

> You shall not utter a false report.
> You shall not follow a multitude to do evil.
> You shall not pervert the justice due to your poor in his suit.
> And you shall take no bribe.

Similar sets of commandments are found in Deuteronomy (16:19–20) and the Holiness Code (Lev. 19:15–16). The items in these ethical codes are self-explanatory and would have been self-evident to ancient Israelites. It is noteworthy that none of these catalogs have a commandment to consult the lawbooks or adhere to the letter of the law. However judicial decisions were argued and rendered, it is evident that conformity to rules of law was not itself a value to be inculcated. Failure to follow the rule of law was not perceived as a threat to justice. From this silence one may surmise that Israelite judges were not expected to consult the legal codes to find the rule that applied to the case before the bar.

If judgments were not rendered on the basis of rules of law, how were they decided? The texts do not make this explicit. What they are concerned with are the corruptions of the judicial proceedings that would result in injustice. The judges and participants are warned to avoid any action that would interfere with the sort of deliberations leading to substantive justice. As shall presently be seen, these deliberations would turn on legal and ethical principles and concepts.

In Exodus 18 (cf. Deut. 1:9–18), Jethro instructs Moses to delegate judicial authority to men who conform to the ethical standards enumerated in the codes of ethics:

> Choose able men from all the people, such as fear God, men who are trustworthy and who hate a bribe.   (18:21)

Their quality of character makes these men fit for deliberating on judicial cases, for a just person is attuned to the sense of justice shared by the legal community. It is noteworthy that legal training is not stated as a requirement for judgeship. Integrity of character takes precedence over technical skill as a qualification for judicial office.

In Exodus 18 the judges are given responsibility over "small matters" and are instructed to go to Moses when confronted with "great matters" (vs. 22) or "hard cases" (vs. 26). One might construe this to mean that judges could decide all cases for which there was a rule but that they were to come to Moses, who received his insight from God (vs. 19), with cases for which no rule existed. This interpretation is unlikely, for the text does not mention rules of law in either description of "small" and "hard" cases. Probably a great or hard case was one in which the judges were puzzled as to what had happened or who was in the right.

Deuteronomy 17 describes a similar system of judicial review. The kind of problem that should be taken to the "Levitical priests, and to the judge" (vs. 9) is stated in verse 8:

> If any case arises requiring decision between one kind of homicide and another, one kind of legal right and another, or one kind of assault and another. . . .

This would be called a problem of conceptual classification; the lay court must seek the guidance of professional legal minds when the case is beyond its sophistication. The text is silent about the procedure of the superior magistrates for deciding such cases. One would have expected a reference to consulting the lawbooks if legal deliberation were a matter of finding and applying rules of law.

Nothing in the codes of judicial ethics, qualifications for judicial office, or instructions regarding judicial review points to a process of judicial deliberation based upon prescriptive rules of law. Rather, the judges are warned to eschew any practice that would impair the rendering of substantive justice and are advised to seek help from professionals when they cannot render it for lack of sophistication.

Narratives of Judicial Deliberation.   The next step is an examination of proceedings of Israelite jurisprudence. Of particular interest is the mode of legal argumentation, where the question is whether judicial decisions were rendered on the basis of rules or of legal and moral concepts and principles. The task would be easier if Palestinian archaeology had unearthed caches of court records comparable to those unearthed in Syria and Mesopotamia. Since scholars are not so fortunate, Israelite practice must be sought in stories reporting or reflecting legal proceedings. This has its dangers, for the literary representation of institutional proceedings is invariably incomplete and possibly distorted. However, one would expect authors to depict court transactions with sufficient realism for their readers to recognize them.

As it would be unfeasible to examine every narrative with a possible bearing on legal argumentation, I have selected a number of well-known accounts, beginning with Abraham's intercession for Sodom. Although this case is not strictly a judicial case, it is modeled after one. Yahweh is specifically designated "Judge of all the earth," and the discussion revolves around guilt, innocence, and punishment. Abraham, as something of a friend of the court, proposes a legal principle for divine consideration and gains the Judge's assent:

> Then Abraham drew near, and said, "Wilt thou indeed destroy the righteous with the wicked? Suppose there are fifty righteous within the city; wilt thou then destroy the place and not spare it for the fifty righteous who are in it? Far be it from thee to do such a thing, to slay the righteous with the wicked, so that the righteous fare as the wicked! Far be that from thee! Shall not the Judge of all the earth do right?" (Gen. 18:23–25)

Abraham's reasoning is that if God destroys the city of Sodom, all will die; there is no possibility of discriminate punishment. The righteous will, consequently, be treated as if they were guilty, which is to Abraham an abomination of justice. It is his view that if the guilty cannot be punished without punishing the righteous, justice is better served by leaving them unpunished. The question is of the relative weight of the law: should the law be biased toward protecting the innocent or punishing the guilty? This sort of question, and the legal principle Abraham proposes, surpasses the question at hand; indeed, every legal system must answer the dilemma with Abraham's principle or its opposite. One can safely surmise that this account reflects a type of legal reasoning which renders decisions on the basis of substantive justice rather than rules of law. That is, it appeals to an unwritten Law to which judicial decisions should conform, even—indeed, above all—those of the Judge of the entire world.

The appeal of the daughters of Zelophehad to Moses (Num. 27:1–11) offers an ample description of legal reasoning. Zelophehad had died leaving five daughters but no sons. Since only males could inherit land according to common practice, Zelophehad's estate (yet to be allotted) would be passed on not to his daughters but to his brothers. His daughters argue against this:

> Why should the name of our father be taken away from his family, because he had no son? Give to us a possession among our father's brethren.   (vs. 4)

The women have argued two interrelated principles: the right of a man to have his name continue, and the right to have his land remain in the possession of his offspring. Moses consults Yahweh, and Yahweh acknowledges their right and offers a solution that satisfies both principles. Thus, the account is a clear example of a case decided on the basis of the intrinsic justice of the claimants' cause.

Of course, one might wonder whether the mode by which Moses arrives at this decision is typical of biblical law. The narrative assumes that he has superior legal authority by virtue of his unique access to the font of justice. This is a "hard case" requiring a divine revelation. For that very reason, however, it is revealing, for it shows that even Yahweh decides the case in terms of the intrinsic justice of the claimants' cause.

There are several examples of judicial hearings before a king in which the king passes judgment only to be told that he has passed judgment upon himself (2 Sam. 12:1–15; 14:1–24; 1 Kings 20:35–43). The account of Joab's procurement of Absalom's pardon (2 Sam. 14) is particularly instructive. A woman from Tekoa appears before David with a cause:

> Alas, I am a widow; my husband is dead. And your handmaid had two sons, and they quarreled with one another in the field; there was no one to part them, and one struck the other and killed him. And now the whole family has risen against your handmaid, and they say, "Give up the man who struck his brother, that we may kill him for the life of his brother whom he slew"; and so they would destroy the heir also. Thus they would quench my coal which is left, and leave to my husband neither name nor remnant upon the face of the earth.   (vss. 5–7)

The woman seeks what might be called an equity decision by pitting the principles of inheritance, lineal continuation, and the right to support from children against the principle of blood vengeance. David grants her son immunity from blood vengeance, and then she reveals the parabolic nature of the case.

The story is important here because the king gives a ruling contrary to every law and principle in Scripture governing murder. In the laws, murder *must* be answered by the execution of the perpetrator:

> Moreover you shall accept no ransom for the life of a murderer, who is guilty of death; but he shall be put to death ... for blood pollutes the land, and no expiation can be made for the land, for the blood that is shed in it, except by the blood of him who shed it.   (Num. 35:31, 33)

Thus, not only does David's judgment not appeal to a rule of law, it is diametrically opposed to a known rule. It is given on the basis of the justice of the woman's cause. As she puts it, David "is like the angel of God to discern good and evil" (vs. 17).

The framing of Naboth (1 Kings 21) exemplifies the way Israelite jurisprudence could be abused and rectified. False charges are leveled against Naboth by two witnesses, he and his heirs (so 2 Kings 9:26) are executed, and his land is confiscated. The charge made against Naboth reads, "You have cursed God and the king" (vs. 10), a charge which is a virtual citation of Exodus 22:28. One might take this as counter-evidence of my description of legal reasoning, but I believe the citation of the law in the charge is evidence of its artificiality. Jezebel, one might imagine, consulted the lawbooks in search of a crime that left no traces and carried the death penalty. Perhaps she believed that refusal to accept Ahab's offer was insubordination (cf. vs. 7) and subsumed it under this law. In any case, one can hardly take her formulation of a false charge as an indication of typical, healthy Israelite practice.

The court's judgment diverges from any known Israelite law or practice. The execution of the offender may be implied by the prohibition, but the execution of his heirs and the confiscation of his land are without legal support or precedent. The sentence must have been requested by the king or Jezebel, and the court, I believe, had the authority to grant it, though their ruling was unjust according to the standards of Israelite law.

Elijah's response to the crimes of the royal house exemplifies the way divine law could rectify abuses. God intervenes to avenge Naboth's death and announces a decision beforehand by a prophet. Elijah charges Ahab with murder and illegal confiscation: "Have you killed, and also taken possession?" (vs. 19). If Elijah had wanted to fit his accusation to the verbal form of the lawbooks, he would have charged Ahab with conspiring to give false witness and to defraud a family of its inheritance. What he does, however, is to go to the substance of the matter. Ahab and Jezebel have violated not rules of divine law but the justice and right to which all Israelites, including royal persons, are subject.

2 Kings 8:1–6 tells of the reclaiming of land after its abandonment. The Shunammite woman had left her land on the instruction of the prophet Elisha (vss. 1–2); when she returned after seven years, she went to the king "to appeal . . . for her house and her land" (vs. 3). When the king heard the facts of the case, he "appointed an official for her, saying, 'Restore all that was hers, together with all the produce of the fields from the day that she left the land until now' " (vs. 6). He hardly takes this action on the basis of some rule of law and may even be breaking custom respecting abandoned land. He decides on the basis of the intrinsic justice of her claim—that she had abandoned the land on instruction from the prophet to avoid a famine.

The narrative of Jeremiah's trial in the temple can draw this re-

view to a close. According to Jeremiah 26, the prophet stands beside
the entrance to the temple and threatens its destruction by God for
the iniquities of the people. Jeremiah's auditors—priests, prophets, and
common people—seize him and convoke an ad hoc trial, charging:

> You shall die! Why have you prophesied in the name of Yahweh, saying,
> "This house shall be like Shiloh, and this city shall be desolate, without
> inhabitant"? (Jer. 26:8–9)

It is unlikely that their charge is based upon a rule of law, for it is
doubtful that a rule condemning the pronouncement of divine judgment within the temple precincts ever existed. Rather, the auditors
are offended by Jeremiah's utterance and simply cite it, in the form
of an accusatory question, as prima facie evidence of guilt, probably
of the crime of blasphemy.

When some royal officials appear, they are allowed to sit as judges, and Jeremiah proceeds to defend himself. He does not deny the
charge but claims that he has God-given authority to speak this
word. The judges with the laity support Jeremiah's claim to innocence by citing the precedent of the prophet Micah, who once proclaimed the destruction of Zion. In this precedent case, the king and
people heeded the prophetic warning and repented, and the implication is that the present generation should do likewise rather than
attack the bearer of ill tidings and thereby incur even greater guilt.
This reasoning prevails and Jeremiah is acquitted.

Jeremiah's trial conforms to the pattern of argumentation found
in the other examples. He has offended the sense of right, or holiness,
of his auditors, and this provokes a criminal charge. He defends himself by appealing to a right inhering in the office of the prophet,
namely, to speak God's word however distasteful it is. The one new
feature of the case is the appeal to precedent in support of the idea
that such a word could be God's. This precedent is not itself a rule of
law or even a judicial precedent but a theological and historical
precedent.

None of the examples report the consultation of the lawbooks by
judges or the justification of a decision by citation (with the exception of 1 Kings 21). Israelite jurisprudence employed argumentation
from principles and concepts either presented by parties before the

bar or articulated by the judges themselves. The law which the judicial system enforced was an unwritten law woven into the fabric of society and discovered in the course of judicial deliberation.

The Purpose of the Lawbooks.   Why are so many rules of law contained in the Torah if Israelite judicial argumentation did not appeal to them? If the picture of Israelite judicial practice and reconstruction of its legal theory are correct, an explanation of the precepts and judgments of Mosaic Law that corresponds to practice and theory must be devised. In the paragraphs that follow, I will endeavor to show that the lawbooks were intended not for judicial application but for instruction in the values, principles, concepts, and procedures of the unwritten divine Law. In actual fact, the biblical lawbooks do not even have the appearance of documents composed to decree judicial rulings. Several salient features suggest that they were more of the nature of moral homilies than legislative codes:

(1) The biblical series and lawbooks are formulated as addresses. This format itself makes what is communicated a mode of persuasive speech. The people, as the addressees, are incorporated into a personal relationship with the divine or (in the case of Deuteronomy) human speaker. They are made personally responsible for their behavior to this lawgiver.

(2) The language of moral suasion pervades the biblical presentation of law. A provision like Exodus 23:4, "If you meet your enemy's ox . . .," clearly attempts to inculcate a high level of moral responsibility in the community. The abundance of motive clauses and homilies in the law testifies to the same purpose.

(3) The apodictic commandments found in the decalogues and scattered through the larger lawbooks are more like moral precepts than legal prescriptions. They are personally addressed to moral agents, and their import is to elicit conformity to the fundamental norms of the social order.

There remains the question of the more technical "judgments" (*mishpatim*) found in the larger lawbooks. This material does have the sound of rulings to be applied in judicial cases, but there is evidence that this appearance is somewhat deceiving. If the intent had been a body of rules to be consulted and employed in legal argumentation, one would expect a striving toward an exhaustive and comprehensive set of rules. No one corpus nor all the biblical corpora taken together exhibit such a striving. In the Book of the Covenant, which contains the largest and purest collection of casuistic law, there are two relatively large and systematic sections: (1) Death and injury (Exod. 21:12–14, 18–36); (2) Theft, lost and damaged property (22:1–15). Neither section exhausts the topic covered; one can, for example, think of numerous judicable cases of death and injury not treated in Exodus 21. The lawgiver recognizes the spottiness of his coverage and directs the addressee to generalize:

> If any harm follows, then you shall give life for life.   (21:23)

> If it gores a man's son or daughter, he shall be dealt with according to this same rule [*mishpat* (principle of justice)].   (21:31)

> For every breach of trust . . . of which one says, "This is it," the case . . . shall come before God.   (22:9)

In essence the judges are being told to make their own judgment in the spirit of the law and according to its underlying principles and customary procedures.

Obviously, harm to body and property is not comprehensive of the whole range of law. The Book of the Covenant has little or no remedial law on such important topics as marriage and sexual relations, inheritance, and commerce and contract. The other biblical lawbooks do supplement it on some of these topics, but none is any more comprehensive, and all of them combined leave large gaps. Clearly the biblical lawbooks are insufficient for regular consultation by judicial authorities.

In addition, the biblical lawbooks contain a healthy sampling of idealistic or utopian provisions. Even within the remedial law of the Book of the Covenant, one finds idealistic provisions, for example, granting a slave freedom for loss of a tooth (21:27). Most of Deuteronomy's slave provisions are idealistic and would have brought the institution to an end if enforced. The Jubilee Year in the Holiness Code is thoroughly utopian. Such idealistic and utopian rulings would not have made their way into the lawbooks if the lawbooks were designed for practical application in judicial cases.

If the judgments of the biblical lawbooks were not drawn up for judicial application, what was their purpose? Any answer will perforce be speculative. My argument suggests that they were created to instruct the judges and the community at large in the legal concepts, principles, and procedures inherent in the unwritten law. One might term them *exercises* in legal thinking. By means of examples, the legal experts of the community inculcated the legal concepts, principles, and judicial procedures that they held to have standing in the legal tradition which was woven into the fabric of Israelite society. The theoretical character of such exercises allowed the authors to indulge occasionally in idealistic and utopian "preaching."

The interpretation of casuistic law as exercises would explain its presence in lawbooks having a tone of moral suasion. Both moral suasion and exercises in legal reasoning can be seen as serving the same purpose, namely, inculcating the values and principles of the legal community. One might say that biblical law sought to create the conscience of the community. The auditors were being instructed in the sense of justice and right expected by their divine sovereign and embedded in the structure of the community.

From Unwritten to Written Law.   A shift in the understanding of God's law can be detected in the literature bearing the stamp of the Deuteronomic school and sustaining the impact of Josiah's reform. The new understanding comes to expression in statements exhorting the addressee to adhere strictly to the words of the legal text and praising persons for doing so.

The evidence for this new understanding appears in a few admonitions in the lawbook of Deuteronomy, for example:

> Everything that I command you you shall be careful to do; you shall not add to it or take from it.   (Deut. 12:32)

This warning against adding to or subtracting from the text betokens an identification of the text with the law. It is of a piece with statements in the sermonic conclusion of the book, for example:

> If you obey the voice of Yahweh your God, to keep his commandments and mandates *which are written in this lawbook.* . . . (30:10, author's translation)

The italicized clause evidences a significant shift in the relation of rules of law and the law; the will of God is now fixed in rules. It may not be going too far to see incipient "statutes" in this understanding of the rules of the lawbook.

The text of the Deuteronomic Law does not exhibit this new conception. Moses' address displays a striking freedom in its adaption and restatement of the materials the author inherited from the Book of the Covenant. The author shows no compulsion to adhere to the letter of the divine law. Moreover, the style and tone of the Deuteronomic presentation of law is so imprecise and homiletical that the very idea of strict adherence is virtually meaningless. It is ironic that Deuteronomy should become the text which gave rise to the understanding of law as a body of written rules.

The verses in the book of Deuteronomy exhibiting this new understanding of law are either isolated elements within the lawbook or a part of the Deuteronomistic framework. I would ascribe all of them to the school which sprang up in Judah following the discovery of the book in the temple and its adoption as the basis of Josiah's reform. The new attitude arose, I would surmise, from the way the book was received, not from any attribute of the book itself.

This surmise is confirmed by the narrative of the Josianic reform. When Deuteronomy was adopted,

> the king . . . made a covenant before Yahweh, to walk after Yahweh and to keep his commandments and his testimonies and his statutes, with all his heart and all his soul, to perform the words of this covenant *that were written in this book;* and all the people joined in the covenant. (2 Kings 23:3)

Most of these expressions exhibit the warm piety of Deuteronomy and have antecedents in older texts; the new element is the identification of divine law with the body of rules in the book. The summary of the reform epitomizes this new literalism:

> Josiah put away the mediums . . . and all the abominations that were seen in the land of Judah and in Jerusalem, *that he might establish the words of the law which were written in the book* that Hilkiah the priest found in the house of Yahweh. (23:24)

The greatest compliment that can be paid Josiah is that he enforced the words of the written law!

The same shift from an unwritten to a written law can be noticed in the classical prophets. The eighth century prophets (Amos, Hosea, Isaiah, Micah) show no inclination to cite the lawbooks. They indict Israel for the violation of the unwritten law—the spirit of justice, righteousness, and loving-kindness. When they seek to define the will of Israel's God, they paint in broad strokes:

> And what does Yahweh require of you
> but to do justice, and to love kindness,
>   and to walk humbly with your God?   (Mic. 6:8)

Nothing could be farther from a fixation on written rules.

Citations and paraphrases of the lawbooks begin to appear in the book of Jeremiah. Many of these citations belong to the portions of the book that are thought to have passed through editors of the Deuteronomic school (e.g., 7:6, 9; 17:19–27), but Jeremiah himself cites a Deuteronomic law (Jer. 3:1, from Deut. 24:1–4). Although his use is allegorical rather than literal, it denotes the shift to a written law. Indeed, allegory is a typical development of cultures which take the written form of traditions to be timeless truth.

Jeremiah may be the first prophet to recognize the dangers of identifying the law with written rules. He charges the scribes with corrupting the law:

> How can you say, "We are wise,
>   and the law of Yahweh is with us"?
> But, behold, the false pen of the scribes
>   has made it into a lie.   (Jer. 8:8)

The new understanding of law, in which the community boasts of the certainty of its laws, is a danger to the divine law that demands substantive justice and righteousness. The more law becomes identified with the rules of law, the greater is the danger of sophistic casuistry, of formal justice that violates substantive justice, and simply of textual tampering and manipulation.

The shift in the understanding of divine law did not immediately take hold in all segments of the religious community. The Holiness Code and Priestly Law do not have statements identifying the divine law with the written rules of law, and it may be that this stream of tradition remained untouched by the thought of the Deuteronomic school. The evidence points in both directions. On the one hand, P's cultic law suggests the shift to a written law. The very idea of incorporating cultic rubrics in the communal law betokens an attraction to written rules to protect practice from change, and the thorough coverage evidences a desire for a complete system. The loss of the temple cult in the Exile probably gave impetus to the transformation of a decision-making process into a fixed body of teaching; thus, the revival of temple worship after the Exile would go by the manual. On the other hand, neither the Holiness Code nor the Priestly Source exhibits a drive toward systematic presentation of judicial law. Indeed, one can discern a concerted effort to avoid judicial legislation. Perhaps the bearers of this stream of tradition assumed, in the spirit of pre-exilic Israel, that judicial decisions were to be rendered on the basis of an unwritten law.

The cultural trend was, nevertheless, toward identifying the written laws with the divine law. It is this conception that led to the canonization of the Torah. Only if one came to believe that the eternal law was contained in the revelation to Moses would one set apart the legal texts—with the rest of the Pentateuch—as inviolable and unalterable. The freedom that once inhered in the unwritten law passed over to the interpreter of the sacred text. Thinking about justice and right, which once was the law itself, became the preoccupation of the interpreter endeavoring to explain and justify the written rules of law.

It is important to grasp just what was entailed by the shift from an unwritten to a written law. By unwritten law is not meant a host of rules and commandments passed on orally, for then the shift to written rules would be a minor change. Rather, the unwritten law is the concepts and principles of justice and righteousness recognized by the legal community. Within such an understanding of law, the commandments, judgments, and motive clauses were formulated (either orally or in writing) to set forth the concepts and principles of the law for the purpose of persuasion and instruction. No attempt to be exhaustive or particularly precise was necessary, for the concepts and principles, not the rules, were to be applied to decisions.

Identifying the law with the written rules of law preserved in the legal texts amounts to a version of the modern theory of legal positivism, according to which the rule, not the reasoning behind it, is authoritative. Hence, each rule is limited to the specific topic covered and can be extended only by some sort of analogy or allegory. To be complete, the law must come as close as possible to a rule for every conceivable case demanding moral decision or judicial action. To be consistent, the lawgiver must possess a genius for system, for this conception of law lacks a mechanism for qualifying each rule by the concepts and principles informing all the rules.

When Israel adopted an understanding of God's law as a set of rules preserved in written texts, they were forced to develop an oral tradition to interpret legal texts according to the principles just outlined. The eternal laws of God, delivered to Moses once for all, had to be adapted, augmented, and rationalized in order to be used in meditation, piety, and jurisprudence. The emergence of this interpretive tradition in post-exilic Judaism charted the course for Judaism and set the stage for the birth of Christianity.

Conflict over the Law

No question divides Jews and Christians more than the nature and purpose of the law of God. Hopefully the thesis of this chapter will explain a facet of this disagreement. Jews hold the actual text of laws in great esteem, meditating upon it, seeking guidance from it, and praising God for having given it. Christians are generally impatient with a body of rules of vast multiplicity. They want them reduced to a manageable size—an essential core, like the Ten Commandments, or a single overriding principle, like the law of love. Jews also have an interest in the summary of the law but balance it with a fascination with the law's manifold provisions.

The Jewish approach to the law developed in the centuries preceding and during the first century of the Christian era. To adapt the revealed laws of Scripture to the various conditions and cultures in which Jews found themselves, there arose an interpretive tradition, indeed, a diversity of interpretive traditions and parties. Rabbinic Judaism came into being in this situation of interpretive ferment and conflict, and it is the rabbinic form of legal interpretation, theology, and piety that became normative Judaism between A.D. 70 and about A.D. 500.

What the rabbis (teachers) did was restate the body of divine law for a religious community lacking a temple, territory, and national institutions. The study of the Torah itself took the place of the sacrificial worship of the temple, and homelife became the primary locus of religious ceremony. The rabbinic traditions that performed the task of adaption were progressively set into written form. The oldest of these is a legal code, the Mishnah, which was subsequently expanded by commentary upon commentary into the Talmud (of which there are two recensions, the Babylonian and the Palestinian).

The interpretative tradition preserved in the Talmud and passed on orally over the centuries is not, as one might expect, a rigid, static, well-ordered system but an ongoing debate over rules and their theological rationale. The rabbis refused to foreclose the discussion even where one interpretation was favored. The process of reasoning itself was the most highly valued aspect of the tradition; in this the rabbis were true heirs of the unwritten law of pre-exilic Israel.

New Testament Criticism of the Emerging Tradition.   Both Jesus and Paul acknowledge the existence of a body of divine laws and shape their thinking in relation to this fact. Jesus affirms, according to the Gospel of Matthew, the timeless validity of the law:

> For truly, I say to you, till heaven and earth pass away, not an iota, not a dot, will pass from the law until all is accomplished. Whoever then relaxes one of the least of these commandments and teaches men so, shall be called least in the kingdom of heaven.   (5:18–19)

Paul likewise states forthrightly that "the law is holy, and the commandment is holy and just and good" (Rom. 7:12).

On the other hand, both Jesus and Paul challenge aspects of the Old Testament law and the interpretation given it by the various competing parties in first-century Judaism. Jesus develops a rather thorough and radical critique of the sacred law in the Sermon on the Mount and elsewhere. For one thing, when the law is equated with a body of rules, the trivial and the important are leveled. This is the import of a number of charges against scribes and Pharisees:

> You tithe mint and dill and cummin, and have neglected the weightier
> matters of the law, justice and mercy and faith; ... You ... [strain] out a
> gnat and [swallow] a camel!   (Matt. 23:23–24)

For another, the Mosaic Law contains compromises with evil. Moses
allowed for divorce, for example, but divorce is contrary to the will
of God:

> For your hardness of heart he wrote you this commandment. But from
> the beginning of creation, "God made them male and female." "For
> this reason a man shall leave his father and mother and be joined to his
> wife, and the two shall become one flesh." ... What therefore God has
> joined together, let not man put asunder.   (Mark 10:5–9)

Jesus would condemn anyone who relaxes the divine law of Scripture
but would qualify the law itself when it relaxes the will of God. In
the Sermon on the Mount, he surveys and radicalizes salient provisions of Old Testament law:

> You have heard that it was said, "An eye for an eye and a tooth for a
> tooth." But I say to you, Do not resist one who is evil.   (Matt. 5:38–39)

In other words, the principle of reciprocal justice is a compromise
with evil. The divine will infinitely surpasses the arrangements by
which human communities secure a tolerable justice and harmony.

Most of Paul's critique of the law is directed at its purpose rather
than its content, but he arrives at a position quite similar to that of
Jesus. He opposes justification by works of law with justification by
faith in Christ. This is an either/or: either one can accept the burden
of complying with the entire body of Old Testament law, or one can
accept the offer of divine righteousness made in the life, death, and
resurrection of Jesus Christ. For the Christian, the body of laws is no
longer obligatory. Jewish converts still may adhere to them to honor
a prior commitment, but Gentiles should not be circumcised and
made responsible for obedience to a set of rules belonging to a national order which has been superseded by the new order in Christ
(see his argument in Galatians 3–4).

While Paul rejects the authority of Old Testament law over Christians, he affirms unequivocally the validity of the divine law in other
passages (see Rom. 7:12 quoted above). Perhaps the solution to this

apparent contradiction in his thinking can be found in his reduction of the valid law to an essential core, the "moral law." When he has occasion to rehearse the content of the divine law, he cites prohibitions from the Ten Commandments (e.g., Rom. 13:9). It may be his intention that this core continue to claim the allegiance of the Christian while the rest would not. The precepts of the moral law themselves are validated by their logical dependence on the one all-encompassing law for Christians, the love commandment (so argues Rom. 13:8–10). It is on this commandment that attention will now be focused.

The Love Commandment in the Teaching of Jesus.   In a number of New Testament texts, the will of God for God's human creatures is summarized by the love commandment. This summary exercised great gravitational force in the early Christian tradition, so much so that it became known simply as the "new law of Christ," under which all moral and legal teaching could be subsumed. It also generated a corresponding theology of love: God is motivated by and manifests an unconditional love in God's dealings with human creatures.

In the paragraphs that follow, I will examine briefly the synoptic texts that enunciate the law of love. In this commandment, I believe, the New Testament has revived the understanding of divine law as an unwritten law. To substantiate this thesis, there must be evidence that the norm of love validates and relativizes the rules of law. It is also necessary to see that the norm of love is woven into the fabric of an actual community.

Biblical scholars and theologians have commonly sought to define the law of love by studying the Greek terms for love. The favored New Testament term for love, *agapē*, is often contrasted to *eros* and *philia*, between which some distinction can be made. *Eros* is a passionate desire for someone or something aroused by the object of love, while *philia* is the affection associated with friendship and family. Unfortunately, the term *agapē* is uncommon in nonbiblical Greek, so its actual use in the New Testament must be examined for its definition.

I will begin with the synoptic Jesus' enunciation of the commandment to love God and the neighbor. By "synoptic Jesus" I mean the personage rendered in the Gospels of Matthew, Mark, and Luke. It would be distracting and irrelevant to the purpose of this study to attempt to go behind the Gospels to the historical Jesus, for it is the New Testament account which has influenced history and which lays claim to the allegiance of the church today.

The Gospel of Mark is generally considered by critical scholars to be the oldest Synoptic Gospel and the source of any tradition shared with Matthew and Luke; hence, its version of the love commandment is a logical beginning. According to Mark 12:28–34, Jesus enunciates the love commandment during the final week of his life, which he spent in Jerusalem. A scribe approaches him in genuine curiosity and asks, "Which commandment is the first of all?" During the New Testament period, there was keen interest among Jewish scholars in the unifying principle of the law, and by "first of all" the scribe indicates his pursuit of this principle. Jesus answers by citing two passages of the Old Testament:

> "Hear, O Israel: The Lord our God, the Lord is one; and you shall love the Lord your God with all your heart, and with all your soul, and with all your mind, and with all your strength." (Deut. 6:4–5)

> The second is this, "You shall love your neighbor as yourself."
> (Lev. 19:18)

The quotation from Deuteronomy begins with a confessional statement affirming the unity and exclusive claim to deity of the biblical God. To such a one belongs the highest loyalty of every human. The commandment to love God with one's total being is a natural consequence of the confession of God's nature. Deuteronomy makes the commandment the summary and in effect fundamental principle of divine law, and Jesus simply reaffirms a scriptural teaching by citing it as the "first commandment."

The love commandment, however, is a *double* commandment. To describe a person's duties to other humans, Jesus cites a statement from the Holiness Code, thereby synthesizing themes of two different legal traditions into a complete summary of the law. In Leviticus 19:18 the commandment to love one's neighbor is set against seeking vengeance or hating fellow Israelites. The lawgiver, assuming that one is attached to oneself and seeks one's own best interests, posits the equal value of others. Leviticus 19:34 extends the duty to resident aliens among Israelites, hence surmounting ethnocentricity to a degree. When Jesus cites the Levitical commandment with the commandment to love God, he elevates it from being one commandment among others concerning relations within the community to an inclusive statement of duties to all human beings.

I have used the word *duty* to explicate the word *love*. To some people these terms may be antithetical, but this is not the case in the New Testament. The love commandment should not be sentimentalized. The very fact that it is commanded indicates that this love is not a spontaneous emotion but an act of will. To be sure, it is an affective state, a sentiment, but not a feeling detached from specific actions. Moreover, the emotive state of love may come and go, whereas the commandment demands constancy. Loyalty and loving concern must be integrated into all one's dealings, not wax and wane.

Though love is used to encompass duty to God and to the neighbor, loving the neighbor is not on a par with loving God. When Jesus commands the love of God, he is not suggesting that a human can enhance God's being or dignity. It is for the good of the human who loves and for God's cause in the world that one should love God, not for any good it might do God. The love of God is a total focus of one's life, an identification of the self with God's cause. The love of neighbor is actually included in the love of God, for human mutuality is God's cause. The neighbor is not a center for the self but one of equal value with the self under God. As an equal, the neighbor claims the same moral concern as does the self.

The scribe's response to Jesus' enunciation of the double commandment is noteworthy (Mark 12:32–33). He approves of Jesus' summary of the law and applies it to a theological issue of the day. One gets the impression that the scribe is saying, This is precisely the position that I have been arguing for years and I am delighted to find an ally. There is even a hint that Jesus and the scribe belong to a "school of thought."

The scribe draws out the implication of Jesus' teaching for cultic practice: "To love [God] . . . and to love one's neighbor . . . is much more than all whole burnt offerings and sacrifices" (vs. 33). The norm of love functions here as the basis for evaluating and critiquing the rules of law, a function reflecting a prophetic stream of Old Testament thought:

> For I [God] desire steadfast love and not sacrifice,
> the knowledge of God, rather than burnt offerings. (Hos. 6:6; also 1 Sam. 15:22; Ps. 51:16–17; and numerous other passages)

Jesus not only approves of this deduction from the love commandment, but he makes a quasi-judicial determination, "You are not far from the kingdom of God," which is an understated way of saying that the scribe is under the sway of the kingdom of God and participates in its order.

The use of the double commandment of love to devalue the cultic law indicates that it revives the understanding of divine law as an unwritten law. The cultic law is valid, now, only to the degree that it serves the love of God and neighbor, and it can be changed or replaced to serve the overriding principle.

Matthew 22:34–40 places the enunciation of the love commandment in a polemical setting. In the midst of the disputes of Jesus' final week, a lawyer of the Pharisaic party tests Jesus with the question, "Which is the great commandment in the law?" (vs. 36), by which is meant the unifying principle of the divine law. Jesus' answer is a slightly abbreviated form of the Markan version of the commandment, concluding with a very powerful theological assertion: "On these two commandments depend all the law and the prophets" (vs. 40). Following hints in Mark 12:31 and 33, Matthew has made the love commandment not only the most important commandment but also the logical basis of every expression of the divine will in Scripture and a norm by which every rule of law can be judged.

The relation of love to the rules and principles of divine law is more fully developed in the Sermon on the Mount. The section where this is done (Matt. 5:17–48) begins with the statement, already quoted, that Jesus does not intend any relaxation of the divine demands but rather their heightening. Then Jesus proceeds to cite Old Testament legal teaching and radicalize it:

(1) Not only should you not kill, but you should not be angry with any person.

(2) Not only should you not commit adultery, but you should not look at a woman with desire.

(3) Divorce was permitted under Mosaic Law, but in fact divorce makes the woman an adulteress.

(4) Not only should you not swear falsely, but you should not swear at all.

(5) The principle of equivalence (an eye for an eye ...) was enunciated in the Mosaic Law, but in fact you should not resist evil.

(6) Not only should you love your friends, but you should love your enemies.

These examples have as their common logic the idea that one must not only fulfill the requirements of justice but exceed them. The last example summarizes the section; it is not accidental that it is a version of the commandment to love the neighbor. It is also radical in requiring unreciprocated love. The spirit of justice and right that characterized the unwritten law of the Old Testament is surpassed in the new law of the kingdom, "Unless your righteousness exceeds that of the scribes and Pharisees, you will never enter the kingdom of heaven" (5:20).

The Sermon on the Mount does not have a section explicitly devoted to the love of God, but chapter 6, covering the religious life, has the commandment in the background. A basic principle is stated at the outset: your piety should not be a show to gain human honor but should be performed secretly for the glory of God. Another is stated later: "No one can serve two masters.... You cannot serve God and mammon" (Matt. 6:24). Any attempt to gain honor among humans or to make this life secure violates total devotion to God. Since total devotion to God is what is commanded in the love commandment, one can regard the teaching of Matthew 6 as the love of God drawn out to a radical extreme.

The Gospel of Luke appears to differ so substantially in its presentation of the love commandment that some scholars have doubted that its version is based upon the Markan passage. However, at a deeper level, one can discern substantive links with both of the passages examined. In Luke the summary of the law comes rather early in the ministry of Jesus (10:25–37) and as in Matthew is located in a polemical setting. A student of the law tests Jesus by asking a question in dispute among scholars: "What shall I do to inherit eternal life?" Although this sounds much different from the question concerning the first, or great, commandment, the questioner undoubtedly expects an answer enunciating the essential law. Jesus surprises him—and the reader—by asking a question that prompts him to answer his own question in an abbreviated version of Mark's double commandment. How surprising it is to have a gravitational center of New Testament teaching credited to someone other than Jesus, indeed to an opponent! Yet it is not quite so shocking if one remembers that Mark had the questioner approve of Jesus' answer. Luke is saying, in effect, that the Jewish community already knows the will of God; all that is needed further is to do it.

The questioner, however, is not finished. He insists on involving Jesus in a legal debate as to "who is my neighbor?", seeking an exposition of the second part of the love commandment. He expects Jesus to draw a circle—say, fellow Jews, or perhaps some larger community—around the scope of obligation. Again Jesus returns the question to the questioner, this time by telling a parable and then asking the questioner to judge who proved neighbor.

The parable is the famous one known as the Good Samaritan. A man is robbed and beaten on the road between Jerusalem and Jericho, and several travelers pass by before one comes to his aid. Now, Jesus says, who proved neighbor? The term *neighbor* has been altered in the question; it is no longer the person to whom one owes duties but the person who performs his duties to others. It is uncertain why Jesus inverted the term; it may be that he wanted to puncture the pride of the questioner. When one contemplates the neighbor as the one to whom a moral agent owes duties, there is a potential for pride in one's moral accomplishments. When the word *neighbor* is a value term equivalent to *merciful*, one is forced to admit a common humanity.

An important aspect of the parable is the identity of the travelers. Those who pass by the victim are a Jewish priest and a Levite, holy men from whom one would expect help. For whatever reason, they fail to meet the need. The one who does help is a member of a heretical Jewish sect toward whom Jews held much hard feeling. The student of the law thus is forced to acknowledge someone outside the people, indeed a religious "enemy," as the true neighbor. In its way, the parable agrees with Matthew's commandment to love your enemies (Matt. 5:43–48).

Jesus sends his questioner off with the exhortation to go and do likewise. At first glance, this seems odd, for the hearer has been forced into the role of victim who receives aid from an enemy. Surely one is not expected to offer oneself as a victim. Obviously, one is expected, rather, to show mercy to whoever is in need, including enemies. The hearers have been prepared to do this by putting themselves in the victim's shoes. When they see someone in need, they should love that person as themselves.

In its way this passage also advances the double love commandment as the unwritten law of God which validates and critiques all rules of law. It inverts all duties among humans by forcing the moral agent out of the pride of moral autonomy into an acknowledgment of the common humanity of actor and beneficiary. For the performance of moral duties to be genuine fulfillment of the law, it must be an expression of the love of neighbor as oneself.

In summary, the double love commandment revives an understanding of divine law as an unwritten law. It does so by reducing the law to a transcendent principle which rules of law must manifest to be valid and in relation to which all rules of law are relative.

The question remains as to whether the unwritten law of love is embodied in an actual community. It has already been noted that love stands in tension with the principles of justice and right forming the basis of Old Testament law. Neither Israel nor any other legal community operates according to the norm of self-sacrificial love. If the idea of an unwritten divine law is revived by Jesus, it is in a new form that exceeds the righteousness of any historical community.

The community to which the law of love belongs must be the kingdom of God, the center of Jesus' proclamation and ministry. In other words, love is the order of the "kingdom" which God will create in the new age. Yet the kingdom is not purely future in the message of Jesus. His first utterance in the Gospel of Mark is the keynote of all that he says and does: "The time is fulfilled, and the kingdom of God is at hand" (Mark 1:15a). The kingdom is future yet breaking forth in the present. People participate in it even now when they "repent, and believe in the gospel" (1:15b).

If the kingdom of God is present as well as future, the law of love which belongs to the order of the kingdom can make claims upon those living in history. When Jesus proclaims the commandment to love God with the totality of one's being and to love one's neighbor as oneself, he is offering an invitation to enter the order of the kingdom. Since life in historical communities is under the sway of a perverted and tenuous justice, those who practice love now are bound to suffer (note Matthew's Beatitudes, 5:3–12). Those who are under the sway of love must abandon their claim to rights in this age to receive them in the kingdom of God. "Whoever would save his life will lose it; and whoever loses his life for my sake and the gospel's will save it" (Mark 8:35).

The Love Commandment in John and Paul. It was said at the beginning of the last section that the love commandment exercised gravitational force in early Christian tradition. It behooves me to show at least that it makes an appearance outside the teachings of Jesus, and so I will deal briefly with the love commandment in the writings of two New Testament writers, John and Paul.

The Gospel of John might best be classified as a meditation on the story of Jesus Christ by an anonymous first-century preacher. In this work, love is not only the subject of commandment, but it is a theological description of God's action in Jesus Christ, of Jesus' action, and of the ethos of the believing community. The love commandment proper is a recurring theme in John 13:34–15:27, introduced as a "new" commandment:

> A new commandment I give to you, that you love one another; even as I have loved you, that you also love one another. By this all men will know that you are my disciples, if you have love for one another. (13:34–35)

The love commandment is hardly new in the sense of having never been uttered before; rather, it is new in the sense of being ever fresh and vital, the beginning of new life. It is also new in its basis of love for one another as an imitation of and a response to Jesus' love and the identification of his community as his. In 15:12–17 the love of Christ is said to be shown forth above all in his dying for his friends.

In the allegory developed in 15:1–11, another expression, "abide in my love," is introduced. Jesus' disciples will abide in his love, as he abides in his Father's love. Love seems to have been elevated to a substantial reality created by the action of the superior party (love of the Father for Christ, of Christ for his disciples). This might be compared to love within a family. The love between parents creates, as we say, a "loving environment" for the children to grow up in. The children entering this preexistent love receive love before they can reciprocate. As they mature, they can continue to participate in or withdraw from the loving environment. By analogy, the love between Father and Son creates a sphere of love which humans can enter (aptly called rebirth) and abide in. In Johannine thought, this love between Father and Son, which extends into the community of disciples, has replaced the kingdom of God proclaimed by the synoptic Jesus. The order of love entered human history in the incarnation and will abide forever (John 14:16).

Although the Gospel of John speaks profusely of God's love of the world, of Christ's love, and of love among the disciples, it is silent about loving outsiders and cautious about humans loving God. John seems to define love as being *between* persons. The commandment of love is never addressed to an individual follower but to the community as a group, who are related to "one another." Hence, there can be no love of outsiders, for outside there exists no "one another." Johannine literature seems to shy away from speaking of humans loving God because humans cannot give anything to God. 1 John 4:10 says outright, "In this is love, not that we loved God but that he loved us and sent his Son. . . ." God can and does give, but humans have a like capacity to give only to each other, not to God. Paradoxically, in 1 John 4:20 and 5:2 the author does speak of loving God as the basis for loving others, very much in the vein of the double love commandment of the Synoptic Gospels.

Paul's letters are the oldest writings in the New Testament. All but Romans were written to deal with specific situations in the life of the churches he had started. In the course of commending, encouraging, and disputing with his readers, he argues points of theology, church practice, and personal morality. The subject of the love commandment comes up now and again, but Paul develops it rather fully in three passages: 1 Corinthians 13, Galatians 5–6, and Romans 12–13.

1 Corinthians 13 is probably Paul's most famous statement on love and might be called a praise (encomium) of love, the supreme virtue of the Christian. The virtues of the religious life are useless without love, though commendable with it (vss. 1–3). Love is known by the spirit of service and respect and avoidance of self-exaltation and insensitivity (vss. 4–7). Spiritual gifts and knowledge will cease with the coming of the new age, but love together with faith and hope will endure (vss. 8–13). Love is the moral quality that must inform all the actions of the Christian because the Christian is living according to the order of the age to come.

Galatians 5–6 and Romans 12–13 treat love as a commandment rather than a virtue. Both propose the same basic thesis: the love commandment sums up the whole law, and loving fulfills the whole law (Gal. 5:14; Rom. 13:9–10). Paul's position is much like Matthew's (Matt. 22:40 in relation to Matt. 5:17–20). Both would affirm that love is the basis of all law and the norm by which every moral duty can be critiqued. The difference between them is a matter of emphasis. Matthew wants to affirm that the law is not abrogated by Christ but confirmed and radicalized; Paul prefers to stress the new freedom in Christ, allowing the Christian to judge according to a Spirit-instructed conscience as to what love prompts and prohibits.

In Galatians 5 Paul warns against yoking oneself to the Old Testament law. Gentile Christians should not be circumcised and thereby incur the duty to obey the written law. Justification by obeying the law is incompatible with justification by faith; either one endeavors to make oneself righteous by moral exertion, or one receives the gift of righteousness by believing. Faith does not license moral turpitude but "works through love" (vs. 6). It is a relationship with God which draws a person out of self-centeredness into God-centeredness and frees the self for others. Like John, Paul is shy about speaking of a human loving God. Faith takes the place, in Paul's thought, of love for God.

Paul tends to employ both the synoptic and Johannine versions of the love commandment. The statement in Galatians 5:13, "through love be servants of one another," expresses John's view that love belongs to a communal context where it is a reciprocal obligation. Paul supports this statement by citing the synoptic (and Levitical) version commanding love of neighbor. In Romans 12:9–13 and 14–21 he applies the love commandment in separate sections to life in the church and life in the world. Love within the church is constituent of the new order which the church seeks to embody; love in the outside world must suffer the disharmony between history and the new age, extending even to enemies and persecutors.

Paul follows the enunciation of the law of love with a contrast between the works of the *flesh*—a term he uses to designate life centered upon the self or other creatures—and the fruits of the Spirit. Even though Paul insists upon the freedom of the Christian from rules of law, moral prohibitions reappear here as symptoms of the perverted life. The fruits of the Spirit are the good works, exhibiting faith and love, that God empowers a believer to do. While Paul commands his readers to live the life of love, he nevertheless holds that any good work is to be ascribed not to the self but to God.

Romans 12:1–21 and 13:8–10 constitute the "exhortation" of Paul's most systematic statement of his theology, and it is quite significant that he summarizes his teaching in terms of love. As I have indicated, much of what he says here follows closely what he says in Galatians 5. In 13:8–10, he develops the idea that the love of neighbor "sums up" the commandments. In chapter 12, love is enunciated as the comprehensive law of the Christian life in verse 9a and explicated in two sections: verses 9b–13, life within the church, and verses 14–21, relations with outsiders.

Romans 12:1–2 can be interpreted as a rephrasing of the commandment to love God. Verse 1 adopts sacrificial language to express duty to God: "I appeal to you . . . to present your bodies as a living sacrifice, holy and acceptable to God, which is your spiritual worship." It is to be remembered that in Mark 12:32–34 the scribe speaking with Jesus draws the conclusion that love of God and neighbor is superior to sacrificial worship. In asking that one's life be made one's sacrifice, Paul's statement seems to be the extension of the scribe's conclusion; that is, Paul has translated love of God into perpetual self-sacrifice to God. Verse 2 speaks of a transformation of the self so that one can know and do the will of God. This sounds very much like a rephrasing of "with all your heart, ... soul, ... mind, ... strength" (Mark 12:30). If it is, Paul sees the centering of the self in the will of God as a transformation from a state of conformity with the present age.

Paul joins the other New Testament authors studied here in representing the love commandment as the summary and fulfillment of the divine law. By insisting upon the Christian's freedom from the yoke of Old Testament law, he endorses a view of God's will that I have called "unwritten law." That is, the transcendent principle of love for neighbor/one another is the source and measure of all duty. Although guidelines and examples of what love demands and excludes can be given, love surpasses every attempt to fix it and requires free, Spirit-instructed decision. Faith in God is the basis for true love of neighbor, for it centers life in God rather than the self.

Recapitulation

During the period in which the legal texts were being composed, the law of God was an unwritten law, that is, the principles and concepts constituting ancient Israel's understanding of justice and righteousness. The codes of judicial ethics show an inculcation of the sense of substantive justice; the examples of judicial deliberation reveal an argumentation from principles and concepts; and the series of commandments and legal codes exhibit qualities that indicate that they were formulated to inculcate the values of the legal community and instruct the judges in the process of legal reasoning.

When the Deuteronomic Law was adopted as the basis of Josiah's reform, a shift occurred in the understanding of divine law. The law became identified with the words of the text. Josiah is even praised for adhering to the letter of the lawbook. Although this new understanding of the law, which I called an ancient version of legal positivism, did not immediately take hold throughout the legal community, it triumphed finally in the canonization of the Torah.

With the emergence of an inviolable, unalterable text of divine law, there sprang up an interpretive tradition to justify, explain, extend, and adapt the written laws to the ongoing life of the community. In the New Testament era, Jewish interpretation was divided into several schools, and out of this debate arose the rabbinic tradition, preserved in the Talmud, which eventually won the day in Judaism.

The New Testament came into being in the same situation. Jesus and Paul both acknowledge and critique the existence of a written divine law and an oral tradition. The double commandment of love is a revival of an unwritten divine law that validated and critiqued all written law and interpretation. In distinction from the Old Testament law, love requires persons to surpass the principles of justice and righteousness in the name of a new humanity and a new world.

SUGGESTED READING

For the policy informing this selection, see the statement introducing the bibliography at the end of Chapter One. Much of what has been said in previous chapters stands in the background of my argument regarding the understanding of law in the Old Testament. The following works are of direct relevance.

Writings which provoked my reflection on Israel's understanding of the law:

Finkelstein, J. J. *The Ox That Gored.* Transactions of the American Philosophical Society, vol. 71, pt. 2. Philadelphia: The American Philosophical Society, 1981.

———. "Ammiṣaduqa's Edict and the Babylonian 'Law Codes'," *Journal of Cunei-form Studies* 15 (1961), pp. 91–104. An earlier presentation of his view.

Writings in the philosophy of law, particularly those describing the nature and method of English common law, have aided the formation of the concept of unwritten law. See the bibliography to Chapter One. The previously cited work by Hans Jochen Boecker, *Law and the Administration of Justice in the Old Testament and Ancient East*, contributes to an understanding of legal argumentation. An earlier monograph by Boecker is *Redeformen des Rechtslebens im Alten Testament*, Wissenschaftliche Monographien zum Alten und Neuen Testament, vol. 14 (Neukirchen-Vluyn: Neukirchener Verlag, 1964). Unfortunately not available in English, this work traces the course of legal process in Israel.

Studies which explore the philosophy of biblical law:

Harrelson, Walter J. *The Ten Commandments and Human Rights*. Overtures to Biblical Theology, vol. 8. Philadelphia: Fortress Press, 1981.

O'Connell, Matthew J. "The Concept of Commandment in the Old Testament," *Theological Studies* 21 (1960), pp. 351–403.

Works in German on philosophical aspects of biblical law:

Horst, Friedrich. "Recht und Religion im Bereich des Alten Testaments." In *Gottes Recht*, pp. 260–291. Theologische Bücherei, vol. 12. Munich: Chr. Kaiser Verlag, 1961.

Richter, Wolfgang. *Recht und Ethos*. Studien zum Alten und Neuen Testament, vol. 15. Munich: Kösel-Verlag, 1966.

Works on the formation of the canon from the written legal (and other) traditions:

Fishbane, Michael. *Text and Texture: Close Readings of Selected Biblical Texts*. New York: Schocken Books, 1979.

Noth, Martin, "The Laws in the Pentateuch: Their Assumptions and Meaning." In *The Laws in the Pentateuch and Other Studies*, trans. D. R. Ap-Thomas, pp. 1–107. Edinburgh and London: Oliver & Boyd, 1966.

Sanders, James A. *Torah and Canon*. Philadelphia: Fortress Press, 1972.

Chapter Seven introduces the subject of law in the New Testament. The following works provide a view of the situation in Judaism and the concept of law in the New Testament. Works covering the debate over the law in Judaism at the time of Jesus:

Davies, W. D. "Law in First-Century Judaism." In *The Interpreter's Dictionary of the Bible*, 5 vols., ed. George Arthur Buttrick and Keith Crim. Nashville and New York: Abingdon Press, 1962–76.

Finkelstein, Louis. *The Pharisees: The Sociological Background of Their Faith*. 3d ed., rev. 2 vols. Philadelphia: Jewish Publication Society of America, 1962.

Moore, George Foot. *Judaism in the First Centuries of the Christian Era: The Age of the Tannaim*. 3 vols. Cambridge: Harvard University Press, 1927.

Neusner, Jacob. *First-Century Judaism in Crisis*. Nashville and New York: Abingdon Press, 1975.

Works on the adaption of Judaism to its hellenistic cultural milieu:

Hengel, M. *Judaism and Hellenism: Studies in Their Encounter in Palestine During the Early Hellenistic Period*. 2 vols. Trans. John Bowden. Philadelphia: Fortress Press, 1974.

Tcherikover, Avigdor. *Hellenistic Civilization and the Jews*. Trans. S. Applebaum. New York: Atheneum Publishers, 1975.

An accessible contemporary translation of portions of the Mishnah with some commentary:

Lipman, Eugene J. (trans.). *The Mishnah: Oral Teachings of Judaism*. New York: Schocken Books, 1974.

Works introducing the Talmud, its legal doctrine, and its methods of reasoning:

Bokser, Ben Zion. *The Wisdom of the Talmud*. New York: Philosophical Library, 1951.

Feldman, David M. *Marital Relations, Birth Control, and Abortion in Jewish Law*. New York: Schocken Books, 1974.

Neusner, Jacob. *Invitation to the Talmud: A Teaching Book*. New York: Harper & Row, Publishers, 1973.

———— (ed.). *Understanding Rabbinic Judaism: From Talmudic to Modern Times*. New York: Ktav Publishing House, 1974.

Schechter, Solomon. *Aspects of Rabbinic Theology*. New York: Schocken Books, 1961.

Strack, Hermann. *Introduction to the Talmud and Midrash*. 5th ed. Philadelphia and Cleveland: Jewish Publication Society of America and Meridian Books, 1960.

The New Testament teaching on law in the context of Judaism:

Daube, David. *The New Testament and Rabbinic Judaism*. London: Athlone Press, 1956.

Davies, W. D. "Law in the NT." In *The Interpreter's Dictionary of the Bible*, 5 vols., ed. George Arthur Buttrick and Keith Crim, vol. 3, pp. 95–102. Nashville and New York: Abingdon Press, 1962–76.

General works on the life and teaching of Jesus:

Bornkamm, Günther. *Jesus of Nazareth*. Trans. Irene and Frazer McLuskey and James M. Robinson. New York, Evanston, and London: Harper & Row, Publishers, 1960.

Conzelmann, Hans. *Jesus*. Ed. John Reumann, trans. J. Raymond Lord. Philadelphia: Fortress Press, 1973.

A selection of studies of the legal teaching of the synoptic Jesus:

Barth, Gerhard. "Matthew's Understanding of the Law." In *Tradition and Interpretation in Matthew*, ed. Günther Bornkamm, trans. Percy Scott, pp. 58–164. Philadelphia: Westminster Press, 1963.

Branscomb, B. H. *Jesus and the Law of Moses*. New York: R. R. Smith, 1930.

Davies, William D. *The Setting of the Sermon on the Mount*. Cambridge: Cambridge University Press, 1977.

————. "Matthew 5:17–18." In *Mélanges bibliques rédigés en l'honneur de André Robert*, pp. 428–456. Paris: Bloud & Gay, 1957.

Grayston, K. "Sermon on the Mount." In *The Interpreter's Dictionary of the Bible*, 5 vols., ed. George Arthur Buttrick and Keith Crim, vol. 4, pp. 279–289. Nashville and New York: Abingdon Press, 1962–76.

Hamerton-Kelly, R. G. "Sermon on the Mount." In *The Interpreter's Dictionary of the Bible Supplementary Volume*, ed. Keith Crim, pp. 815–816. Nashville: Abingdon Press, 1976.

The law of love in the New Testament:

Furnish, Victor Paul. *The Love Command in the New Testament*. Nashville: Abingdon Press, 1972.

Perkins, Pheme. *Love Commands in the New Testament*. Ramsey, N.J.: Paulist Press, 1982.

Schottroff, Luise, Reginald H. Fuller, Christoph Burchard, and M. Jack Suggs. *Essays on the Love Commandment*. Ed. and trans. Reginald H. and Ilse Fuller. Philadelphia: Fortress Press, 1978.

A selection of studies of Paul's teaching on the law:

Beker, J. Christiaan. "The Enigma of the Law: Instrument of God or Servant of Sin?" In *Paul the Apostle: The Triumph of God in Life and Thought*, pp. 235–254 et passim. Philadelphia: Fortress Press, 1980.

Hübner, Hans. *Law in Paul's Thought*. Edinburgh: T. & T. Clark, 1982.

Sanders, E. P. *Paul and Palestinian Judaism: A Comparison of Patterns of Religion*. Philadelphia: Fortress Press, 1977.

Schoeps, H. J. "Paul's Teaching About the Law." In *Paul*, trans. Harold Knight, pp. 168–218. Philadelphia: Westminster Press, 1959.

On the subject of law, treated in all New Testament theologies:

Bultmann, Rudolf. *Theology of the New Testament*. 2 vols. Trans. Kendrick Grobel. New York: Charles Scribner's Sons, 1951–55. Vol. 1, pp. 259–269.

Conzelmann, Hans. *An Outline of the Theology of the New Testament*. Trans. John Bowden. New York and Evanston: Harper & Row, Publishers, 1969. Pp. 220–228.

Chapter Eight

LAW
AND
COVENANT

Whenever one studies law, sooner or later one encounters constitutional questions, which is to say, questions of authority and sovereignty. Who has authority to make law? How is authority distributed within the legal community? How is the duty to obey justified? We have in fact been dealing with these questions tangentially throughout this study. The identification of biblical law as divine law is a case in point. The lawbooks and series, with the exception of Deuteronomy, have Yahweh, the God of Israel, as speaker, and all assume that he alone has authority to make law in Israel. Moses is only a mediator who communicates what he has received from God. The judicial officials derive their authority to enforce the law from God, who is the supreme judge as well as lawgiver. Such a structure of authority can be called a theocratic constitution.

The biblical term for the Israelite constitution is *covenant* (Hebrew *berith*). The term is found in most of the accounts of the giving of law (Exod. 19:5; 24:7, 8; 31:16; 34:10, 27, 28; Lev. 24:8; 26:9, 15, 25, 44, 45; Deut. 4:13; 29:1, 21). The same term is employed in Scripture to designate a variety of other formal relationships: perpetual friendship (1 Sam. 23:18), political alliance (1 Kings 20:34), harmony between nature and humans (Hos. 2:18), association between God and an individual (Gen. 15:18) or a king (2 Sam. 23:5) as well as between God and Israel. These usages have in common a performative action instituting harmony and beneficial order between parties.

Several decades ago a number of biblical scholars thought they had discovered significant formal parallels to the covenant between Yahweh and Israel in documents recording international treaties.

These scholars held that the biblical material was similar to and modeled upon Hittite treaties of alliance between an emperor and his subject states, called suzerainty treaties or suzerain-vassal treaties.

This thesis, although still held by many scholars and taught in most textbooks, has been seriously challenged by subsequent studies. It has been pointed out that no one biblical text has all the component parts of a suzerainty treaty; the critic has to piece together passages from different sources to arrive at a complete form. Moreover, the biblical material does not really correspond in substance to the purported treaty parallels. Biblical law, for example, does not resemble the provisions of a treaty in form or content, for treaties govern relations between states, whereas biblical law governs relations within a state. Such flaws vitiate the treaty thesis and prompt me to leave it out of the exposition of the covenant texts.

The search for parallel forms among ancient Near Eastern texts has not turned up anything to replace the suzerain-vassal treaty. Perhaps future investigation will discover new formal parallels to the covenant traditions or solve the problems with the identification of the covenant as a treaty. Until that time, a general categorization and a careful analysis of the structure of the covenant texts must suffice.

The texts recount the execution of a performative act, which consists of verbal statements, perhaps accompanied by solemn gestures, that create the state of affairs described. When a person with the proper authority gives someone a name, that is henceforth the person's name; when a person in authority commands someone, the one commanded is duty-bound to obey. Making a promise is a performative act in that the promisor is bound to pursue a course of action, and the actions of the promisee can be predicated upon the certainty that the course of action will be pursued.

The making of a covenant was a formal act of promising between parties. Each party obligated itself to order its actions in a way consistent with the relationship between them. Sometimes specific duties were enunciated in a covenant; sometimes simply loyal friendship and peace were the terms. Sometimes sanctions for noncompliance were stated, and sometimes they were implicit or indefinite. In all cases, the act of making a covenant created the situation of mutual obligation the covenant described.

The covenant between Yahweh and Israel formally established a relationship in which Yahweh was Israel's God, and Israel was Yahweh's people. The relationship was mutually exclusive: Yahweh would not become the God of another people, and Israel would not recognize other gods. Within the relationship, Yahweh possessed the requisites of sovereignty, namely, the power to command and enforce his commands, and Israel obligated its members to obey. The people of Israel became subjects of a divine sovereign and reaped the benefits of being so favored.

In the following three sections, I will identify the accounts of covenant making in Exodus through Deuteronomy and follow this up with an examination of the structure of the covenant texts.

The Accounts of Covenant Making

It is necessary to recognize that the literature recounting what happened at Sinai and later on the plain of Moab is a combination of the work of authors from different times and places. This fact is well established in critical biblical scholarship. Although the division of a text into sources may be disturbing and confusing to the casual reader, it is a great help to those who read the Bible closely. The Sinaitic narrative is disjointed, uneven, inconsistent, and overfilled; and its large-scale sequences can only be grasped, paradoxically, by breaking it up into separate, coherent strands. The editors who combined the separate accounts, in seeking to preserve all witnesses to what happened at this moment of extreme importance in Israel's history, were willing to sacrifice narrative coherence for what was to them a higher value. While grateful to them for their conservatism, the reader must to some degree reverse the process of amalgamation to grasp sequences and concepts.

The account of what happened at Sinai runs from Exodus 19 to Numbers 10. The preponderance of this material belongs to the author known as the Priestly writer (P), who wrote during the Babylonian exile (587–450 B.C.), drawing on the traditions of the priests of the Jerusalem temple. To P can be ascribed Exodus 19:1–2b; 24:15–31:17; 35:1–40:38, all of Leviticus (counting the Holiness Code, Lev. 17–26, as a part of P), and Numbers 1:1–10:28. The narrative that remains after subtracting P is the older

Sinaitic account—Exodus 19:2c—24:14; 31:18—34:35; and Numbers 10:29–36.

This older account contains the portions of the story with which the average person is most familiar. The people arrive at Sinai and prepare for a theophany. God appears amidst spectacular disruptions in nature and proclaims the Ten Commandments. In fear the people elect Moses as mediator, and he ascends the mountain to receive a lawbook (the Book of the Covenant). He returns and reads aloud the laws, receives a pledge of obedience from the people, and guides them through a covenant ratification ceremony. Then he and a delegation of elders ascend the mountain for a theophanic meal. Moses ascends the mountain again to receive the tablets of the Ten Commandments, rebellion breaks out in camp, he returns, shatters the tablets in anger, and institutes a variety of punishments. Just as it seems that Israel is about to leave Sinai, Moses is again upon the mountain before Yahweh; he requests and receives a personal theophany, at which time another covenant is struck and more commandments are proclaimed. Moses returns to the camp and, after much consternation over the radiance of his face, proclaims the commandments to the people.

This older Sinaitic account is obviously a composite of at least two strands, probably four. The two sources recognized by most critical scholars are the Yahwist (J) and Elohist (E). The Yahwist derives from the period of the united monarchy (c. 1000–930 B.C.), from the milieu of the Davidic royal court; the Elohist can be traced to the Northern Kingdom from the middle of the ninth century. I believe that the additional strands of a narrative framework attached to the Book of the Covenant and an independent story of rebellion during Moses' absence can also be isolated.

It will not be necessary to divide the older Sinaitic account into its component sources here. In examining the structure of the texts, I will employ a paradigmatic form to which all adhere and contribute. Throughout this section examples will be drawn from the three main sources identified, but I will not confuse the reader by identifying each passage by source. The intent is to identify not the nuances of each source but the basic structure and concepts informing the oldest level of the Sinaitic tradition.

The Priestly account of the events on Sinai relates the construction of the portable sanctuary (tabernacle) and the arrangement of the camp. In Exodus 25—31 Moses receives the blueprints for the sanctuary, and in 35—40 it is constructed. Leviticus 1—10 outlines the sacrifices to be offered there and recounts the installation of its priests. Leviticus 11—15 provides rules for keeping the sanctuary and surrounding camp free from ritual contamination, and chapter 16 institutes a festival for removing whatever contamination has occurred. Then follows the promulgation of the Holiness Code (Lev. 17—26/27), which functions within the narrative to shape the ritual and moral life of the holy people. With the timeless structure of the people of God now set forth, they are ready to depart; Numbers 1—10 records a census and establishes the order for marching and camping.

It is noteworthy that P has no story of the act of covenent making proper. Some scholars believe that the Abrahamic covenant (Gen. 17) was the only covenant making with Israel in the original Priestly narrative; others speculate that this episode was dropped during editing in favor of the older Sinaitic version. In either case, P now relies upon the older account to put the covenant in force. It contributes to Sinaitic tradition the idea that Israel was a religious community with a sanctuary and ritual at its center.

The book of Deuteronomy must also be included among the covenant accounts. To be sure, it does not recount, except in retrospect, the events at Sinai nor the beginning of the national community, but it can be regarded as a "renewal" of the covenant by the first generation that was not present at Sinai (called "Horeb" in Deuteronomy). Deuteronomy's law harks back to the Ten Commandments and the Book of the Covenant, and the sermons that introduce the lawbook (viz., Deut. 6—11) are constructed from the liturgical formulas and concepts of the older Sinaitic account.

Deuteronomy is commonly broken into two sources: the original document with sermons, law, and concluding blessings and curses; and the narratives that set the original in a historical context. The author of the original is designated the Deuteronomist (D); the narrator, the Deuteronomistic Historian (Dtr.). It is the latter author who specifically designates the event as a covenant renewal (Deut. 29:1). The assembly on the Plain of Moab is the first of a series of covenant-making events that reenact and renew the covenant made at Sinai.

The accounts of covenant making and renewal are, taken together, valuable testimony to views of the covenant from various periods and locations. Israel's constitutional history from the period of the Judges through the monarchy down into the Exile is telescoped into this combined account. When one examines it for constitutional theory, one is able to reconstruct not just the understanding of one period or group but a complex of theory fused together to form the comprehensive constitution of the people of Israel.

The Structure of the Older Covenant Texts

To describe the structure—the "logical architecture" of the relationship created by the act of covenant making—of the older Sinaitic covenant texts, one needs to look carefully at its leading conceptual components: the roles of the parties entering into covenant, Yahweh and Israel; the function of the proclamation of law within the covenant-making act; and the act of ratification.

The Identification and Authority of Yahweh. The statements concerning Yahweh in the covenant texts (1) identify him by name and describe his character and (2) grant him authority to command this people and enforce his commands.

(1) The proclamation of the divine name is accentuated in several texts (Exod. 20:2; 34:6). In 34:6–7, after a repeated declaration of his name, a description of Yahweh's moral character reveals

> a God merciful and gracious, slow to anger, and abounding in steadfast love and faithfulness, keeping steadfast love for thousands, forgiving iniquity and transgression and sin, but who will by no means clear the guilty, visiting the iniquity of the fathers upon the children and the children's children, to the third and the fourth generation.

By such self-description, Yahweh testifies to his own worthiness to be Israel's God and at the same time projects what can be expected of him in that capacity. The declaration endeavors to strike a balance between severity and graciousness, enhancing the majesty of the law by assuring punishment, yet affirming Yahweh's freedom over strict justice. Exodus 20:2 is God's self-introduction, by name, and auto-biographical identification:

> I am Yahweh your God, who brought you out of the land of Egypt, out of the house of bondage.

This historical recollection both identifies God and reveals God as gracious and effective. God has proven worthy of Israel's loyalty and obedience and can be counted on to act in the same way in the future.

Recollection of Yahweh's deeds also identifies him in Exodus 19:4:

> You have seen what I did to the Egyptians, and how I bore you on eagles' wings and brought you to myself.

This may be called a *demonstration formula* ("You have seen . . .") in that the events mentioned testify to Yahweh's power over foes and his care for this people. He is worthy to be Israel's God and can be trusted to manifest the same character in the future. The future itself takes the place of past history in one passage:

> Before all your people I will do marvels, such as have not been wrought in all the earth or in any nation; and all the people among whom you are shall see the work of Yahweh; for it is a terrible thing that I will do with you. (Exod. 34:10)

In this demonstration formula, Yahweh's identity is, as it were, outstanding, yet to be demonstrated. The people must accept him on faith.

The various theophanies themselves play a central role in identifying the divine partner to the covenant. This is implicit throughout the Sinaitic account and made explicit several times. The Book of the Covenant begins with a demonstration formula referring to the theophany to the people:

> You have seen for yourselves that I have talked with you from heaven. (20:22)

Yahweh's vocal manifestation demonstrated his reality and his concern for Israel. When the seventy elders are allowed to see their God, they come away with a conviction of God's sublimity and favor toward them (24:10–11). The divine appearance to Moses exemplifies the freedom of God's grace:

> I will be gracious to whom I will be gracious, and will show mercy on whom I will show mercy. (33:19)

When Moses receives this demonstration of divine favor, he pleads that like favor be shown the people henceforth (34:9).

(2) The covenant texts establish Yahweh's right to command Israel and to enforce his commands. In Exodus 19:3b–8, Yahweh offers his covenant on the condition that the people will acknowledge his authority:

> If you will obey my voice and keep my covenant, you shall be . . . (vs. 5)

The people accept this offer by pledging to obey him:

> All that Yahweh has spoken we will do. (vs. 8)

This exchange establishes the sovereignty of Yahweh over the people of Israel.

No other text is so explicit in granting Yahweh authority, but numerous texts assume his prerogative to command Israel. In both the Decalogue in Exodus 20:1–17 and the commandments in 34:10–27, Yahweh establishes his authority simply by exercising it. The section following the Decalogue interprets God's fearful theophany to the people as the engendering of respect for the law and the lawgiver:

> Do not fear; for God has come to prove you, and that the fear of him may be before your eyes, that you may not sin. (Exod. 20:20)

The conclusion of the commandments in 34:10–27 declares them to be the implementation of the relationship:

> In accordance with these words [commandments] I have made a covenant with you [Moses] and with Israel. (34:27)

The covenant texts do not distinguish between Yahweh's authority to command and his authority to enforce his commands. It was undoubtedly assumed that the one entailed the other. Israel is warned now and again of Yahweh's punishment for wrongdoing, as in Exodus 34:7, where he is described as a judge "who will by no means clear the guilty, visiting the iniquity of the fathers upon the children."

The Status and Vocation of Israel.   The human party to the covenant is promised a unique standing before God if they will acknowledge God's authority over them. This unique standing can be called Israel's *status*, and their obligation, Israel's *vocation*. The classic statement of election and covenant is Exodus 19:5–6:

> Now therefore, if you will obey my voice and keep my covenant, you shall be my own possession among all peoples; for all the earth is mine, and you shall be to me a kingdom of priests and a holy nation.

Yahweh offers to single out Israel as uniquely his own. As owner of the entire earth, he has the right to dispose of all peoples according to his pleasure; hence, he is justified in setting a people aside as a "private treasure." This special relationship to the Lord of the earth is Israel's status. Their vocation is indicated by the pair of designations, "kingdom of priests" and "holy nation." Each combines a political and a religious term to indicate Israel's peculiar character—a political entity with Yahweh as their ruler, in other words, a theocracy. The conditional clauses at the head of the passage stipulate that being Yahweh's kingdom involves obedience to his commands. The duty to obey is simply the reverse side of being a political entity under divine rule.

Other covenant texts conceptualize Israel's unique status and vocation somewhat differently. The dialogue between Moses and Yahweh in Exodus 33:12–16 turns upon the divine presence in Israel's midst. When Yahweh assures Moses, "My presence will go with you, and I will give you rest" (vs. 14), Moses responds:

> If thy presence will not go with me, do not carry us up from here. For how shall it be known that I have found favor in thy sight, I and thy people? Is it not in thy going with us, so that we are distinct, I and thy people, from all other people that are upon the face of the earth?   (vss. 15–16)

This text accentuates Israel's cultic identity in distinction from the more political conception of Exodus 19:5–6. Israel is like a sanctuary in the midst of a profane world. No explicit mention is made of Israel's vocation. Exclusive recognition of Yahweh and obedience to his will are demanded in associated covenant texts (Exod. 34:14, 17, 27), but these texts are not directly linked to the presence of Yahweh in the midst of the people. Exodus 33:12–16 implies that Israel must be able to bear Yahweh's holy presence (cf. Exod. 34:9; 33:1–3).

The account of a theophany to seventy elders in conjunction with a meal (Exod. 24:9–11) also makes the divine presence a clue to Israel's status. Nothing is said specifically of Israel's uniqueness in this passage, but the human party is granted an audience with "the God of Israel," who graciously protects them from the harmful effects of seeing God. Again, Israel's vocation is not explicitly described.

The covenant texts speak of the human party, the people of Israel, as though already constituted as a collective entity. On further reflection, however, one realizes that the very act of entering the covenant constitutes them as a people. Their common loyalty to Yahweh and acknowledgment of his sovereignty binds them together. Without a focus of loyalty and locus of authority, the group is no more than a collection of individuals and families. Thus, the act of covenant making not only establishes a relationship between God and a people but creates a people to be in that relationship.

The Function of Law Giving in Covenant Making.   Each of the strands of the older Sinaitic narrative contains a legal text. Critical scholars have often argued that law and narrative do not belong together, but the case is not compelling. A logic can be discerned for the proclamation of law within the act of covenant making. Specifically, the proclamation of law is (1) an exercise of Yahweh's authority and (2) an institution of the moral and legal order necessary for establishing and maintaining community.

(1) In announcing his law, Yahweh exercises the authority of lawgiver granted him by the covenant and binds his subjects to an actual order of justice and right. This proposition can be inferred from the order of passages in Exodus 19–24: in response to the offer of a covenant with Yahweh, the people agree to obey him in principle (Exod. 19:8); then the law is communicated (chs. 20–23) and read to the people (Exod. 24:3), after which they again pledge to obey Yahweh. Thus, Yahweh exercises the authority to give law granted to him in principle and elicits a second acknowledgment of

his authority after the people learn what he expects. The other covenant texts do not distinguish between authority in principle and its exercise but simply have God establish authority by exercising it.

(2) For what purpose is divine law proclaimed? It will be recalled that much of the law in the older series and lawbook can be classified as moral suasion, and the rest as exercises in legal reasoning. The proclamation of legal texts serves to inculcate the values, norms, principles, and concepts of the divine law governing the people of God. The conscience of the community is instructed in the justice and right expected by its ruler.

The purpose of the unwritten divine Law to which the written law testifies is to establish peace and justice in the people of God. As the focus of loyalty, Yahweh draws the community together; as the locus of authority, he weaves justice and right into the fabric of the social order for its good.

Yahweh not only commands the law but promises to enforce it, acting through the community's judicial officials and as a supplement to them. In singling out the guilty for punishment, he acts for the benefit of the people as a whole. His punishment lends majesty to the law and heals the breaches in the community caused by violators.

Theologically stated, the law is a gift of grace, not a condition for it. Yahweh imposes his law to establish harmony and justice among his subjects. His commandments are of a piece with his saving acts, for both create community. By obedience to the commandments, the people are conformed to the social order already established among them. Acts of disobedience which tear at this order must be countered by punishment to mend the fabric of community.

The Ratification of the Covenant.   As a formal act of promising, covenant making involves a performative act of putting the promises into effect, of binding the parties to their word. The technical term for such a performative act is *an act efficacious in form*, meaning that the expression of certain words and gestures, usually established by custom (like shaking hands or signing a document), *effects* the relationship between the parties. In the following paragraphs, I will identify the efficacious acts depicted in the covenant texts and draw implications for the concept of covenant.

Exodus 19:8 has the people accept Yahweh's offer of the covenant relationship by pledging to obey him. This utterance itself could be a binding declaration, but the related text in Exodus 24:3–8 has the people pledge obedience twice in a ritualized context which enhances the solemn, sacred force of the words. The people are not fully bound to their word until blood is sprinkled upon them with words declaring the covenant to be in effect:

> Behold the blood of the covenant which Yahweh has made with you in accordance with all these words.   (24:8)

It should be noted that this text is the most democratic ritual of ratification in the tradition. The people are allowed to assent explicitly to entrance into covenant. Their word, in conjunction with the sacrifices and blood rite, conveys them into relationship with Yahweh.

The account in Exodus 34 stands at an opposite extreme. Yahweh puts the covenant into effect unilaterally:

> And [Yahweh] said, "Behold, I make a covenant. . . . In accordance with these words I have made a covenant with you and with Israel." (34:10, 27)

Neither Moses nor the people have been given the opportunity to assent or any other role in ritual ratification. Indeed, Exodus 34 has no account of a ritual beyond the proclamation of the covenant (34:32), for the solemnity and efficacy of Yahweh's word needs nothing to enhance it. The one point of agreement between the two accounts of ratification is that the act of obligating Israel to obey Yahweh's law puts the covenant relationship into effect. In fact, both accounts describe the covenant in virtually identical words: "Yahweh has made a covenant with you [Israel] in accordance with these words [law]."

Exodus 24:9–11 is the other ratification ritual in the older Sinaitic narrative. The action is a sacred meal, eaten by seventy elders representing the people, at which the elders are allowed to see God. One may surmise that the conjunction of the meal, signifying the solidarity of the human community, and the gracious audience with the "God of Israel" puts the covenant relationship into effect. The broad participation in such a unique and exclusive event betokens a democratic spirit, though the human party does not explicitly own their God. This last ratification ceremony differs from the other two by its startling silence regarding Israel's duty to obey their God. The sacred bond established by theophany, rather than a formalization of sovereignty, gives efficacy to the promises.

None of the older accounts of ratification make express provision for the breach of covenant. Obviously no provision would or could be made for divine breach (though divine breach of covenant is the subject of a number of laments, e.g., Ps. 44). On the other hand, provision for Israel's collective disobedience is expected. The covenant-making accounts do issue threats to those who violate the divine law, but nothing is said of the dissolution of the *community's* relationship to God. God will enforce divine law against members of the community for the benefit of the community as a whole, but the possibility of collective guilt and punishment is at most implicit in the older covenant texts. It clearly is not a source of motivation for obedience.

The Structure of the Priestly and Deuteronomic Covenant

The writings of P and D, rather than presenting specific covenant texts, disperse covenant language and concepts in narrative, sermon, and law. Both documents will be examined for evidence of the structural components identified .in the older covenant texts. The treatment is only extensive enough to confirm continuities and fully draw points of discontinuity.

The Identification and Authority of Yahweh.

The Priestly Source does not recount an act of covenant making between Yahweh and Israel at Mount Sinai. Hence, it lacks formal declarations of Yahweh's name, character, and deeds. On the other hand, it gives God's self-identification in the covenant with Abraham (Gen. 17:1) in a similar form and includes both a self-introduction and a covenant formula in the call of Moses:

> I am Yahweh. . . . I will take you for my people, and I will be your God. (Exod. 6:2, 7)

The Holiness Code employs the self-introduction formula with legal passages. In Leviticus 19, for example, "I am Yahweh (your God)" concludes practically every legal paragraph (vss. 4, 10, 12, 14, 18, 25, 28, 30, 31, 32, 34, 37). The formula is probably intended as a reinforcement of the commandments, reminding the people of the divine majesty behind the law. The statement "You shall be holy; for I Yahweh your God am holy" (Lev. 19:2), which gives the Holiness Code its name, also recalls the identification of the divine partner of the covenant.

The sermons of Deuteronomy transpose the formal declarations identifying the divine party to the covenant into a loose, homiletical form. Exodus 34:6–7 (and 20:5–6), for example, in Deuteronomy becomes:

> Know therefore that Yahweh your God is God, the faithful God who keeps covenant and steadfast love with those who love him and keep his commandments, to a thousand generations, and requites to their face those who hate him, by destroying them. . . . You shall therefore be careful to do the commandment . . . which I command you this day. (Deut. 7:9–11)

The identification of the divine partner of the covenant has been modified to support a call for obedience. The author does much the same thing with the recitation of Yahweh's deeds.

The Status and Vocation of Israel.   The Priestly Source lacks a formal declaration of the status and vocation of Israel in the Sinaitic account. However, P enunciates the covenant formula in its call of Moses (Exod. 6:7a), and the concepts and homiletical statements of the Holiness Code and Priestly Law conform to traditions in the older Sinaitic account. P's idea that Yahweh dwells among his people in the portable shrine resembles the theology of Exodus 33:12–16. Yahweh's dwelling among them sets Israel apart from the nations of the world (compare Lev. 18:3, 24–30; 20:23–26). Their vocation is to be holy like their God (Lev. 19:2).

The introductory sermons of Deuteronomy describe Israel's status and vocation in terms very similar to Exodus 19:5–6:

> For you are a people holy to Yahweh your God; Yahweh your God has
> chosen you to be a people for his own possession, out of all the peoples
> that are on the face of the earth.   (Deut. 7:6)

There is a slight terminological variation, but the basic structure
of the Exodus prototype seems to be retained: Israel has the status
of Yahweh's treasured possession and the vocation of being his
holy community. There is one important difference between
Deuteronomy and the Exodus prototype. The Deuteronomic
Moses refers to Israel's status and vocation as already in effect;
moreover, their status is the object of the verb *choose*, with
Yahweh as subject. In other words, Israel's status and vocation
are not entered into by an act of covenant making in the present
but were created by Yahweh in past history.

The Function of the Law.   As in the older account, the proclamation of the law in the Priestly Law and Holiness Code is an
exercise of the authority of the divine party to the covenant. This
logic can be discerned in sequences of homiletic statements like Leviticus 18:2–5:

> Say to the people of Israel, I am Yahweh your God. You shall not do as they
> do in the land of Egypt . . . Canaan. . . . You shall do my ordinances and
> keep my statutes and walk in them. I am Yahweh your God.

The self-identification of God is the reason for obeying the law and
indicates that the law is an exercise of God's authority.

Deuteronomy couches the proclamation of law in the address of
the human leader, Moses, so it is not literally an exercise of divine
sovereignty. Nor does Moses exercise sovereignty; rather, he assumes
the role of a teacher and preacher who is re-presenting the law
promulgated by God in the past.

Deuteronomy speaks for both traditions and the older sources as
well when it ascribes a beneficial purpose to the law:

> And now, Israel, what does Yahweh your God require of you, but to fear
> Yahweh your God, to walk in all his ways, to love him, to serve Yahweh
> your God with all your heart and with all your soul, and to keep the com-
> mandments and statutes of Yahweh, which I command you this day for
> your good?   (Deut. 10:12–13)

The divine law is God's provision for a just and righteous community, and the obedience required of its members completes God's saving work.

The Holiness Code and Deuteronomy also know of God's law as a potential source of communal judgment and warn explicitly of curses befalling the entire people for disobedience (Lev. 26; Deut. 28). Such curses presuppose a concept of collective guilt for mass violations, such as apostasy and institutional corruption, or for serious offenses of individuals which escape judicial and cultic remedy. Undoubtedly the concept of collective guilt has much older roots, but it reaches theological conceptualization only in this later covenant tradition material. When it does, the law becomes a two-edged sword: it is a saving gift for peace and justice in the community, but it is also the norm against which the community can be judged from on high.

From Ratification to Renewal.   Neither D nor HP has accounts comparable to the acts of ratification in the older Sinaitic accounts. I propose the thesis that D and HP replace ratification with a call for renewed resolve to fulfill the demands of the covenant. Consider Deuteronomy 26:17–19:

> You have declared this day concerning Yahweh that he is your God, and that you will walk in his ways, and keep his statutes and his commandments and his ordinances, and will obey his voice; and Yahweh has declared this day concerning you that you are a people for his own possession, as he has promised you, and . . . that he will set you high above all nations that he has made, in praise and in fame and in honor, and that you shall be a people holy to Yahweh your God, as he has spoken.

If one can penetrate these ponderous and overloaded phrases, one finds the makings of a ratification ritual in which each partner owns the other. Israel says, "Yahweh is our God (literally, *is to us God*), and we will walk in his ways, etc."; and Yahweh says, "You are to me a people of treasured possession, etc." Such a dialogic ceremony clearly recalls Exodus 19:3–8; 24:3–8. Even the key designations of Israel's status and vocation echo those of Exodus 19:5–6. In both, too, the pledge to obey Yahweh identifies Yahweh as the ruler of this people.

It must be admitted, however, that the pledge to obey is much expanded in Deuteronomy and has practically smothered the declarations of belonging. Such is the trend of Deuteronomic thought—that the relationship between Yahweh and Israel is not really entered into in the present but is renewed, at the most. D seeks renewed resolve to obey the law in force prior to the declarations made here.

Deuteronomy does not end with this formal renewal of resolve but continues on into the blessings and curses of chapter 28. The purport of the entire Deuteronomic address is to persuade the present generation of Israel to choose life rather than death, to redouble their efforts to obey Yahweh before it is too late. They owe him a debt of gratitude for their election and the good things he has bestowed and therefore should fear the consequences of breaking the covenant into which they were born.

The Holiness Code also concludes with blessings and curses (Lev. 26). Its author in like manner seeks to motivate the people by appealing to their desire to remain in Yahweh's favor and their fear of punishment. In distinction from Deuteronomy 28, the curses of Leviticus 26 are arranged sequentially and continue through exile to repentance and rebirth. The chapter was probably drafted after the Exile to urge the people to repentance. If so, it is comparable to the call to repentance in Deuteronomy 30:1–10, which was added to the basic stock of Deuteronomy by the Deuteronomistic Historian.

The Priestly Source has no account of covenant making at Sinai but does recount earlier acts involving Noah and Abraham. In these accounts, P alters the common Hebrew expression *cut a covenant,* or *strike a covenant, (make a covenant* in RSV) to *establish a covenant* (Gen. 9:9; 17:7). This altered phrasing suggests a unilateral act of God (compare Exod. 34:10, 27). If the Abrahamic covenant is the only covenant making in P between God and the people, it can be inferred that P understood the covenant relationship to have already been put in force by God before the communal order was founded at Sinai. Thus, P agrees with D that Israel should renew their resolve to conform to an order established in the past.

To summarize, the older Sinaitic accounts depict acts that put the promises into effect, while the later documents seek to renew resolve to obey the law already in force in Israel. The older traditions portray the giving of law as Yahweh's exercise of authority to establish peace and justice among his people, while the Deuteronomic Law and Holiness Code offset the law's saving purpose with its potential to provoke judgment. All covenant traditions share language and concepts describing the partners of the relationship, but the early Sinaitic sources have the roles come into being in the very act of covenant making, whereas D and HP assume the roles derive from the past action of God.

A New Covenant

The Jewish synagogue can lay claim to the covenant between God and Israel at Sinai, but the Christian church must venture its claim to the covenant via a "new" covenant ratified in the death of Jesus Christ. The idea of a new covenant is already embedded in the history of the Sinaitic covenant. This newness is then raised up into the promise of a future covenant in the prophetic message.

The New in the Covenant. The idea of newness inheres in the act of covenant making. To make a covenant is to begin a relationship that did not exist before and make promises toward a future of unlimited duration. The accounts of covenant making may betoken ceremonies held at regular or irregular intervals in which a "new" covenant was made between Yahweh and Israel to consolidate a new arrangement. Joshua 24, above all, recounts an event that sounds very much like the initiation of a new constitution incorporating hitherto unrelated tribes and traditions and establishing a center for the new organization.

The tradition as it comes to us has tended to subsume the new covenants under renewal of the covenant made at Sinai. This is understandable, for every new covenant was between the same parties, was executed in the awareness of the earlier event, and was modeled upon earlier traditions. The newness of each act of covenant making tended to be forgotten as time went on, and the traditions from various covenants gravitated to the event at Sinai. Eventually the covenant making at Sinai was elevated to a once-for-all event establishing a permanent relationship between Yahweh and his people. Since more than one such timeless event was impossible, all other acts of covenant making were reduced to the status of renewals.

The adaptability of the covenant tradition is also a token of newness. The capacity of the covenant to continue as a constitutional framework for the people of Israel through changing political structures reveals a dynamic, self-surpassing quality. In the period beginning with Moses and ending with Saul and David, covenants between Yahweh and Israel functioned as the political constitution for a theocratic community, Israel. Yahweh was the focus of loyalty and locus of authority in a loose confederation of clans and tribes.

With the advent of the monarchy, the covenant lost a measure of its direct political import and became a framework for legitimating and critiquing monarchical power. The king ruled a territorial state loyal to him and under his authority. For legitimation he claimed Yahweh's election; those who were loyal to Yahweh should be loyal to his anointed. However, the priority of the covenant between Yahweh and Israel limited a king's claim to loyalty and restricted his authority in the realm of law to that of an appeals judge and administrator (compare Jehoshaphat's administrative innovations, 2 Chron. 19:8–11).

When the people split into two kingdoms, a dual constitution emerged—Israel, the people of Yahweh, and the two kingdoms, Israel and Judah. A citizen of either kingdom was also a member of the people of Yahweh; the potential for conflicts of loyalty is obvious. Each kingdom claimed to embody the people of Yahweh, but each had to acknowledge that the neighboring kingdom could also make such a claim. The division of the kingdom of God into two kingdoms was a built-in check on royal pretensions.

The next period of constitutional history begins with the fall of the Northern Kingdom and ends with the exile of Judah. On the one hand, the fall of the Northern Kingdom allowed Judah to identify itself as the people of God and its king as God's sole ruler. On the other, it reinforced the prophetic message of doom. Deuteronomy addresses this situation. For its author, the covenant relationship was secured in the past, and the present is the occasion for renewing resolve to abide by it—the future of the people of Israel hangs in the balance. In reformulating the law and covenant for this moment of crisis, D "spiritualizes" the covenant, making obedience chiefly a matter of heart and will. To be sure, the covenant is to be enacted in the public arena, but there is a distinctively Camelot air to D's picture of public life. Even D's major institutional reforms are more the occasion for homily than for enabling legislation.

When Josiah adopted Deuteronomy as the basis for reform, he and the people joined in a covenant to obey the newly discovered Mosaic Law (2 Kings 23:1–3). This act certainly revives the political import of the covenant despite D's rather unpolitical spirit. In harmony with D's view that the covenant between Yahweh and Israel is already in force, Josiah's act of covenant making does not institute or renew the relationship between Israel and Yahweh but instead formalizes their resolve to obey Yahweh and, in particular, to perform the written law of Deuteronomy.

The Exile represented a genuinely new situation in Israel's history. Suddenly Israel was not a territorial entity nor a body politic. This was both crisis and opportunity. The people scattered about the Near East could melt into their surroundings or renew their identity. Both the Holiness Code (in Lev. 26:34–45) and the Deuteronomistic Historian (in Deut. 30:1–10) issued a call for repentance; the suffering the people experienced was divine judgment for covenant violation, and the survivors should take this experience to heart and redouble their efforts to obey Yahweh. The repentance of the exiles would be the beginning of a new era in which faithfulness and obedience would flow freely from an inwardly transformed people.

For the people of the new era, the Priestly Source designed a new political structure centered around the temple cult and guided by the quest for holiness. Israel was in fact reborn after the Exile as a religious community with a common loyalty to the temple, the dwelling place of Yahweh. Thus, the covenant had adapted once more to the turns of history, becoming the constitution of a religious community dispersed among the political kingdoms of the world.

New Covenant as Promise. The newness of the covenant takes a new and radical turn in classical prophecy. Amos, Hosea, Isaiah, Micah, Zephaniah, Jeremiah, and Ezekiel join in indicting and sentencing the people of Yahweh for their violation of the divine will for justice and righteousness. Most of them also promise a new beginning that would accomplish the divine purpose in choosing Israel. Many of their words of hope could be said to be in substance the promise of a new covenant, though the expression is absent; Jeremiah (31:31–34) actually does employ the expression and thereby introduces into the stream of prophetic promise a concept with a strong power of attraction. The exposition of this key passage will be sufficient illustration.

Jeremiah's prophecy of a new covenant has passed through a process of oral transmission that modified its language but not its conceptual content. His description of the new covenant is highly dialectical. The new covenant will not be like the old, which was broken despite Yahweh's marriage to Israel. The new covenant, by implication, will be unbreakable, something accomplished by communicating the law in a new way. It will be put within the people, written on their hearts. There will be no need in the new covenant, as there was in the old, for teaching and motivating, for the knowledge of Yahweh will be miraculously implanted and sustained.

The new covenant remedies the defects in the old but retains its basic structure. The obedience of Israel to Yahweh's commands remains all-important. Only when Israel in fact obeys the law fully and automatically can the covenant formula "I will be their God, and they shall be my people" (31:33) be declared in truth. For Jeremiah this statement is no longer a formal principle of the covenant, establishing authority and obligation and promising remedy for violations; it has become a statement of substance or fact which must be true in every sense before it is true at all. When Americans say "with liberty and justice for all" in the pledge of allegiance, they are declaring a formal principle and communal commitment. If they were to apply the Jeremianic test of truth, the statement would prove false.

The act that implants and sustains the knowledge of Yahweh is forgiveness: "for I will forgive their iniquity, and I will remember their sin no more"(31:34). One could construe this narrowly, namely, that forgiveness clears the slate for a new beginning. I believe that the conjunction *for* requires that the act of forgiveness be instrumental in implanting the knowledge of Yahweh. Perhaps the awareness of living out of God's forgiveness transforms the heart by a special quality and degree of gratitude. If so, the new covenant incorporates the failure of the old in the very structure of the new.

The newness of Jeremiah's new covenant is the newness of covenant making per se, the inaugurating of an enduring relationship raised to an ultimate, unconditional level. The breaking of the covenant will be eliminated by a transformation of the heart and will of the human partner. The intention of the old covenant will remain, and the experience of failure will be incorporated into the new by Yahweh's forgiveness.

The New Covenant in Christ

The expression "new covenant" gives the New Testament its name. No other expression could summarize so succinctly the new reality that the New Testament announces. This is somewhat lost in the English word *testament*; the Greek word *diathēkē* means both "covenant" and "will and testament," and English translation tradition mistakenly latched on to the latter meaning.

The substance of Jeremiah's new covenant is found in Jesus' proclamation of the kingdom of God. The coming kingdom of God will involve a transformation of the physical universe and a conversion of the human heart. The law will be implanted in the heart so that humans will be able to obey God completely and unconditionally. The future kingdom is present in history in a hidden form, erupting now and again in earnests of the coming revelation. Those who acknowledge the claim of the law of the kingdom (radical, self-giving love) enter it now. The capacity to acknowledge and obey the law of the kingdom is given by God.

Jesus did not use the expression "new covenant" for the relationship between God and the citizens of the kingdom. There is, however, one utterance of Jesus that does mention it. In the communion liturgy passed on by Paul, Jesus is purported to have said:

> This cup is the new covenant in my blood. Do this, as often as you drink it, in remembrance of me.   (1 Cor. 11:25)

The accounts of Mark and Matthew are quite similar:

> This is my blood of the covenant, which is poured out for many (for the forgiveness of sins).   (Mark 14:24; Matt. 26:28)

The word *new* is not in the best of the New Testament manuscripts, but there can be little doubt that "new covenant" is intended.

The association of the new covenant with blood harks back to the ratification of the Sinaitic covenant: "Behold the blood of the covenant which Yahweh has made with you" (Exod. 24:8). Christ's blood, shed at his execution, is interpreted typologically as the "blood of the (new) covenant." Since the cup of wine is identified as Christ's blood, the drinking of the wine has the same effect as the sprinkling of blood on the people; that is, the covenant is put in force, incorporating the participants into a people with God as their ruler.

The two Synoptic Gospels add another typological reading. The blood is "poured out" for many, which means that Christ's death has the significance of a vicarious sacrifice. Matthew adds "for the forgiveness of sins" to underline that the sacrifice was specifically for atonement. Paul makes this emphasis by identifying the bread as "my body which is broken for you" (1 Cor. 11:24). In endeavoring to maximize the meaning of Christ's death, the New Testament authors pile image upon image as if to say that all God's saving work has been accomplished in this event. Although the association is probably unconscious, the atonement theme recalls Jeremiah's new covenant—forgiveness as the act by which God will implant knowledge of God within the people.

In the new covenant in Christ, his shedding of blood at once ratifies the promises establishing the people as God's people and enacts the forgiveness by which the new covenant is sealed upon the heart. The event of covenant making is first of all an event in history—the crucifixion of Christ—subsequently translated into a cultic ritual. The ritual, perhaps, has the significance of a covenant renewal, as it incorporates participants into the covenant made once for all for "many."

The "many" of Mark and Matthew could refer to believers who are forgiven by accepting forgiveness, to all who participate in the kingdom, believers or not, or to all humans (cf. Rom. 11:32). This ambiguity is inevitable, for neither the New Testament authors nor the teachers of the church should decide how far God's mercy extends.

The New Testament is quite emphatic that the new covenant is not to be limited to a people among the peoples or a nation among the nations. The new covenant, in including people called from all nations, surmounts all divisions between humans. The ritual of baptism develops this theme more explicitly (Gal. 3:27–28), and the church has quite rightly interpreted this rite as entrance into the new covenant, replacing circumcision in the old. This interpretation, however, is not made explicit in the New Testament and therefore falls outside the purview of this chapter.

There remains a serious problem in the claim that Christ's death establishes a new covenant. According to Jeremiah, the people of the new covenant will have the law implanted in their hearts, and they will obey God without fail. This description does not fit the Christian church. Paul himself had to fight a losing battle against sin in the members of his churches, and things have not gotten better. In Paul's thought, the Spirit is supposed to enable the will of Christians to obey God, in accordance with Jeremiah's word, but Paul must exhort his people to "walk by the Spirit" by which they "live" (Gal. 5:25). It sounds very much as though the New Testament falls back into the track of the old covenant, wherein "I will be their God, and they shall be my people" is a statement of principle and commitment, not of accomplished fact. Honesty requires the church to admit that it is in this sense no closer to the kingdom of God than the Israel which lived and lives under the first covenant.

SUGGESTED READING

Although there is a good deal of overlap between the scholarship in biblical law and the scholarship in the concept of covenant, the latter has a rather different bibliography. The following works introduce major contributions to the analysis of the covenant tradition, particularly the thesis that the covenant "form" corresponds to that of the ancient suzerain-vassal treaty.

The studies that put the formal identification of the covenant as a treaty on the scholarly agenda:

Baltzer, Klaus. *The Covenant Formulary: In Old Testament, Jewish, and Early Christian Writings.* 2d ed., rev. Trans. David E. Green. Philadelphia: Fortress Press, 1971.

Mendenhall, George E. *Law and Covenant in Israel and the Ancient Near East.* Pittsburgh: The Biblical Colloquium, 1955.

———. "Covenant." In *The Interpreter's Dictionary of the Bible,* 5 vols., ed. George Arthur Buttrick and Keith Crim. Nashville and New York: Abingdon Press, 1962–76.

A worthwhile history of the covenant concept from the treaty perspective:

Hillers, Delbert R. *Covenant: The History of a Biblical Idea.* Seminars in the History of Ideas. Baltimore: Johns Hopkins University Press, 1969.

Close readings of covenant texts from the treaty perspective:

Fensham, F. Charles. "Clauses of Protection in Hittite Vassal-Treaties and the Old Testament," *Vetus Testamentum* 13 (1963), pp. 133–143.

Hillers, Delbert R. *Treaty-Curses and the Old Testament Prophets.* Biblica et Orientalia, no. 16. Rome: Pontifical Biblical Institute, 1964.

Muilenburg, James. "The Form and Structure of the Covenantal Formulations," *Vetus Testamentum* 9 (1959), pp. 347–365.

Newman, Murray Lee, Jr. *The People of the Covenant: A Study of Israel from Moses to the Monarchy.* New York and Nashville: Abingdon Press, 1962.

Other close readings of covenantal texts that have influenced my presentation:

Smend, Rudolf. *Die Bundesformel.* Theologische Studiën, no. 68. Zurich: EVZ-Verlag, 1963.

Wildberger, Hans. *Jahwes Eigentumsvolk: Eine Studie zur Traditionsgeschichte und Theologie des Erwählungsgedankens.* Abhandlungen zur Theologie des Alten und Neuen Testaments, no. 37. Zurich/Stuttgart: Zwingli Verlag, 1960.

Works critical of aspects of the formal identification of the covenant as a treaty:

Gerstenberger, Erhard. "Covenant and Commandment," *Journal of Biblical Literature* 84 (1965), pp. 38–51.

McCarthy, Dennis J. *Treaty and Covenant: A Study in Form in the Ancient Oriental Documents and in the Old Testament.* Analecta Biblica, no. 21. Rome: Pontifical Biblical Institute, 1963. This work introduced skepticism as to the conformity of Sinaitic texts to the treaty form but affirmed the conformity of Deuteronomy.

Perlitt, Lothar. *Bundestheologie im Alten Testament.* Wissenschaftliche Monographien zum Alten und Neuen Testament, vol. 36. Neukirchen-Vluyn: Neukirchener Verlag, 1969. This work revived Wellhausen's thesis that Deuteronomy introduced the concept of covenant and covenant law into biblical tradition.

A thorough survey of this and many other debates over the concept of covenant:

McCarthy, Dennis J. *Old Testament Covenant: A Survey of Current Opinions.* Growing Points in Theology. Richmond: John Knox Press, 1972.

A selection of monographs and articles on the concept of covenant:

Buss, Martin J. "The Covenant Theme in Historical Perspective," *Vetus Testamentum* 16 (1966), pp. 502–504.
Clements, R. E. *Prophecy and Covenant.* Studies in Biblical Theology, no. 43. Naperville: Alec R. Allenson, 1965.
Eichrodt, Walther. "Covenant and Law," *Interpretation* 20 (1966), pp. 302–321.
Fensham, F. Charles. "Covenant, Promise and Expectation in the Bible," *Theologische Zeitschrift* 23 (1967), pp. 305–322.
Huffmon, Herbert. "The Exodus, Sinai and the Credo," *Catholic Biblical Quarterly* 27 (1965), pp. 101–113.
Thompson, J. A. "The Near Eastern Suzerain-Vassal Concept in the Religion of Israel," *The Journal of Religious History* 3 (1964–65), pp. 1–19.
Tucker, Gene M. "Covenant Forms and Contract Forms," *Vetus Testamentum* 15 (1965), pp. 487–503.
Whitley, C. F. "Covenant and Commandment in Israel," *Journal of Near Eastern Studies* 22 (1963), pp. 37–48.

On theophany in the Sinai event:

Kuntz, John Kenneth. *The Self-Revelation of God.* Philadelphia: Westminster Press, 1967. Pp. 72–103.

Various theological works of interest:

Buber, Martin. *Kingship of God.* 3d ed. Trans. Richard Scheimann. New York and Evanston: Harper & Row, Publishers, 1967.
Muilenburg, James. *The Way of Israel: Biblical Faith and Ethics.* Religious Perspectives, vol. 5. New York: Harper & Brothers Publishers, 1961.
Patrick, Dale. *The Rendering of God in the Old Testament.* Overtures to Biblical Theology, vol. 10. Philadelphia: Fortress Press, 1981. Pp. 96–100 in particular.
Rylaarsdam, J. Coert. "Jewish-Christian Relationships: The Two Covenants and the Dilemmas of Christology." In *Grace Upon Grace: Essays in Honor of Lester J. Kuyper,* ed. James I. Cook, pp. 70–84. Grand Rapids: Wm. B. Eerdmans Publishing Co., 1975.

WHAT IS
THE MEANING OF
THIS LAW?

In the preceding chapters, I have endeavored to study biblical texts historically, but the question of what the text means for the modern reader should not be suppressed. It is quite natural to ask why one is expending considerable effort studying texts from an ancient legal community. So that the question of appropriation of the text and the exposition of its historical meaning may not be confused, this discussion is set off as a postscript. The title is drawn from the Revised Standard Version translation of Deuteronomy 6:20. It is the question the Israelite male child is expected to raise as he begins to appropriate the religious traditions of his people. What is this law for? Why was it given to us? Why are we expected to obey it? What is its place in the scheme of things? In answer the father is to tell the story of the divine lawgiver and his people (Deut. 6:21–25). The people were enslaved to the Egyptians, and Yahweh liberated them and gave them directions for living that would assure their continued existence. By living accordingly, the people would be right with their God.

What is the meaning of this law for the twentieth-century reader? A lot has transpired since the Deuteronomic Moses addressed Israel. The text of Deuteronomy has become Scripture. Nations and empires have arisen and fallen. Cultures have flourished and withered. Judaism and Christianity have waxed and waned. The law of God which was once proclaimed "today" has become the text of "yesterday."

One way to appropriate biblical law is simply to accept it as the legal tradition of an ancient people which had a profound impact on Western civilization. The value of studying any ancient culture is to enrich the understanding of the creative power of the human spirit.

The study of biblical law is particularly rewarding because of the uniqueness and creativity of the biblical authors in this realm of culture. Moreover, the living religious communities which regarded the Bible as sacred Scripture shaped the world view and values of Western civilization. The study of biblical law, consequently, is a study of the roots of modern Western law which rank with the contributions of Greek and Roman law.

Another way to appropriate biblical law is to acknowledge it as the original formulation of the will of the living God. The legal texts of ancient Israel were preserved and edited for the religious community that arose from the ashes of national destruction. The Bible in its present form, thus, was not intended to be used as evidence from the ancient past but was intended to be the living word of the living God for the living people of God (Judaism). The law contained in the Bible is meant to become an address to the members of that community and can be an address to the people which claims to be the "new Israel" (Christianity).

Biblical Law as a Historical Tradition

J. J. Finkelstein's *The Ox That Gored* is a superb example of the use of creative historical imagination in the interpretation of biblical law. In a comparative study of the Israelite and ancient Mesopotamian treatment of the legal topic of the goring ox, Finkelstein argues that the biblical system of law elevated the human world above nature and accorded the individual human self an infinite value. By contrast, Mesopotamian law subjected human society to nature and the individual to society.

The different world views and value systems are exemplified in the treatment of death or injury due to a goring ox. In Exodus 21:28, the ox that kills a human must be destroyed because it has violated the hierarchical order of reality (God–human–animal). The parallels in the Laws of Eshnunna and the Code of Hammurabi have no such provision because their cultures did not acknowledge this hierarchical order. In the matter of the owner's liability, all codes allow the owner to avoid legal liability if the ox had not been known to gore. If it was known to gore, all codes impose legal liability for negligence on the owner, but with a difference. The Mesopotamian laws stipulate compensation to the family of the victim assessed according to the victim's social status; they assumed that a human being can be assigned a monetary value. The biblical law imposes the death penalty on the owner because the biblical lawgivers had a deep aversion to setting a monetary value on human life. Since no bloodguilt attached to the owner, a ransom could be substituted for his death, but the life of the owner (executed or ransomed) was the only thing commensurate with the life of the deceased.

Finkelstein follows the influence of this scheme of values on the Western law of the Middle Ages and afterward, demonstrating that a "trial of animals" is not a primitive idea of an animistic sort but is an excessively literal application of the concept of a hierarchical order of reality and the infinite value of each human being.

He treats Israel's theology in the same way. The biblical God, in contrast to the Mesopotamian deities, is both radically transcendent and extremely accessible. "The conception is more readily comprehended if it is perceived that the biblical god is the human moral ideal personified and apotheosized" (*Ox That Gored*, 11). That is, the biblical God is the idea of the uniquely human freed of all finite limitations. The individual human has access to the center of the universe, which is an absolutized image of the self. This being is the locus of sovereignty, the "source of the series of imperatives which command the ordering of human society and the rest of visible creation in ways designed to give greatest effect to [the] ideal qualities [of man]" (ibid., 46).

Finkelstein's work represents a thoroughly historical interpretation of biblical law and theology. Even God is explained as a product of the human imagination as it creates a world of meaning and value. One who would appropriate biblical law along these lines would celebrate the power of the human spirit to create a moral universe. If it created the systems of the past, it is free to abandon those inherited from the past and invent new ones.

Biblical Law as the Word of God

The appropriation of biblical law as the word of God is diametrically opposed to Finkelstein's reduction of God to a projection of the human self, but it need not exclude his insights into the world view and value system enshrined in biblical law. Over against Finkelstein the theologian would maintain that the theology informing biblical law grew out of Israel's encounter with the holy. The Deuteronomic Moses, in the passages cited at the beginning of the chapter, can be paraphrased as saying: the people of Israel came into being by the deliverances of Yahweh, whose power and justice shattered the predictable course of human events (in the Exodus and Conquest). The mysterious Creator took on an identity in the events of Israel's history. This identity is also revealed in the encounter with the sacred order of justice and right embedded in the community's law.

The biblical legal tradition can best be understood as a reform of the ancient legal traditions of the Fertile Crescent under the pressure of Israel's unique experience of deity. The legal traditions inherited by this people were being constantly pulled in the direction charted by the action of Yahweh in their history. The law itself was a mode of that action in drawing the people together in loyalty to the divine sovereign and providing an order of justice and right to facilitate life together as a people.

The religious communities that recognize the biblical God as God indeed can still hear the divine address in biblical law. This law belongs to the identity of the God who once promulgated it. The people who worship this God must acknowledge the claim of God's commandments on their conscience. When the Jewish synagogue or Christian church proclaims this law, it identifies itself with the Israel that originally heard the words. The repetition of the action creates a unity that spans the ages.

In what sense are the provisions of this law binding on the members of the communities that recognize the biblical God? Jews and Christians through history have given divers answers. The fundamentalists of every age, both Jewish and Christian, have insisted on strict adherence to the letter of the law, though they have never achieved consistency. The rabbis understood the task to be one of adapting the rules to changing moral sensibility and social circumstances. The philosophical have attempted to rationalize the law, some going so far as to sublimate its provisions into a system of moral maxims. Christian charismatics have dismissed all externalities for pure spontaneity, while Jewish mystics have transformed external obedience into sacramental mysteries. Many Christians have subscribed to the Ten Commandments and ignored the rest, while others have thought Jesus' dual commandment of love a sufficient substitute.

The Jewish community has struggled with the question more seriously than Christians because divine law is at the heart of their faith. The study and performance of Torah are the spiritual discipline that nurtures the religious Jew. A piety focused on discovering the will of God in the written Scripture and oral tradition (Talmud) must continually decide what God, through the specific injunctions, requires of God's own; a person's salvation depends upon it.

The Christian church has the question complicated by the dialectical quality of its tradition. The Matthean Jesus both affirms the validity of the Mosaic Law and radicalizes the demands of God to conform to the in-breaking kingdom of God. Whereas the Old Testament requires the people of Israel to meet their neighbors halfway, to comport themselves according to a common sense of decency, and to practice a public piety, those belonging to the kingdom of God are required to abandon self-interest, surpass the righteousness of common decency, and practice a hidden piety. The Old Testament lawgivers did indulge in counsels of perfection and utopian schemes, but even then their desire was for a more just equilibrium of interests within the social order. The New Testament law of love requires the citizen of the kingdom to transcend all sinful impulses and renounce the right to receive justice in this age. The church has swung back and forth between the poles of equal justice and self-sacrificial love, between the Old Testament and the New, throughout its history and has often fallen short of both.

Obviously, the issue cannot be resolved here. Indeed, it is doubtful that one should even seek to develop an answer that would be satisfactory to all parties. An idea has emerged in this study, however, that may satisfy those who endeavor to take Scripture seriously but not literally—the idea that the written law is a witness to an unwritten law (see Chapter Seven). The series and codes can be understood as testimony to the justice and righteousness God requires of God's people. If one were to adopt this perspective, one would be bound not to the actual provisions of the law but to the principles and values informing them. The search for God's will would be grounded in the God already known, yet open to new insight into the order of justice and right that is the norm of all law.

Witnesses to the Law

As a follow-up to the proposal to interpret the legal texts of Scripture as testimony to an unwritten divine law, I wish to conclude with a few principles and values that can be gleaned from the series and codes here examined. These gleanings are neither systematic nor exhaustive but exemplary of the kind of interpretation I am proposing.

The Ten Commandments. This series (Exod. 20:1–17; Deut. 5:6–21), along with related ones (viz., Exod. 34:14, 17; Lev. 19:1–18), is a personal address of Yahweh to his people. The address format fits the narrative setting—an oral address of God to the people. The religious communities which recognize the biblical God exhibit true instincts when they read the Decalogue as a constituent part of the liturgy. The text provides a splendid opportunity to re-enact the event of law giving.

The expansiveness and comprehensive scope of the Ten Commandments makes them uniquely appropriate for liturgical proclamation. The Commandments taken together cover the subjects of primary concern to the Old Testament legal tradition. Yahweh's status in Israel is protected in the "first table"; the individual's person, family, property, and remedial rights, in the "second table." In addition, each commandment is open ended in that it can be expanded to cover cases unforeseen when it was formulated. The second commandment, for example, was extended from the making of images of Yahweh to include any worship of a creature; it was also developed into a theological critique of the religious imagination. The sixth commandment might be construed as narrowly focused against the extreme act of murder; however, as a commandment it would discourage any course of action that might end in killing. Leviticus 19:17–18 can be interpreted as an expansion of the commandment against killing: "You shall not hate your brother in your heart, but you shall reason with your neighbor, lest you bear sin because of him. You shall not take vengeance or bear any grudge against the sons of your own people, but you shall love your neighbor as yourself."

Not all of the Ten Commandments retain the cogency they had for ancient Israel. Abusing God's name was much more serious when it was thought that verbal statements of all sorts were efficacious in form. The commandment still witnesses to the importance of treating the sacred with proper respect and keeping one's word, but profanity per se is not an offense equal to apostasy or murder. For Christians, the sabbath commandment has lost its original force. The observance of the sabbath is surely more important than many believers think, but it is not on a par with the rest of the Commandments.

Despite these erosions of time, the Ten Commandments retain their original force in their overall lineaments. They provide a direct encounter with the biblical God in which God enacts sovereignty over the people. God's order of justice and right is stated in such a comprehensive and open-ended fashion that it is capable of encompassing every circumstance in which people might find themselves.

The Book of the Covenant.   Large portions of this most ancient of the biblical codes are personally addressed, but the book does not suggest itself as a candidate for regular liturgical use. It was once proclaimed orally, but it is too time-bound to be used thus today. While the Decalogue is comprehensive and open ended in a very brief compass, this collection deals with a great variety of concrete issues. The Decalogue is itself a set of principles and values, whereas this code embodies principles and values in specific rulings.

The Book of the Covenant seems to have set the pattern and standard for biblical lawbooks. It established a precedent for the scope of divine law and introduced the concepts and principles and even specific provisions which would continue to be enunciated and enhanced in subsequent legal compositions. It also inaugurated the address format and homiletical style of biblical legal documents; the later codes retained the format and heightened the apologetic, homiletical qualities discernible within it.

This lawbook is distinctive in the type of laws it includes. Only this biblical code enters into cases of liability, damages, and ownership disputes. Such subjects are dealt with because the code came into being in Israel's earliest era, a time when the covenant between Yahweh and Israel was the actual constitution of the Israelite legal community. Judicial subjects of a relatively technical nature were as much under the sovereign will of Yahweh as serious offenses and moral and religious duties. One of its primary theological contributions is its capacity to unite the most technical and "secular" legal topics with moral and religious injunctions into a single system of law.

The law and homilies of the Book of the Covenant are informed by a unique system of values. One of the values identified in Finkelstein's findings is the sacredness of the individual human being. The lawgiver shies away from assigning monetary value to a human life even when that would have been the simplest, most realistic course to take. When theft, loss, and damages are treated, he uses monetary compensation exclusively; none of the laws governing property (except slaves) have penalties involving the execution or physical punishment of the culpable. The rule is restitution with compensation. According to Finkelstein, this pattern indicates that it

> is not merely that wrongs against the person are of greater gravity than wrongs against property. It is rather that the two realms belong to utterly different mental sets. Different scales are used to weigh the wrongs, and the corrective measures prescribed are of two distinct qualitative orders. (*Ox That Gored*, 37)

Almost all of the laws of this code prescribing capital punishment are predicated on the infinite value of human life (Exod. 21:12, 16, 20, 22–23, 29; 22:2–3) or the sanctity of the hierarchical order (Exod. 21:15, 17; 22:19, 20). That the Book of the Covenant (and all Old Testament law) frequently takes recourse to capital punishment has given Israelite law a reputation of vindictiveness and indifference to the value of human life, but in fact the value scheme informing these laws accords human life infinite value. The famous or infamous dictum of "life for life" is an expression not of "vengefulness" but of moral symmetry: the only thing one who is liable for a death can "give" equal to what one "took" is one's own life.

In the contemporary debate over the legitimacy of capital punishment, the Old Testament is frequently enlisted as the authority for taking life, but it would be more appropriate to read it as a witness to the infinite value of every human life. It would require us to ask: What punishment would preserve the infinite value of every human being? Is it more just to pursue moral symmetry ("life for life") or to honor the killer's infinite worth by showing mercy? Is the majesty of the law shown more respect by punishment equal to the crime or by reservation of the ultimate punishment for God?

The Book of the Covenant is a witness to the divine order of justice and right as it impinges on a given period of history. It is of special value for its formulation of a thoroughgoing theocratic law. The communities that recognize the biblical God can glean from it the world view and values that inform its laws and incorporate these in their theology, ethics, and social teaching.

The Deuteronomic Law.   This lawbook is the culmination of the impulse toward homily in biblical law. The whole is personally addressed, and the law proper is embedded in hortatory phrases and motive clauses sealing the law on the hearts of the people. Unlike the other biblical codes, it is a human word—Moses speaks in his own name—interpreting God's word. In sum, the presentation of law has taken the form of a sermon, and its most natural place in the life of synagogue and church is as a text for sermons.

The sermonic rhetoric of Deuteronomy is both emotional and rationalistic. The author understands the purpose of religious practice to be the cultivation and expression of the "inward" attachment of the heart. Sacrifices are to be occasions for rejoicing and fellowship; practically nothing is said on sacrifices and rituals done for their own sake. It is not accidental that the school highlights the proclamation of the law as a cultic action (cf. Deut. 31:9–13; 33:10a). The language of the cult is meant to instruct and motivate the people in their religious and communal living.

The Deuteronomic homily on the divine law stresses rigorous enforcement of laws governing serious offenses and compassionate concern for the welfare of the needy and defenseless. Although these demands may seem contradictory to a citizen of modern America, they are a complementary pair in Deuteronomic Law. One test of the justness of a society is its capacity to protect and enhance the lives of those at the bottom; another is its capacity to establish and defend the moral order against serious violations. A large portion of this law is devoted to instilling the responsibility of persons of means for the welfare of the neighbor in distress—the poor and needy, the widow and orphan, the slave and the day laborer, the Levite and resident alien, even the helpless beast. Much of the remainder is dedicated to urging the judges and people to purge the evildoer from their midst to restore the moral equilibrium of society and to avoid collective guilt before God.

At the head of the list of serious offenses stands the demand for exclusive loyalty to Yahweh. Overt apostasy was treason against the divine sovereign. The identity and unity of the people of Israel was at stake in such violations. Israel was to be unique among the nations, recognizing only the one God known in its history and shaping its religious practice to accord with God's identity. To the modern Western reader, this passion for religious orthodoxy, strongest in the Deuteronomic Law but present in all biblical law, is shockingly intolerant. Polytheism was basically tolerant and pluralistic, whereas monotheism was neither. Biblical monotheism made religious truth a life and death matter. Only the one God was to be accorded reality, so all competitors must be eliminated and misconceptions of the one God stamped out. Any person or group which proved disloyal to this God or which understood God to be one of the gods had to be destroyed to avoid communal contamination and collective guilt.

The long history of religious persecution within and between the religious communities recognizing the biblical God has taught them the lesson of tolerance, and the secularization of the modern state has nullified their power to punish deviance. The coercion of conscience to achieve religious unanimity has been renounced as contrary to true religious faith. Unquestionably this is a great gain, but there is a concomitant loss: the passion for truth has weakened in religious communities, and Western society has substituted political ideology for religious orthodoxy. Deuteronomy's principle of a people passionately committed to the one true God is surely still binding on the synagogue and church, but some means other than persecution must be devised to enforce the principle.

The voice that speaks in Deuteronomy is urgent. The people of God are in danger of incurring the wrath of God for their violation of divine law. Terrible devastation, exile, perhaps even extinction is on the horizon and can only be avoided by a national renewal of allegiance and obedience to God. The work has retained its sense of urgency and immediacy for Jews and Christians through the ages, repeatedly challenging religious people to take responsibility for the justice and equity of their societies and for the seriousness of their religious communities' commitment to the one true God.

The Holiness Code and Priestly Law. The Holiness Code is probably the least accessible Old Testament lawbook for the religious communities that recognize the biblical God. It is literally buried away in that little-read portion of the Pentateuch, the Priestly Source, from which it is not easily distinguished. Its fate is to be treated as a part of P, and the fate of both is not a happy one. Although the priestly stream of tradition has gained the respect of scholars in recent years for its antiquity and intellectual sophistication, its conceptions and spirituality are too foreign to the modern temperament to appeal to many nonspecialists.

The priestly stream of tradition exhibits a distinctive theology and system of values. Yahweh exercises his rule of his people through his presence in the sanctuary, interacting with them in the sacrifices and other rituals presided over by the priesthood. All of communal life is to be shaped to conform to the holiness imparted to the people by the presence of the deity in their midst. Although it has been cogently argued that this priestly theology is quite ancient, it does not appear to have attained public acceptance until the Babylonian exile and restoration of the temple cultus. P may be considered the constitution of the post-exilic Jewish religious community.

One way to grasp the distinctive world view of the Holiness Code and Priestly Source is to compare their views to Deuteronomy's. The differences between them stand out in their treatment of the sanctuary and sacrifice. The Deuteronomic Law speaks amply of the sole legitimate altar but provides virtually no directions for the arrangement of the sanctuary, for maintaining its holiness, or for distributing duties among the ranks of clergy. Theologically speaking, only Yahweh's name dwells at the sanctuary, not Yahweh himself. The Priestly Law has something to say about every detail of tabernacle construction, arrangement, maintenance of holiness, and priestly duties. Yahweh himself dwells in the holy of holies, and all space must be organized accordingly.

For the Deuteronomic lawgiver, a layperson is to go to the sanctuary to rejoice and give thanks. The quintessential sacrifice is the sacrificial meal, which is to be shared with the family and the needy. For the priestly stream of tradition, the quintessential sacrifices are the holocaust and the offerings that atone for guilt. Within this system, sacrifices have an essential place in the maintenance of the sacral order, and the most important are gifts from which the offerer reaps no material (i.e., nutritional) benefit.

The Holiness Code and Priestly Law are the only legal traditions in the Pentateuch to prescribe rites solely for atoning for guilt. Both the reparation and purgation offerings generally fall into this category, and the Day of Atonement brings these year-round rituals to a climax. Deuteronomy is quite conscious of individual and collective guilt, but it has virtually no cultic rituals for purging and expiating it; rather, it thinks in practical terms of repentance and the enforcement of law. For the priestly stream of tradition, the practical actions must be supplemented by rituals that remove the "pollution" caused by violations of sacred law. The pollution attaches to the land (H) and sanctuary (P) and must be removed, or God will be driven to punish the people and/or abandon the holy dwelling place.

The theological contribution of the priestly tradition is its conversion of the experience of the divine presence into the foundation and motivation of moral life, judicial action, and cultic order. The holy is experienced as awful mystery, as a supernatural reality wholly superior to humans in power and goodness. The qualitative difference between the divine and human wills has both amoral and moral aspects. The amoral aspect of holiness underlies the arrangements of the sanctuary, the separation of the priests from the people, the laws of cleanness and uncleanness, and so forth. When the Holiness Code commands Israel to be holy, it means, in part, abiding by the separation of the holy and the profane. It also means, however, fulfilling the moral commandments and preserving a just and righteous community. Every willful wrong introduces pollution into the holy community and brings God into contact with that which God hates. Thus, the Holiness Code and Priestly Law are able to synthesize the amoral and moral qualities of holiness within their theology and law.

From the vantage point of its doctrine of holiness, the author of the Holiness Code is able to contribute to the biblical legal tradition moral and social teachings of the highest order. His sensitive, probing statement of the fundamental commandments (Lev. 19) is a highpoint of the presentation of divine law. It is fitting that the famous commandment to love the neighbor as oneself is the capstone of the chapter. The Code also provides the most exhaustive teaching respecting the most intimate sphere of life, sexual intercourse; and from its sacral view of the land, it offers a profound theory of land ownership and citizenship in Israel. Such specific contributions are invaluable to the presentation of divine law.

Perhaps the value of the Holiness Code and Priestly Law for the synagogue and church is to be found precisely in the foreignness of their theology and spirituality. This tradition constitutes a counterbalance to the subjectivistic, rationalistic spirituality of Deuteronomy. Surely the theology and ethics of the synagogue and church need the concept of objective holiness and sacred value. Of course, the priestly cultic order cannot be adopted without modification, but that is true to a greater or lesser extent of all the theological and legal concepts studied in this book.

SUGGESTED READING

Most of the works listed below are drawn from previous chapters, and the bibliographies of the early chapters contain many works relevant here. Of note are J. J. Finkelstein, *The Ox That Gored*, previously cited, and Rudolf Otto, *The Idea of the Holy*, trans. John W. Harvey (New York: Oxford University Press, 1958).

Works discussing the theological meaning of the law:

Eichrodt, Walther. "The Law and the Gospel," trans. Charles F. McRae, *Interpretation* 11 (1957), pp. 23–40.

Hals, Ronald M. *Grace and Faith in the Old Testament*. Minneapolis: Augsburg Publishing House, 1980. Pp. 57–69.

Hoppe, Leslie J. "The Meaning of Deuteronomy," *Biblical Theological Bulletin* 10 (1980), pp. 111–117.

Noth, Martin. " 'For All Who Rely on Works of the Law Are Under a Curse.' " In *The Laws in the Pentateuch and Other Studies*, trans. D. R. Ap-Thomas, pp. 118–131. Edinburgh and London: Oliver & Boyd, 1966.

von Rad, Gerhard. *Old Testament Theology*. 2 vols. Trans. D. M. G. Stalker. Edinburgh and London: Oliver & Boyd, 1962–65. Vol. 2, pp. 388–409.

Zimmerli, Walther. *The Law and the Prophets: A Study of the Meaning of the Old Testament*. Trans. R. E. Clements. New York: Harper & Row, Publishers, 1965.

An article by the author:

Patrick, Dale. "Political Exegesis." In *Encounter with the Text: Form and History in the Hebrew Bible*, ed. Martin J. Buss, pp. 139–152. Semeia Supplements. Missoula: Scholars Press, 1979. Sketches the way a biblical text can be relevant to theological construction.

Index of Biblical Passages

Index of Subjects